Council of Europe (CoE)

The Authors

from left to right: Agnes von Maravić, Maren Lambrecht-Feigl, Elise Cornu, Tim Lisney, Irena Guidikova, Tanja E. J. Kleinsorge, Nikolaos Sitaropoulos.

The Authors

from left to right: Schnutz Rudolf Dürr, Rüdiger Dossow, Sylvie Affholder, Hugh Chetwynd, Matthieu Birker.

Tanja E. J. Kleinsorge, née Klein, was born in Münster, West Germany, on 5 July 1969. She studied Slavic Studies, History, Political Science and Law at the Westfälische-Wilhelms-Universität Münster from 1988 to 1991. She continued her studies with a scholarship at Georgetown University, Washington DC, and graduated with a Master of Science in Foreign Service in May 1993 with the Dean's Award for Academic Excellence and a Certificate in Russian Area Studies. She started her career with the Council of Europe (CoE) on 1 August 1993, working for the Parliamentary Assembly, first in the Secretariat of the Political Affairs Committee, then in the Secretariat of the Committee on Legal Affairs and Human Rights. She has since gained an additional Master of Arts in History, Law and Political Science from the FernUniversität Hagen in Germany by correspondence. After serving as the Head of the Secretariat of the Parliamentary Assembly's Committee on Equal Opportunities for Women and Men for seven years, she currently works as the Head of the Secretariat of the Social Affairs, Health and Sustainable Development Committee.

Sylvie Affholder was born in Neuf-Brisach, France, on 10 February 1970. She studied International Relations at the Institut d'Etudes Politiques in Strasbourg, France, from 1989 to 1993, including a year at the Erlangen–Nürnberg University, Germany. She holds a Master's in Political and Cultural Construction of Europe (1994) from the Robert Schuman University, Strasbourg and a Master's in European Advanced Interdisciplinary Studies (1995) from the College of Europe in Natolin, Poland. She joined the CoE in May 1995 as coordinator of the Congress twinning programme 'Network of Local Democracy Agencies in southeast Europe' and a member of the Stability Pact Unit for southeast Europe. She became, in addition, Deputy Secretary to the Chamber of the Regions and to the Committee on Social Cohesion in 1998. She joined the Secretariat of the Parliamentary Assembly as Co-**secretary** of the Committee on Equal Opportunities for Women and Men, and project manager of the parliamentary dimension of the CoE Campaign 'Stop domestic violence against women'. She currently serves as Secretary to the Assembly's Monitoring Committee.

Matthieu Birker, born in 1980 in Epinal, France, studied Law in France and Germany and holds a PhD in Human Rights Law from the University of Strasbourg, France. He has been an advisor to the Commissioner for Human Rights of the CoE since September 2012. He covers human rights challenges related to data protection as well as the impact of counter-terrorism measures on human rights, and is desk officer for four CoE Member States. Prior to this position he was a researcher and a junior lecturer in French and International Public Law at the University of Strasbourg. From 2008 to 2010, he was a junior member of the Fundamental Rights Agency Legal Experts. He has also worked for a non-governmental organization (NGO) specialized in migrants' human rights protection. He has published a number of articles and case comments in the field of European Human Rights Law.

Charlotte Altenhöner-Dion, born in 1969 in Alexandria, Egypt, studied Law in Germany and France and holds an LLM in International Law from Georgetown University, US. She worked for ten years for the United Nations High Commission for Refugees (UNHCR), mainly in Central Asia and the Balkans, and gathered further experience in the international protection of human rights in Honduras, Colombia, Rwanda and Geneva, among others with the United Nations High Commissioner for Human Rights (UNHCHR). After some non-governmental work in the United Kingdom (UK) and the Netherlands, she joined the Organization for Security and Co-operation in Europe High Commissioner on National Minorities (OSCE-HCNM) in 2008, and the Secretariat of the Framework Convention for the Protection of National Minorities of the CoE in 2010. Since 2016, she has been working for the Media and Internet Governance team in the Directorate General of Human Rights and Rule of Law.

Hugh Chetwynd was born in Malvern, England, on 2 October 1967. He studied Modern History at the University of East Anglia, England, from 1986 to 1989 and obtained a Master of Science from the University of Bristol, England, in 1992 in Domestic Politics and Foreign Affairs. In June 1993 he joined the CoE, initially working on democratic, legal and human rights reform programmes in Albania before transferring in September 1995 to work on local democracy issues in the countries of Central and Eastern Europe. In September 1997, he joined the Directorate General of Human Rights to work on human rights co-operation and awareness programmes, primarily in southeast Europe. In August 2002, he was appointed as Deputy and later Special Representative of the Secretary General of the CoE to Bosnia and Herzegovina. In May 2005, he returned to Strasbourg after being appointed Head of Division of the Secretariat of the European Committee for the Prevention of Torture (CPT), where he currently continues to work.

Elise Cornu was born in 1974 in Grasse, France. She studied Law at the University of Nice-Sophia Antipolis and the University of Aix-Marseille III, France. In 2004, she obtained Doctor of Law from the University of Strasbourg, France. She joined the CoE in 2002. She worked for nine years in the Directorate of Legal Advice and Public International Law (as Head of the Treaty Office from 2009 to 2013) and four years in the Secretariat of the Parliamentary Assembly (as Head of Secretariat of the Committee on Equality and Non-Discrimination from 2015 to 2017). Since 2018, she is Head of Division, in charge of legal affairs and human rights, in the Secretariat of the Committee of Ministers (CM).

Rüdiger Dossow, Dipl.-Jur., LLM, a native of Nuremberg, Germany, studied Law at the University of Erlangen-Nuremberg, the Hague Academy of International Law, the University of Virginia School of Law and the School of Professional Education of the Paris Bar. After legal practice with Rogers & Wells in New York and Beiten Burkhardt Mittl & Wegener in Nuremberg, he joined the CoE early in 1994, where he consecutively dealt with transfrontier co-operation and local democracy, the European Conference of Ministers for Regional Planning, and media law and policy. In 2002, he was seconded as Legal Advisor to the Special Representative of the European Union (EU) in Skopje in charge of implementing the Ohrid Agreement on reconciliation and subsequently worked for the Political Affairs Committee of the CoE's Parliamentary Assembly, in particular on Chechnya, Nagorno-Karabakh, Kaliningrad, Belarus, Georgia, the United Nations (UN) and the future of democracy. As Secretary to the Assembly's Committee on Culture, Science, Education and Media for twelve years, he worked on Assembly reports concerning journalists in conflict zones, media and terrorism, freedom of expression and information on the Internet, cyber-terrorism, protection of media freedom and safety of journalists, freedom of expression and respect for religious beliefs as well as on Islam, Islamism and Islamophobia. He is currently Secretary to the Assembly's Committee on Migration, Refugees and Displaced Persons.

Schnutz Rudolf Dürr, born in 1964, studied at the Law Faculty of the University of Graz (Magister of Law), Austria, and the Diplomatic Academy in Vienna. In 2002, he obtained Doctor of Law from the University of Vienna. After working for three years at the Ministry of Foreign Affairs of Austria, he joined the Venice Commission of the CoE in 1994. Within the Venice Commission's Secretariat he is the head of the Constitutional Justice division, in charge of providing support to constitutional courts and equivalent bodies. He prepares Venice Commission's opinions on constitutional amendments and laws relating to the courts' activity, in addition to amicus curiae opinions for the courts, and publishes their case law in the Commission's *Bulletin on Constitutional Case-Law* and the database CODICES. Since 2014, he is the Secretary General of the World Conference on Constitutional Justice.

Andrew Forde was born in Galway, Ireland, on 23 May 1983. He is an honours BSc Computer Applications (Information Systems) graduate of Dublin City University, Ireland (2004). Following various periods of work in the area of human rights both in Ireland and overseas (particularly in the field of children's rights in the Caribbean and South Asia) he went on to obtain an LLM in International Human Rights Law from the Irish Centre for Human Rights at the National University of Ireland, Galway (2006). He was awarded a Gold President's Award in 2003 and currently is also Chairman of the Gold Award Holder's Association (Tar Éis Óir) in Ireland, which aims to promote personal development and community involvement of young people through realizing self-defined challenges. He joined the Office of the CoE Commissioner on Human Rights as an advisor in January 2007 and worked as part of the Commissioner's South-Eastern Europe task force. Andrew has since spent time in the Balkans working for the OSCE Mission in Kosovo[1] and for the Irish Human Rights Commission, and as the Deputy Head of the CoE Office in Pristina. He is currently on sabbatical.

Matjaz Gruden was born on 24 November 1965 in Ljubljana, Slovenia. He studied Law at the University of Ljubljana and graduated in 1990 with a thesis on the European Community (EC) as a member of international multilateral agreements. He continued his studies at the College of Europe in Bruges, Belgium in 1990–1991, where he obtained a degree in Advanced European Legal studies. From 1992 to 1995 he worked at the Ministry of Foreign Affairs of Slovenia, first in Ljubljana and in the last three years as a diplomat in the Slovenian Mission to the EU in Brussels. He joined the CoE in 1995 as a co-secretary of the Political Affairs Committee of the Parliamentary Assembly. He also worked as an advisor to the President of the Parliamentary Assembly, Lord Russell-Johnston (1999–2002), headed the Assembly's Communication Unit and served as the Secretary to the Monitoring Committee. Between 2005 and 2009, he worked as a special advisor and spokesperson to the Secretary General of the CoE, the Rt. Hon. Terry Davis. From 2009 to 2014, he was the Deputy Director of the Private Office of the Secretary General Thorbjørn Jagland. In 2015, he was appointed Director of Policy Planning, and Director of Democratic Participation in 2018.

Irena Guidikova was born in Bulgaria on 22 March 1968. She received a Master's in Politics from Sofia University, Bulgaria, in 1992 and a Master's in Political Philosophy from the University of York, UK, in 1994. Since the end of 1994, she has been a staff member of the CoE in the following positions: manager of a youth research programme; project officer for a project on democratic institutions and the future of democracy and member of the Private Office of the Secretary General.

1. Throughout this text, all reference to Kosovo, whether to the territory, institutions or population shall be understood in full compliance with United Nations Security Council Resolution 1244 and without prejudice to the status of Kosovo.

Having served as Head of Division for the World Forum for Democracy, she is currently responsible for inclusion and anti-discrimination programmes.

Jack Hanning, a European of British extraction, was until May 2007, Director of External Relations at the Strasbourg-based CoE. Born in Birmingham in 1942, he was educated at Malvern and Jesus College, Oxford. Fluent in four languages, he has spent most of his working life promoting European unification and cultural understanding first as a teacher of languages, then as a translator, and later as a journalist. After joining the CoE, he was successively press spokesperson to several Assembly Presidents and then to Secretary General, Catherine Lalumière, before heading the Organization's Press and Public Relations Department. Since 2000, he has specialized in external and multilateral affairs. He has taught at Strasbourg University and at the University of Syracuse. He is now Secretary General of the European Association of Schools of Political Studies of the CoE and the Representative of the European Movement International to the European Institutions in Strasbourg.

Mario Heinrich was born in Bayreuth, Germany, in 1945. He studied Law at the Universities of Würzburg, Paris and Berlin. He also did his military service in between. In 1974, he passed his second state examination in Law in Munich. In 1981, he obtained Doctor of Law from the University of Würzburg. Between 1972 and May 1974 he was employed in a lawyers' office in Bayreuth. From June 1974 he worked in the Secretariat of the Parliamentary Assembly in different functions. He recently retired from his last position of Secretary to the Committee on Rules of Procedure, Immunities and Institutional Affairs.

Antti Koreakivi was born in Oulu, Finland on 9 October 1967. He is a graduate of Helsinki University and Columbia University Law Schools. He worked as Legal Advisor for the Lawyers' Committee for Human Rights in New York before joining the CoE's Directorate of Human Rights in 1997. From 1998, he has dealt with national minority issues, most recently as the Head of the Secretariat of the CoE's Framework Convention for the Protection of National Minorities. He currently works for the Office of the High Commissioner on Human Rights (OHCHR).

Maren Lambrecht-Feigl, née Lambrecht, born in Germany on 16 June 1969, studied Urban and Regional Planning at the University of Dortmund, Germany, where she graduated, after various internships and work periods in France and Switzerland, as an Engineer of Territorial Planning in 1996. She started her career as a project manager at the University of St Gall, Switzerland, on a major research project on Sustainable Development for the Swiss Federal Office of Regional Development. From 1998 until 2006, she worked as a project manager, then senior project manager at the Alsace Development Agency regional development agency, where she was in charge of accompanying foreign direct investment projects (in particular from Japan, Canada and Germany), and elaborating major regional development projects, including for Franco-German cross-border co-operation. In 2006, she joined the CoE, first working as Secretary to the European Committee on Local and Regional Democracy, then as of 2009 as Secretary of the Committee on Social Affairs, Health and Sustainable Development of the Parliamentary Assembly in charge of files relating to children's rights, social rights more generally, as well as local and regional democracy and governance questions. Since March 2018, Maren has been a Programme Officer in the CoE Children's Rights Division with a portfolio, including legal and policy responses to violence against children, children's rights in the digital environment and child participation.

Manuel Lezertua was born in Bilbao, Spain, in 1957. He studied Law in the University of Deusto, Spain, where he obtained a diploma in Law, with honours, in 1980. He taught Spanish in Northumberland University in 1980–1981 before joining London University where he was awarded a Master's in Law in 1982. In 1985 he succeeded, with honours in the first phase of a PhD in Law in the Law Faculty of the University of the Basque Country. He obtained different awards in languages, such as the Proficiency in English and translation English-Spanish Diplomas by Cambridge University in 1981, Diplôme d'Etudes françaises by the University of Toulouse and Bilbao School of Modern languages and the Basque Academy Diploma in 1978. Manuel Lezertua worked as a consultant in the Department of Health in 1982 and was subsequently recruited in 1983 by the Department of Justice in the Government of the Basque Country. He joined the CoE in 1985 where he has occupied several posts: lawyer at the European Social Charter (1985–1988), lawyer at the European Commission for Human Rights (1988–1992), Principal Administrator in the CM (1994–1996, in charge of Human Rights issues), Head of Economic Crime Unit (1996–1999), Executive Secretary of the Group of States against Corruption (GRECO), 1999–2003), Head of the Crime Problems Department (2003–2004) in the Directorate General of Legal Affairs, and Director of the Office of the Commissioner for Human Rights from 2004 until 2007. Between 1992 and 1994, he worked as a lawyer for the Constitutional Court of Spain. Following some years as Director of Legal Advice and Public International Law (Jurisconsulte), he worked as the Director in the CoE Congress of Local and Regional Authorities until 2016, when he was appointed Human Rights Defender of the Basque Region, Spain.

Tim Lisney, born in London, UK, graduated in French at the University of Kent in Canterbury, England. He joined the CoE in 1989 from the British Library, to work as a librarian and database manager, before moving to the secretariat of the Committee of Ministers, setting up their website and working on equality and information policy issues. In 2000 he took charge of the Council of Europe Archives, moving to the Congress of Local and Regional Authorities in 2005, where he is currently Secretary to the Governance Committee.

Agnes von Maravić, born in 1977 in Bayreuth, Germany, studied Public Policy and Administration at Potsdam University and Sciences Po Lille, France. After graduation in 2003, she worked in the non-governmental sector based in Kyiv, Ukraine, and later moved to Düsseldorf University, Germany, to research civil society and regional politics in the post-Soviet space. In 2006, she joined the CoE, where she started working on judicial reform in Ukraine and Georgia. In 2008, she transferred to the Children's Rights Division. From 2012 to 2014 she used the opportunity of a sabbatical in Canada to attend international public law courses at the University of Edmonton, Alberta. Since 2017, she has been working for the CoE's Secretariat of the Framework Convention for the Protection of National Minorities.

The Authors

Elda Moreno was born in 1965 in Cartagena, Spain. In 1989, she obtained a degree in Law from the University of Murcia, Spain, and worked for two years as a lawyer in the fields of human rights, family and social law. In 1991, she moved to France to specialize in International and Environmental Law at the University of Strasbourg. During her studies, she co-operated with NGOs, wrote for various journals and magazines and won several writing contests. She started her career in the CoE in 1995 as Head of the Centre Naturopa, where she led a pan-European programme for the promotion of nature conservation. Between 1999 and 2001, she worked in the Directorate General of Legal Affairs for the protection of regional and minority languages. In 2001, she became a member of the Private Office of the Secretary General and the Deputy Secretary General of the CoE, whom she advised on legal and political issues related to human rights, legal co-operation, culture, education, youth and communication. From January 2006 to September 2009, Elda Moreno was the coordinator of the new programme 'Building a Europe for and with Children', with the mandate of promoting the rights of the child and eradicating violence against children in the then forty-six Member States of the CoE. In September 2009, she was invited to join again the Private Office of the Secretary General and the Deputy Secretary General as a special advisor on transversal matters. From 2014 until 2016, she worked for United Nations International Children's Emergency Fund (UNICEF), after which she returned to the CoE to lead the Children's Rights and Sports Values Department in the Directorate General of Democracy.

Christina Olsen was born on 8 October 1970 in Vicenza, Italy. She obtained her degree in Law from the University of Padua, Italy, in March 1996, and passed the Italian national bar exam in Trieste in 1999. She continued working as a lawyer for two different legal firms, specialized in international commercial law before being recruited by the CoE on 15 March 2001, where she worked in the CoE Treaty Office until recently. She now works on violence against women in the Directorate General of Democracy.

Simon Palmer, born in southern England in 1947, read English and French Literature at Cambridge University and joined the CoE in 1983 after an initial career in the private sector. He was appointed to the Secretariat of the CM in 1990 and in 1996 assumed responsibility for the Committee's work on the supervision of the execution of the judgments of the European Court of Human Rights (ECtHR), a position from which he recently retired.

Christophe Poirel, having graduated from the Institute of Political Science in Paris and having obtained a Master in Public Law, joined the CoE in 1989, where he worked for fifteen years in the human rights field. After moving to the Secretariat of the CM in 2004, he was Deputy Secretary to the Committee from 2010 to 2018, when he was appointed Director of the Human Rights Directorate.

Nikolaos Sitaropoulos was born in Samos, Greece, on 3 January 1967.
He is Head of Division in the Department for the Execution of Judgments of the ECtHR. Former Deputy to the Director and Head of Division at the Office of the

CoE Commissioner for Human Rights (2009–2018), advisor to the CoE Commissioner for Human Rights (2007–2009) and lawyer and head of unit in the Department for the Execution of Judgments of the ECtHR, CoE (2004–2007). From 2000 to 2004 he held the post of legal officer at the Greek National Commission for Human Rights. He is a member of the Bar in Greece since 1996. He holds a PhD in Law from University College London (1995), an LLM in International Human Rights Law from the University of Essex (1991), England, and an LLB from the School of Law of the Aristotle University of Thessaloniki (1988), Greece. He has published on subjects relating to international and European human rights, immigration and refugee law, international humanitarian law, as well as minority, nationality and anti-discrimination law.

Mateo Sorinas Balfegó was born in Tarragona, Spain, in 1946. In 1968, he obtained a Master of Physics from Universidad Complutense, Madrid. He taught Physics and Mathematics in Las Palmas from 1969 to 1977. He joined the CoE in 1978 where he occupied several posts in the Secretariat of the Parliamentary Assembly: Co-Secretary of the Committee on Environment, Regional Planning and Local Authorities (1978–1986), Secretary of the Committee on Migration, Refugees and Demography (1986–1992), Secretary of the Political Affairs Committee (1992–1994), political counsellor in the Private Office of the President of the Assembly (1992–1996), Head of the Central Division (1994–1997), Director of the Political and Legal Affairs Department (1997–2002), Director General (2002–2006). From February 2006 and following his election by the parliamentarians until his retirement in 2011, Mr Sorinas was Secretary General of the Parliamentary Assembly.

The Authors

Table of Contents

List of Abbreviations

ALDA	Association of Local Democracy Agencies
ALECSO	The Arab League Educational, Cultural and Scientific Organization
CAHDI	Committee of Legal Advisers on Public International Law of the Council of Europe
CAHENF	Ad hoc Committee for the Rights of the Child
CDDH	(Council of Europe) Steering Committee for Human Rights
CEB	Council of Europe Development Bank
CETS	Council of Europe Treaty Series
CIS	Commonwealth of Independent States
CM	Committee of Ministers (of the Council of Europe)
CoE/COE	Council of Europe
CPT	European Committee for the Prevention of Torture and Inhuman or Degrading Treatment or Punishment
CSCE	Conference on Security and Co-operation in Europe
EBRD	European Bank for Reconstruction and Development
EC	European Community
ECHR	European Convention on Human Rights (also known as: the Convention for the Protection of Human Rights and Fundamental Freedoms)
ECML	European Centre for Modern Languages
ECRI	European Commission against Racism and Intolerance of the Council of Europe
ECSC	European Coal and Steel Community
ECSR	European Committee of Social Rights
ECtHR	European Court of Human Rights
EDQM	European Directorate for the Quality of Medicines and Health Care
EEC	European Economic Community
ENTO	European Network of Training Organisations

List of Abbreviations

EP	European Parliament
EPAS	Enlarged Partial Agreement on Sport
ETUC	European Trade Union Confederation
EU	European Union
EUF/UEF	European Union of Federalists
GRECO	Group of States Against Corruption
HCNM	High Commissioner on National Minorities
ICRC	International Committee of the Red Cross
ILO	International Labour Organization
INGO	International Non-governmental Organization
IOE	International Organization of Employers
IPU	Inter-Parliamentary Union
ISESCO	The Islamic Educational, Scientific and Cultural Organization
LDA	Local Democracy Agencies
MONEYVAL	Committee of Experts on the Evaluation of Anti-money Laundering Measures and the Financing of Terrorism
MP	Members of Parliament
NALAG	National Association of Local Authorities of Georgia
NATO	North Atlantic Treaty Organization
NCPs	Neighbourhood Co-operation Priorities
NGO	Non-governmental Organization
NPM	National Preventive Mechanism
OECD	Organisation for Economic Co-operation and Development
OEEC	Organization for European Economic Co-operation, forerunner of the OECD
OHCHR	United Nations Office of the High Commissioner for Human Rights
OPCAT	Optional Protocol to the United Nations Convention against Torture
OSCE	Organization for Security and Co-operation in Europe
PACE	Parliamentary Assembly of the Council of Europe
UK	United Kingdom of Great Britain
UN	United Nations
UNECE	United Nations Economic Commission for Europe
UNESCO	United Nations Educational, Scientific and Cultural Organization
UNGA	United Nations General Assembly
UNHCHR	United Nations High Commissioner for Human Rights
UNHCR	United Nations High Commission for Refugees
UNICE	Union of Industrial and Employers' Confederations of Europe
UNICEF	United Nations International Children's Emergency Fund

UniDem	Universities for Democracy
UNMIBH	United Nations Mission to Bosnia and Herzegovina
UNMIK	United Nations Interim Administration Mission in Kosovo
US	United States
WADA	World Anti-doping Agency
WEU	Western European Union
WHO	World Health Organization
WW I	First World War
WW II	Second World War

List of Abbreviations

Preface

Reading up on the work of an international organization such as the CoE can be a daunting task. All the more reason therefore to be grateful when people who work for, or are otherwise connected with, that organization pen their personal views on its various challenges. Each contribution in this collection has a different aim and outlook, resulting in an enriching and entertaining mosaic illustrating the organization's 'soul', 'vision' and surrounding reality better than could any statute or activities report.

The reader will understand the organization's origin, evolution and functioning, as the latter has been formed and reformed over its six decades of existence – influenced by, and influencing, a continent in dizzyingly rapid flux.

And how this Europe of ours has indeed changed during this time: the icy, terrifying division of the Cold War; the first East-West contacts in the 'détente' decades of the 1960s and 1970s; the renewed tensions of the 1980s; and, finally, the fall of the Berlin Wall and the entirely new – and altogether more promising – Europe of today.

Throughout these times the values guiding the CoE – democracy, human rights and the rule of law – have stood as beacons for the people of Europe, who know that without them international peace and prosperity are doomed to fail. The contribution of the CoE to the promotion and strengthening of these values – working in co-operation with other international institutions and in particular the EU and the Organization for Security and Co-operation in Europe (OSCE) – has been and continues to be essential.

What makes this book so interesting is that it focuses as much on what remains to be done as on what has been achieved. The chapters on bodies such as the European Committee for the Prevention of Torture (CPT), the CoE Commissioner for Human Rights, the Venice Commission and the Congress of Local and Regional Authorities – all created by the Council's two statutory organs, the Committee of Ministers (CM) and the Parliamentary Assembly – clearly illustrate how these were responses to new realities and challenges, aiming to build a more just, open and free society. As we all know, the values we cherish have to be defended by each one of us, and by every generation. New challenges arise along Europe's path every day, and the CoE exists precisely in order to tackle them.

To read the various essays that make up this collection, written by people who go about their business on Europe's behalf with enthusiasm and commitment, has been a real pleasure for me, as I am sure it will be for readers. In brief, to understand the work of the CoE is to understand the yearnings of a continent intent on overcoming its tragic and divided past, and heading for a future where, though united, it will retain its diversity.

To conclude – and in recognition of the fact that an undertaking as important as this book will always have a personal initiative at its origin – I wish to thank Tanja Kleinsorge for having started it all and seen it through so successfully together with her many co-writers – too many to mention by name but too worthy not to thank collectively.

Mateo Sorinas Balfegó
Former Secretary General of the Parliamentary Assembly of the Council of Europe

General Introduction

Irena Guidikova

§1. A Definition of Europe

1. 'Europe' is a wild card in contemporary geopolitics. Whether used as a buzzword or as a swearword – no populist speech or learned analysis of global politics or economics can overlook the 'phenomenon Europe' and the weight of … well, how many countries and how many million Europeans?

To answer this question, let us look at some point in 'the beginning' of 1949, 70 years ago. A continent was to be rebuilt from the wreckage of the war through the vision of a few grand statesmen and the will of millions of people. A forum was to be created for the dialogue of nations against the background of growing East-West tensions. A symbol was to be found to seal the newfound hope for European unity. The Council of Europe (CoE) was born; the flag with the twelve stars (in 1955) and the Ode of Joy (in 1971) became the landmarks of a continent reunited.[2]

2. With the birth of the CoE, the concept of 'co-operation' won – temporarily – over the concept of 'integration'. Belgium, France, Luxembourg, the Netherlands and the United Kingdom (UK), accompanied by Ireland, Italy, Denmark, Norway and Sweden signed the Founding Treaty (Statute) of the CoE. The organization had an ambitious mandate: it had to do no less than 'achieve a greater unity between its Members for the purpose of safeguarding and realizing the ideals and principles which are their common heritage, and facilitating their economic and social progress'. This first 'unification experiment' proved so successful in rebuilding trust between formerly divided countries that only six years later the most ardent supporters of integration – Belgium, France, Italy, Luxembourg, the Netherlands and the Federal Republic of Germany – signed, on 9 May 1951, the Treaty Establishing the European Community (EC).

2. In 1983, the European Parliament in turn adopted the flag devised by the Council of Europe and recommended that it become the European Communities' emblem. The European Council gave its approval in June 1985. With the Council of Europe's consent, the Communities' institutions began to use the flag at the beginning of 1986.

3. Ever since, these two strands of Europe's modern biography have coexisted, one seeking unity, the other a union – to the puzzlement of citizens constantly bombarded with a simplistic notion of one 'Europe'. In the era marked by 'Brexit' and family quarrels around refugee quotas which threaten to break down the European Union (EU), some see a reform making the EU more like the CoE – an organization of NATIONS (in other words, an intergovernmental alliance, not a supranational entity) – as the key to Europe's survival.

Clearly, there is some logic in speaking about Europe when referring to the ultimate goal, a goal which is common to the CoE and the EU: lasting peace and prosperity on a continental scale. But while political and economic integration pursued by the EU are a fast but risky track to this goal (when the economy does not deliver growth and more welfare for all, the EU's democratic deficits come to the fore and citizens demand more say, with all the risks of populist mobilization this entails), the CoE represents the slow, incremental, organic process of joining at the grassroots – the building of Europe in the hearts and minds of its people.

4. Both approaches are legitimate and effective, albeit in different areas. Deep integration works better in fields such as competition or industrial policies where regulatory instruments can determine 'the rules of the game'. Less intrusive means such as international treaties, peer reviews and pressure, training and good practice – the CoE's tools *par excellence* – are probably more suitable when it comes to reinforcing citizenship and democratic governance. Of course, this division is somewhat artificial and simplistic. The CoE has binding, directly executable treaties such as the European Convention on Human Rights (ECHR), while the EU often has recourse to 'soft standards'. But the basic difference of approach, of a philosophy of being and action, is nevertheless there.

5. Let's try a somewhat unexpected, hopefully non-offensive analogy. While joining the CoE can be compared to joining a self-help group – you seek to share and learn from others while remaining in full control of your life – joining the EU can probably be compared to joining a monastic order – you share a belief and abandon, in its name – your will and possessions.

Like self-help groups, the CoE functions on the principles of trust and solidarity. Mimicking the complex systems of governance in its Member States, it involves an array of interconnected institutions: a Committee of Ministers (CM), a Parliamentary Assembly, a Congress of Local and Regional Authorities, an International Non-governmental Organization (INGO) conference. A Development Bank, a Human Rights Commissioner and a set of technical monitoring and co-operation bodies complete the picture.

6. But above all, Europe's watchdog of human rights and fundamental freedoms, the CoE hosts the unique mechanism for human rights' protection, which is the European Court of Human Rights (ECtHR).

Indeed, to many Europeans, the CoE is little more than the ECtHR. The Court is a key pillar in the CoE's edifice. But the mandate and endeavours of the organization throughout its six decades of existence testify to a much broader agenda and contribution.

§2. European Integration Based on Shared Values

7. The CoE has been a pioneer in many critical areas for European integration. It has conceived and developed the notion of a European cultural identity, enshrined in the European Cultural Convention, which entered into force only a few years after the creation of the organization itself.

The very notion of the CoE is based on the idea of a European cultural identity, which represents the countries' common heritage. Europe is a land of many cultures and its cultural diversity is constantly enriched through the input of people coming from other continents. The CoE seeks to convey the notion of pride of diversity and its value for peace, prosperity and social cohesion.

8. The CoE believes that the common cultural tradition of all countries in Europe gives them the potential to develop structures and practices, which would qualify them for membership in the club of democracies. Before becoming members of the CoE, in the framework of the European Cultural Convention (work on cultural, educational and youth policy, multilateral projects, events and exchanges) countries in Central and Eastern Europe developed a political culture guaranteeing the respect for human rights and the rule of law. Accession to the European Cultural Convention was the 'anti-chamber' – the first step towards the integration of new democracies in Central and Eastern Europe.

9. In multicultural societies, the CoE is encouraging the development of public policies, which stimulate creativity and ensure access to cultural life for all. It is working towards a strategic policy framework for the management of cultural diversity as a means for sustainable social and human development.

§3. The CoE as a Standard-Setting Organization

10. The CoE can be described as a standard-setting organization, although these standards do not all have a binding character. Over 200 international treaties, hundreds of recommendations and policy guidelines provide precious advice to public authorities in a range of areas – from animal welfare to the fight against corruption, cybercrime and counterfeit medicine. The CoE has developed, through the years, a recognized expertise in a range of fields such as anti-corruption and money laundering, the protection of national minorities, social cohesion, the protection of cultural heritage and diversity, quality standards in education, intercultural youth work and exchanges. More recently, the Council has ventured into emerging fields such as hate speech and discrimination, including the rights of sexual minorities, cybercrime, bioethics, trafficking in human beings and organs, as well as e-voting, and has assumed global leadership in areas of traditional concern where adequate instruments and concerted policy action was lacking, such as protecting women and children from violence. The challenges of globalization and the information society require constant adaptation of the institutions of governance and public policies to ensure that European societies uphold their fundamental values. A key strength for the Council is its ability to translate shared values and principles into legal standards, shaping a European legal space which is in the process of gradually being extended to Europe's neighbourhood and even beyond, with most new Conventions drafted by the Council being open to countries worldwide.

11. Some examples of the CoE's pioneering work concern the protection of victims of trafficking in human beings, and dealing with public provocation to commit acts of terrorism and the recruitment and training of terrorists as well as combating violence against women and domestic violence, and Roma inclusion. In some fields, such as diversity management, the CoE has truly pioneered flagship initiatives such as Intercultural cities which are global in scope and combine policy-standards development with 'soft monitoring' of policy implementation.

The negotiation of standards is a complex process since they often seek to strike a balance between concerns about security/order and the protection of human rights. Their ratification and implementation – which are far from being guaranteed – are a test for the vitality of European countries' attachment to the values of human rights and dignity. The CoE is constantly taking up new challenges facing its Member States, such as match-fixing, and negotiates treaties or other instruments to deal with them. In areas of utmost global importance and high complexity such as the governance of the Internet and artificial intelligence, the CoE is leading as a watchdog, making sure that human rights standards count in global debates and agreements. For instance, the CoE has been instrumental in bringing a strong Human Rights dimension to the Global Compact on Refugees.

12. Although it has not really established formal standards in this respect, the CoE monitors and assists democratic development and good governance. This monitoring is shared between the Organization's key bodies – the CM, the Parliamentary Assembly and the Congress of Local and Regional Authorities. The Venice Commission is the CoE's advisory body on constitutional matters. It also helps to ensure the dissemination and consolidation of a common constitutional heritage and provides 'emergency constitutional aid' to states in transition. The CoE is also increasingly acting as a leading organization in the field of democracy innovation and change, identifying, analysing and diffusing ideas and initiatives which are likely to ensure democratic stability in the era of mobile communications, social media and global population movements. The World Forum for Democracy is one of the Organization's key actions in this respect, and its Participatory Democracy Incubator encourages the adoption of deliberative and participatory democracy practice in cities across the continent.

13. One of the CoE's key challenges is to strengthen democratic culture and transmit European values to the next generations. It is necessary to safeguard the fundamental principles of liberal democracy and transmit them to future generations. While its basic principles remain unchanged, institutions and practices of democracy must follow the evolution of European societies. The future of democracy depends on its capacity to adapt to a world of growing interdependence and rapid socio-cultural changes, to provide new opportunities for citizen participation, to increase the transparency of decision-making and the accountability of public authorities. The first reports by the Secretary General on the State of democracy, human rights and the rule of law in Europe, issued in April 2014 and April 2015 respectively, have marked a new stage of maturity and consolidation of the work of the CoE in its main fields of action. The reports are a consolidated analysis of human rights, democracy and the rule of law in Europe, based on the findings of the CoE's monitoring bodies and acts as a basis for determining the Organization's future priorities.

§4. The Human Dimension of the CoE

14. Citizens of all ages and walks of life participate in many aspects of the CoE's work – a proof that Europe's oldest project for continental unity is fundamentally about people and their commitment to a common future.

The 'human dimension' of the CoE's work is fundamental. Laws and institutions have no firm foundation if people are not ready to acknowledge their intrinsic value. The CoE's flagship projects like the European Year on Citizenship through Education, or the youth campaigns 'All different – all equal', have been designed to reach a broad range of actors and mobilize them to ensure the endurance of a democratic and human rights culture and the uprooting of racism, xenophobia, anti-Semitism, Islamophobia and all other forms of intolerance. The Council's Forum on the Future of Democracy has become a platform for exchange, innovation and inspiration for modernizing democratic practice, for broadening and deepening democracy.

15. Several major organizations and institutions pursue similar goals on the European scene. The CoE, the EU and the OSCE all have broad, sometimes overlapping mandates. All these organizations are naturally keen to react and adapt to the developments of the modern world, and therefore to continuously enlarge their fields of action. This fact of life does create ambiguity and uncertainty. One can even sometimes think of an identity crisis – illustrated by the fate of the European Constitution. But identity crises are not really the issue – honestly, who can possibly insist that people must understand that the CoE and the European Council are totally separate institutions? It is not about existential fears either – does it really matter that a couple of thousand international civil servants and several hundred thousand, CoE 'stakeholders' (governmental experts, Members of Parliament (MPs), local elected representatives and Non-governmental Organization (NGO) members directly involved in CoE activities) worry that the Council's generous, but vague mandate is being gradually eroded by the EU?

§5. The CoE and Other European Clubs

16. The real issue is that the EU is, and will remain for a long time, a club excluding some countries belonging to the European continent. And that European culture, outlook, values, world view, has a clear political meaning in the context of a world composed of 'civilizations'. Is there a reason to reduce Europe to twenty-eight when speaking about human rights, democracy and the value of diversity?

Does it matter whether behind these notions stand 500 or 800 million citizens? The EU is sometimes accused of having neglected its humanist, democratic values for the harsh realities of the common market. An increasingly closer partnership between the CoE and the EU is both giving the CoE the means to support democratic consolidation and reforms in its newer Member States, which are not EU members, and is giving the Union new credibility and operational capacity in the field of human rights and democracy.

17. Sometimes, there can be an impression that there is a rivalry and competition in the family of European institutions. But why should the pluralism of platforms for European political dialogue and co-operation be in itself a problem? Both the CoE and the OSCE are working in areas such as democratic elections, the fight against racism or trafficking in human beings. Apart from the obvious differences of membership, working methods and instruments, the diversity of European organizations and institutions encourages, a priori, the pluralism of ideas and approaches. The unresolved issues continent- and worldwide are sufficiently broad and complex to leave room for the initiative, experimentation and contributions of different organizations.

18. Of course, there is a limit to the resources our societies can devote to European co-operation and integration infrastructure. But a monolithic European architecture can quickly lead to dogmatism – the complex problems of our time require flexibility and a variety of platforms for co-operation. Europe needs an architecture which helps overcome divisions which still persist on our continent. This architecture should enable Europe to carry out a political dialogue with other parts of the world, establish close relations of confidence with its neighbours and position itself clearly as a moral leader committed to the building of a peaceful and sustainable future for an increasingly interdependent world.

§6. Accomplishing the Task of Pan-European Unity

19. The CoE is accomplishing the challenging task of pan-European unity in the context of massive geopolitical reshuffling. This experience could be instrumental in developing new partnerships with Europe's neighbouring regions. The CoE has demonstrated an astonishing capacity to grasp the challenges of a rapidly changing geopolitical environment, and to respond to them timely and effectively, while adapting its structures and methods to the new requirements. The democratic transformation of Central and Eastern Europe led not only to a spectacular increase in the CoE Member States which grew from twenty-one to forty-seven in only fifteen years. It also helped the CoE to evolve from a detached standard-setter, the guardian of a pan-European legal space, into an organization capable of promoting development and change through direct involvement with institutions and civil society organizations. The Council is now facing an illiberal slideback in some of its oldest members, and among the most solid of the continent's democracies. To prevent this populist surge from undermining the democratic institutions and individual freedoms, the Organization needs to renew its discourse and seek new alliances with forces beyond Member States – with businesses, civil society and cities.

20. To convey Europe's humanistic legacy and our shared values to all members of European societies and beyond, to coin collective responses to the challenges of a new century so as to enable everyone to live in security, freedom and dignity: such is the mandate of the CoE for the coming years.

Part I. The Process that Led to the Creation of the CoE and Its Assembly

Mario Heinrich

§1. Introduction

21. The COE of 1949 was the first political Organization of Europe. It was part of a quartet of four organizations including the Brussels Treaty Organisation (later the Western European Union (WEU)), the Organization for European Economic Co-operation (OEEC) (later the Organisation for Economic Co-operation and Development (OECD)) and North Atlantic Treaty Organization (NATO) which the Western Allies set up after no agreement on the reconstruction of Greater Europe in the fields of economy and security could be reached with the Soviet Union between the Potsdam Conference and the end of 1947. The CoE is also the first treaty-based International Organization into which a Parliamentary Assembly composed of members of national parliaments was integrated as a statutory organ. That is why, of all the CoE's bodies, the Assembly was the most original one. Strasbourg was chosen as the seat of the CoE and its Assembly. Thus, the success story of European parliamentarism began in Strasbourg in August 1949.

It may be added that the COE was also characteristic for the 'Anglo-French period' (mainly 1947–1950) of the process of creating European unity.

§2. Proposals Made for a European Organization or a European Assembly Before the Second World War

I. Projects and Developments Before the Twentieth Century

22. It is not easy to retrace who made the first serious proposal to create a COE and a European Parliamentary Assembly. When Winston Churchill made his statement as Honorary President of the Congress of Europe in The Hague in May 1948, he spoke about where the idea of United Europe had originated and said:

> There are many valid modern patents. But we may all yield our pretensions to King Henry of Navarre, King of France who with his great Minister Sully between the years 1600 and 1607 laboured to set up a permanent committee

(Council) representing the fifteen […] leading Christian states of Europe. This body was to act as arbitrator on all questions concerning religious conflict, national frontiers, internal disturbances and common action against any danger from the East which in those days meant Turks. This he called 'The Grand Design'. We are the servants of the Grand Design.[3]

23. The permanent committee or Council ('Conseil Général de l'Europe'[4]) and the subordinate provincial councils according to the Sully Plan may have inspired the name of European Council or COE.[5] While it is true that one or two of the older European political projects, dating from before the nineteenth century (e.g., that of William Penn of 1693), mentioned a European Diet (Parliament),[6] they had no chance of being implemented.

In connection with the efforts to achieve a new European order[7] after 1814/15 (Vienna Congress) there was agreement to conclude a Quadripartite Alliance and on holding, when appropriate, meetings to discuss matters of common interest and measures aiming *inter alia* at preserving peace in Europe and the prosperity of the people. In 1818, this Alliance was enlarged to include France. Count Metternich, one of the main architects of this system, referred to a moral solidarity among the Powers. One of his ideas was to create in Vienna a 'Centre d'information' as a kind of permanent organization. In some jokes he was called 'The Secretary General of Europe'.[8] The guiding principle of the Alliance was the balance of power, a fixed relationship of forces between the five Great Powers. They were to act as a 'Directoire' of Europe or as a 'European Council'. This system was restoration with monarchy shielding itself against revolutionary assault by establishing a firm international order (Franco Valsecchi). But no great power then had proposed to set up any kind of European Organization, least of all an Assembly. François Mitterrand[9] has referred to the Congress of Vienna as a remodelling of the European map without caring about people and their aspirations.

---

3. Already on 13 Dec. 1940, Churchill had referred to the 'Grand Design', *see* below.
4. Philippe Dieudonné, *Un Conseil de l'Europe au XVIIe siècle in 'Notre Europe' (periodical)*, Nos 9–10 (Strasbourg: Société européenne d'Editions et de Publications, 1951), 69–73, at 72.
5. Carl Jacob Burckhardt, *Vier historische Betrachtungen* (Zürich: Manesse Verlag, 1953), 26, 27; *European Movement (editor) and the Council of Europe* (London: Hutchinson & Co. Publishers, 1950), 24.
6. Lord Gladwyn, *The European Idea* (London: Weidenfeld & Nicolson, 1966), 29.
7. Interestingly, on the island of St-Helena, Napoleon had tried to justify his work as follows: the object of his vast conquests had been to build a new Europe, a Europe of national states. His aim had been to emancipate the peoples, to liberate nationalities. Only by a new order based on nationality could the balance of power […] be established […]: 'My reign is over and my system discarded, but there can be no stability in Europe save by an agglomeration of the great peoples' (Mémorial de Sainte-Hélène, 11 Nov. 1816); for more details *see* the report by Professor Franco Valsecchi for the Council of Europe: Working Group on History and Political Institutions (Doc. TR/Etude (55)2, 5 and 6).
8. Werner Näf, 'Versuche gesamteuropäischer Organisation und Politik in den ersten Jahrzehnten des 19. Jahrhunderts', in *Staat und Staatsgedanke, Vorträge zur neueren Geschichte* (Bern: Stümpfli Verlag, 1935). Further details are to be found in: Georges-Henri Soutou, *L'Europe de 1815 à nos jours*, 2nd edn (Paris: Presses Universitaires de France, 2009) and in Jacques-Alain de Sédouy, *Le concert européen, aux origines de l'Europe, 1814–1914* (Paris: Éditions Fayard, 2009).
9. Opening speech at the Conference on Security and Co-operation in Europe, Paris, 19 Nov. 1990.

24. Conscious of a European mission, the French Emperor Napoleon III considered the Congress of Paris of 1856 to settle the Crimean War as a kind of peace tribunal to cure Europe of her ills. Following the conclusion of Alliances among members of the European Concert and the appearance of non-European powers such as America, the Concert was re-aligned in groups with attachments outside Europe, foreshadowing a system no longer European, but worldwide (Franco Valsecchi). Also in the nineteenth century there were several private initiatives for more unity in Europe, including by Victor Hugo.

25. According to several authors 'by 1870 no more intergovernmental treaty-based relations existed between the major States, capable of forming Europe as a whole. These States were rather isolated, being placed side by side and the power game was open'.[10] Interestingly, already in 1870s and 1880s proposals of different importance were made for international parliamentary assemblies and even a Senate representing the national parliaments of Europe.[11] In particular the proposals by Victor Hugo were well received. However, all these ideas and proposals were never officially supported by European Governments.[12] In 1889, the Inter-Parliamentary Union (IPU) was created and in 1905 the IPU appointed a committee to consider the question of an international parliament. Six years later, in 1911, the Empire Parliamentary Association was established, which became the Commonwealth Parliamentary Association in 1948.

II. The Situation after the First World War

26. After the First World War (WW I), the idea of a European Organization was germinating. However, the victorious powers gave preference to the League of Nations which was not fully representative at world level, as great powers like the United States (US) and (initially) the Soviet Union were not a member of it. At its peak, League membership rose to sixty-three States, but in the course of its existence seventeen States either withdrew or were expelled, including Japan, Germany, Italy and the USSR. Proposals of the UK and the South African Prime Minister Smuts for integrating a kind of parliamentary Assembly in the League, but also a draft for a covenant suggesting a world parliament, did not materialize.[13] For US President Wilson it was important to involve public opinion in the work of the League, but he did not give details how this should be done.[14]

27. According to Lord Gladwyn[15] (Gladwyn Jebb), the lack of efficiency of the League of Nations became ever more evident and this made thoughts turn again to

10. Werner Näf, *Abrüstungsverhandlungen im Jahr 1931* (Bern: Lang, 1931).
11. Franco Valsecchi in Council of Europe document TR/Etude (55)2, 18.
12. L'idée de l'Europe avant 1914 by Professor du Réau, at the French Senate Colloquy on 'L'Europe au Parlement, de Victor Hugo à nos jours' (Paris, 6 Apr. 2007), 24 of the report of the Colloquy.
13. For the details *see* Per Fischer, Europarat und parlamentarische Aussenpolitik, München 1962, 16–20.
14. Mount Vernon speech of 4 Jul. 1918.
15. Lord Gladwyn, *The European Idea* (London: Weidenfeld & Nicholson, 1966), 38.

the possibility of a purely European arrangement involving some elements of federalism. This concept was promoted mainly by Count Coudenhove-Kalergi from 1922 and by French and British intellectuals. In 1923, Coudenhove-Kalergi published a remarkable book on 'Pan-Europa' and created a Pan-European Union (Movement). He proposed a federal system not dissimilar to that of the US and hoped to persuade national parliaments to renounce the necessary degree of sovereignty. In order to achieve this, he planned to educate public opinion. By 1925, Edouard Herriot (later also Aristide Briand), Léon Blum, Konrad Adenauer and Paul Löbe, Karl Renner, and President Benes were members of the Paneuropa-Union.

III. The Years of Peace Diplomacy in Europe (1925–1933): The League of Nations and European Organization

28. The first serious proposal at official level for a European Organization in liaison with the League of Nations was made by Edouard Herriot (French Prime Minister, Minister and, in August 1949, first (provisional) President of the Parliamentary Assembly of the Council of Europe (PACE)) in 1924 and, in particular, on 25 January 1925, before the then French Chamber of Deputies. He said:

> It is my greatest wish to see the realisation of the United States of Europe. And if I have devoted my energies [...] to the League of Nations, I have done so because in this great institution I have seen the first rough draft of the United States of Europe.

In a speech before the Assembly of the League of Nations on 5 September 1929, the French Prime Minister and Foreign Minister Aristide Briand made the following proposal:

> I think that among the peoples constituting geographic groups, like the peoples of Europe, there should be some kind of federal bond. It should be possible for them to get into touch at any time, to confer about their interests to agree on joint resolutions and to establish among them a bond of solidarity which will enable them, if need be, to meet any grave emergency that may arise. That is the link I want to forge.

29. When presenting his plan, Briand apologized for his boldness in putting the problem of a European Federation before the League.[16] The underlying expectations of Briand's plan were to achieve a better organization of Europe and European stability in the economic and political fields and to promote a kind of European Germany.[17] Briand was asked to prepare a memorandum for the governments, which would then be discussed in the Assembly of the League. The preamble of Briand's memorandum of 1 May 1930 refers to the principle of a moral European unity

---

16. Wilhelm Cornides, 'Der Strassburger Europarat in der Perspektive der Vorschläge Briands von 1929', *Europa-Archiv* 17 (1949): 2417.
17. Gérard Unger, *Aristide Briand – le ferme conciliateur* (Paris: Éditions Fayard, 2005), 558, 559.

and underlines the collective responsibility in view of the dangers which threaten European peace from a political, economic and social angle because of the general state of non-coordination of Europe's general economy. Briand refers to a permanent regime of conventional solidarity in the form of a regional understanding under the Covenant of the League of Nations.

30. The Treaty to be elaborated should create a 'European Conference', composed of representatives of all twenty-six European Member States of the League, a permanent political committee as executive organ and a secretariat with the seat in Geneva. The treaty was to be very concise and express well the objectives of:

- the peaceful organization of Europe;
- the examination of all questions which interest in the first line the community of European peoples; and
- the possible adoption of a common policy.

In order to show the subordination of the European Federation under the League of Nations, the Treaty was initially to be open to accession by European States of the League of Nations only. Furthermore the treaty was to confirm the sovereignty of the States.

31. A prominent place is given in Briand's memorandum to the question of security and to the fear of the weakest nations to be dominated by the industrialized countries. The text advocates a European Union to be followed by a common market. Furthermore, the memorandum proposes spheres for European co-operation and one of these fields is inter-parliamentary relations. Most replies by governments to Briand's memorandum were disappointing.[18] On a proposal from France and Yugoslavia, the governments finally accepted to discuss the plan in the Assembly of the League of Nations under the condition that it no longer refers to a federal bond or a European Union but to a close co-operation between European Governments. A study commission for European Union was appointed on 17 September 1930. It was chaired by Briand almost until his death in March 1932 and then, for some months, by Herriot, before it discontinued its work in the same year. The committee's work focussed on economic questions and two international conferences were organized on wheat trade. Furthermore, the committee dealt with the project of a customs union between Austria and Germany which was abandoned in September 1931 after having met with considerable opposition.

32. The Briand Plan does not refer to any European parliamentary Assembly. Some indications on the parliamentary dimension of European relations at that time

18. For the details *see* Antoine Fleury & Lubor Jilek, *Le plan Briand d'Union féderale européenne* (Bern: Éditions Lang, 1998) and the Colloquy on 'L'Europe au parlement, de Victor Hugo à nos jours' organized in the French Senate on 6 Apr. 2007, and in particular the lectures on 'Briand and Europe' and 'the Europe of the League of Nations'.

are contained in the book entitled 'Europe' (1930) by Edouard Herriot. He mentioned in addition to the co-operation in the IPU, the contacts among parliamentarians of Northern Europe, the inclusion of parliamentarians in governmental delegations to international meetings (e.g., in delegations to the Assembly of the League of Nations, such as UK Labour M.P. Barnes in the first Assembly) and the co-operation of the services for foreign documentation of national parliaments.

33. The very limited results achieved by the plan are mainly explained[19] by the mistrust of the governments not wishing to abandon even small parts of their sovereignty. Furthermore it is argued that the years 1926/1927 would have been much more favourable for a follow-up to the plan than 1930 which was marked by the economic crisis. Also by 1930, the situation in Germany had changed (death of Stresemann in October 1929, success of the opposition in the German elections of 1930).

IV. Some Considerations on the Echo of the Briand Plan and Further Action in Favour of Peace and Co-operation in Europe until WW II

34. From 1932 one finds hardly any appeals of active European statesmen for a united Europe. At the moment where the European idea proved impossible to be realized among the European Member States of the League of Nations, it became popular and had an impact at regional level. Several private Organizations were set up in France, Switzerland and the UK such as the Federal Committee for European co-operation, the European Parliamentary Union, the European Customs Union, Europa-Union (Switzerland), Federal Union (UK). Also the intellectuals in several European countries and Coudenhove-Kalergi did not give up their European dreams and projects. Already in an Article of 1933 on European Human Rights Coudenhove-Kalergi underlined that the European idea was liberty, that the new Europe claimed European human rights and that the treatment of minority rights was a central problem of European renewal.[20]

35. In February 1933, a Permanent Council of the Entente between Yugoslavia, Czechoslovakia and Romania was set up, in 1934 a Balkan Entente was created (Yugoslavia, Greece, Romania, Turkey) and in the same year the Baltic Council (Estonia, Latvia, Lithuania) became operational. In connection with the preparatory work for the CoE, Briand was quite often referred to. At least two German articles deal with the Briand Plan's influence on the CoE project.[21] Furthermore, Edouard Bonnefous[22] argues that Briand had in mind a 'European Council'. However, there

19. Edouard Bonnefous, *L'idée européenne et sa réalisation* (Paris: Editions du Grand Siècle, 1950), 68.
20. In *Paneuropa*, No. 4/1933, 97–101.
21. Ellinor von Puttkamer, 'Der Briand Plan – Vorbote der europäischen Einigung?', in *Festschrift für Carl Friedrich Ophüls aus Anlass seines 70. Geburtstags*, ed. Hallstein, Ophüls & Schlochauer (Karlsruhe: Verlag C.F. Müller, 1965), ss 143–151; Wilhelm Cornides, 'Der Strassburger Europarat in der Perspektive der Vorschläge Briands von 1929', *Europa-Archiv* (1949): 2417–2420.
22. Edouard Bonnefous, *L'idée européenne et sa réalisation* (1950), 68.

is no reference to be found to such a 'Council' in the generally available material of the League of Nations and in the standard biographies on Briand. A similarity between the Briand Plan and the CoE is that for both projects a study commission for European Union was set up, chaired in both cases (at least temporarily) by Edouard Herriot.

36. From 1937, the action for peace in Europe and in the world by the League of Nations and President Roosevelt (Chicago speech on peace-loving nations) and of the churches was important. March 1937 saw two major encyclicals of Pope Pius XI, one entitled 'with deep anxiety' (concerning Germany) and the other 'divini redemptoris' (concerning atheistic communism). At an international conference in Oxford in July 1937, a Christian Ecumenical Organization was created, called the World Council of Churches. The conference affirmed that the principle of absolute sovereignty of state or nation and as ultimate standard of judgment and conduct is incompatible with the Church's belief in the sovereignty of Jesus Christ alone.

37. On 17 May 1939, Coudenhove-Kalergi's Paneuropa-Union organized a major meeting in Paris. One of the participants, Duff Cooper, former First Lord of the Admiralty and later again Minister in the UK War Cabinet, underlined the need for a European Union, based on France and the UK, which shared a common destiny. Coudenhove-Kalergi then insisted on a moral renewal of Europe to vanquish the political and economic crisis.[23]

§3. Initiatives Taken During WW II until the Potsdam Conference

I. General

38. The outbreak of the Second World War (WW II) was the event which made the view prevail that Europe must be united, particularly in the UK. As from 1939, the governments of the US[24] and the UK[25] either defined war aims or commissioned preparatory work for a post-war order. This included also the idea of a European Organization ('a European Council with a common fund contributed by its member states') referred to as early as 3 November 1939 in an article by a 'special correspondent' (Max Nicholson) in *The Times*.[26] It favoured a movement towards a federal solution as an escape from the necessity of fighting a major European war

23. Richard Coudenhove-Kalergi, *Kampf um Europa* (Zürich: Atlantis Verlag, 1949), 211; in his article 'La paix de demain' in Politique étrangère No. 4/1939, Coudenhove-Kalergi proposes that Europe should return to the traditional concept of European values and to the principles of democracy, two of which should apply in the whole of Europe: the control of governments by the people and the respect of human rights; only in that case a Europe united by the concept of common civilization could develop.
24. Harley A. Notte, *Postwar Foreign Policy Preparation 1939–1945* (Washington: 1949), 458. In January 1940, a special committee was established to handle post-war planning.
25. *The Memoirs of Lord Gladwyn*, (London, 1972), 95.
26. IIn a broader European context also the radio addresses by Lord Halifax and Prime Minister Chamberlain of November 1939 are of interest.

every twenty-five years. Nicholson considered that it was the task of Britain and France to assert the tested values of Western civilization and to give new life to its cultural inheritance from Greece and Rome, from Christianity and modern science. The maintenance of inheritance may, according to Nicholson, be said to hang on four principles:

- the upholding of freedom of opinion, faith, and speech;
- the upholding of the rule of law, both nationally and internationally;
- the use of the state as an instrument not of domination but of public service; and
- the raising of standards of life and of living, universally and not merely for a restricted group.

Interestingly, the manifesto on the peace aims of the UK Labour Party,[27] refers to a new world order and not to a European Organization:[28]

> The Peace settlement must establish a new association or Commonwealth of States the collective authority of which must transcend, over a proper sphere, the sovereign rights of separate States. […]. The present close co-operation between the British Commonwealth, France and their allies in the political and economic spheres should be the nucleus of this wider association, membership of which should be open and advantageous to all nations […] great and small […].

39. It would not appear that in that context the proposal of a European Parliament or Assembly was made. However, in the remarkable British literature on a European Federation or Organization between 1939 and 1941 several authors (scientists, members of research institutes, writers on politics) presented in 1939/1940 draft constitutions for a federation including a federal parliament ('People's House', European second chamber, European Assembly, European Parliament) or general projects for a Federation with a parliament.[29]

40. Archbishop William Temple of York (and then Canterbury) proposed that the League of Nations should include regional (continental) models for the whole continent. According to Philip M.H. Bell and John Pinder,[30] a wide discussion on a

27. The Times of 9 Feb. 1940, 8.
28. *See* however, a text by Clement Attlee, Leader of the Labour Party, of November 1939 which contains the sentence 'Europe must federate or perish,' quoted in Walter Lipgens (ed.), *Documents on the History of the European Integration Volume 2, Plans for European Union in Great Britain and in Exile, 1939–45* (Berlin & New York: De Gruyter Verlag, 1986), 167.
29. Ivor Jennings, 91; Otto Kahn-Freund, 99; Ronald Mackay (who later become a member of the CoE Assembly), 105; William Beveridge, 89; Margaret Storm Jameson, 173; *see also* Pinder, 26; all these references are included in: Documents on the History of the European Integration vol. 2, edited by Walter Lipgens.
30. Lipgens, 24.

European Federation was thought desirable to inspire public opinion and to stimulate support for the war by offering the British people a vision of the post-war world. Furthermore, it was hoped to enlist the support of neutrals by displaying the ideals for which the Allies were fighting.

41. It is recalled that in connection with the reflections on a European Federation or Organization, the idea of elaborating an international or European bill of rights took shape. Furthermore, among the basic principles for these federations with federal parliaments[31] are to be found common civilization and the common foundation of European culture, the need of a democratic constitution of Member States.[32] It is not necessary and possible to describe all proposals and currents which were relevant concerning European reorganization after the war. However, some additional information will be given on the planning and other considerations at the level of the UK and US Governments, of France and of some other selected international actors.

II. The UK, France, the US and the Soviet Union (1939–1941)

A. The UK and France

42. The UK influence on preparing and building post-war Europe was probably predominant until 1950. A theme, which in 1939/1940 seemed to strengthen the cause of European unification, was the widespread belief that France and Britain were developing a close wartime union which would form a natural basis for a united Europe.[33] On the proposal of Jean Monnet, who was in London, and due to military developments, the UK made on 16 June 1940 a dramatic gesture to keep France in the war.

43. The British War Cabinet made an offer of 'indissoluble union' between Britain and France to the French Government in Tours. According to the draft declaration, France and Great Britain were no longer to be two nations but one Franco-British Union. During the war there was to be a single War Cabinet. The two parliaments were to be formally associated. France was to keep her available forces in the field, on the sea and in the air. However, the majority of the then French Government rejected the draft declaration as they believed that the war was already lost. Some experts see in this declaration the beginning of the European integration process at intergovernmental level. Those who looked for a wider European Federation found in the Union of France and England the only practical nucleus of their dream.[34]

31. Lipgens, 186.
32. Lipgens, 175, 183.
33. Philip M.H. Bell in Lipgens, 158.
34. Trevor Salmon & Sir William Nicoll, *Building European Union – A Documentary History and Analysis* (Manchester & New York, 1997), 16, 17.

In this connection it might be recalled that perhaps the first governmental plan of post-war co-operation was that announced by the UK and France on 28 March 1940. They agreed to continue after peace a community of action in all spheres to safeguard their security and to effect the reconstruction, with the assistance of other nations, of an international order which will ensure the liberty of peoples, respect for law and the maintenance of peace in Europe.[35]

44. In the UK War Aims' Committee, Leo S. Amery and Stafford Cripps made proposals for a COE.[36] In the War Cabinet, Prime Minister Winston Churchill proposed at least since 13 December 1940 a powerful CoE, composed of England, France, Italy, Spain and Prussia and of four Confederations in Northern Europe, Central Europe, for the Danube States and the Balkan States. The Council would be competent for the supreme legislation and it would be flanked by an Economic Council. All air-fleets of Member States would be internationalized and all members of the European Council would have to contribute to a European air-fleet. Russia would be included in a reorganization of the East and in this context the whole Asian problem would have to be dealt with. There should be no reparations. A difficult question was how to give the Council the possibility to sanction any member which had been condemned by the other members. This project was described as the 'Grand Design', similarly to the above-mentioned plan of Sully.[37]

45. After France fell in 1940 and in particular after 1941, when the Soviet Union and the US entered the war, the assumption that France and the UK would have the predominant influence on an eventual peace settlement no longer seemed valid.[38] And obviously, the US and also the Soviet Union played an ever-greater role in this respect.

B. The United States

46. Although there was already before 1940, a certain interest in the US in European co-operation, the main efforts of that country were concentrated on bringing together a large alliance based on the same values against the axis powers.[39] The first step was the agreement with the UK on an Atlantic Charter on 14 August 1941 which fixed common principles on which both countries would base, in their national policies, their hopes for a better future of the world. Second, came the Declaration by the United Nations (UN) of New York (1 January 1942) signed by

35. *See* editorial comment by Clyde Eagleton, 'A Pattern of World Order', *The American J. of Intl L.* October (1942), 620–663 (622).
36. *See* Alfred William Brian Simpson, *Human Rights and the End of Empire* (Oxford: Oxford University Press, 2001), 224 et seq.
37. Robert J. Colville, *Downing Street Diaries*, German edn (Berlin: Siedler Verlag, 1988/1991), 226, 227.
38. Bell & Pinder, in Lipgens (ed.), 24.
39. For the details *see* Pierre Melandri, *Les Etats-Unis face à l'unification de l'Europe 1945–1954* (Paris: Editions Pédone, 1980); John Lamberton Harper, *American Visions of Europe* (Cambridge: Cambridge University Press,1996).

twenty-six States. The declaration underlined the need to defend life, liberty, independence and religious freedom and to preserve human rights and justice. There has been some criticism that both declarations did not refer to peaceful settlement of disputes, to a possible new International Court (post-war international judicial system), to legislative or administrative machinery necessary to handle international problems and the financing of institutions to maintain world order.[40]

C. The Soviet Union

47. During WW II the Soviet Union was associated to and informed of all major initiatives of the Allies concerning a new European Order.

In December 1941 Anthony Eden, then Foreign Minister in the UK War Cabinet, travelled to Moscow. His talks with Marshal Stalin also dealt with the conditions and organization of peace and security after the war, including the machinery for keeping peace. Obviously the Soviet Government and the UK could make no final decisions at the meeting without intimate consultation with the US and the other Allies.[41] During the meeting with Eden, Stalin raised the question of 'how were we to keep peace and order in Europe after the war?'. Stalin suggested a council of the victorious powers with a military force at its disposal. The Soviet Union would have no objection if some countries wished to federate (*see* Anthony Eden, The Eden Memoirs, the Reckoning, Cassell, 1965, pp 334–335; Martin Mc Cauley, The origins of the Cold War 1941–1949, 2nd edition, 1995, pp 115–116).

48. The Soviet Union adhered to the principles of the Atlantic Charter and joined in the UN declaration of 1 January 1942. On 26 May 1942, the UK and Russia concluded a Treaty of Alliance in the war against Hitlerite Germany and her associates in Europe and of collaboration and mutual assistance thereafter. They agreed *inter alia* to work together in close and friendly collaboration after re-establishment of peace for the organization of security and economic prosperity in Europe. When Ernest Bevin become UK Foreign Secretary in 1945, he made particular efforts until late 1947 to keep the USSR informed of regional projects for Europe, starting with a discussion with Stalin at Potsdam.[42]

Lipgens[43] reports that despite the above commitments, the Soviet policy was to secure maximum territorial gains and keep the neighbours as small, weak and disunited as possible.

---

40. *See* editorial comment by Clyde Eagleton, *supra*, *The Am. J. of Intl L.* (1942), 624 and 666; it is interesting that in those days a review of the League of Nations' Covenant was still contemplated (668).
41. Anthony Eden, *Freedom and Order* (London: Faber & Faber, 1957), 144.
42. *See* Simpson, 549.
43. *See* Lipgens, Documents, 10.

III. Post-War Planning in the US and the UK in 1942

49. 1942 was the turning point of the war. With the increasing momentum of allied victories, the structure of the peace settlement assumed increasing urgency and significance.[44] Post-war planning work, including schemes of individual rights, was particularly intense in the US (by the aforementioned Special Committee established in January 1940). A draft Bill of Rights, however, without an enforcement mechanism, was produced in December 1942. In this connection a proposal was made to incorporate the Bill in the Statutes/Constitution of a possible European Federation. In the summer of 1942, a close US-UK co-operation on post-war settlement was initiated at the level of Under-Secretaries of State, including Gladwyn Webb, later Lord Gladwyn. Both the UK and the US then had sympathy for a possible European regional organization also with the aim to preserving freedom in Europe. This co-operation led to the preparation of a draft Four Power Plan.

50. According to Lord Gladwyn[45] the main strategic considerations of the Western Allies were the following:

- the preservation of the great power coalition after the war;
- the need to avoid the domination of the world by two different ideologies, the grim confrontation of the two super powers and possible cold war;
- after the war the Great Powers would take account of their worldwide interests and responsibilities and be able and willing to enter into worldwide commitments in order to prevent any other nation from again troubling the peace;
- to give the Big Powers all the scope they want in their respective regional/continental spheres;
- to avoid a division in the British and Soviet spheres of interest;
- trying to enlist the favour of Germany; therefore some European Organization responsible for security and welfare of Europe as a whole should be achieved, which would come under a world organization.

51. Concerning Europe there were other possible concepts, such as an Anglo-French alliance to conduct it. In this connection, the draft declaration on Union between the UK and France as proposed in June 1940 was referred to. In May 1942, President Roosevelt told the Soviet Foreign Commissioner Molotov in Washington that after the war the US, Russia, Britain and possibly China should police the world and enforce disarmament by inspection. Molotov replied 'that this had the full approval of the Soviet Government'.[46] According to Lord Gladwyn,[47] the UK War Cabinet had indication of official American thinking on post-war settlement in July 1942. This contemplated a military occupation of Germany, and its possible dismemberment. The Rhine and the Ruhr and Bavaria, as separate entities, should associate themselves with the West and the rest of Germany would rather look to

44. Philip M.H. Bell, in Lipgens, 205.
45. Lord Gladwyn, Memoirs, 130–134.
46. Lipgens, 9.
47. Lord Gladwyn, Memoirs, 111.

the Soviet Union. This concept included a world organization after the war based on the United Nations as a whole and directed by the four big powers, the 'four policemen' as Roosevelt called them (US, USSR, Britain, China), completed by regional organizations, led by a big power. One of the main UK aims in that time was to organize, possibly with the co-operation of the US, some measure of unity in Western Europe. In the view of the UK such a Western Bloc could act as a counterpoise to the US and America. Eastern Europe could be guided either by some association with Russia in the background or by Russia herself.[48] It was in particular Winston Churchill who was fearful of the USSR and had little enthusiasm for Roosevelt's plans for a world organization and rather favoured some form of a Council of Europe.[49]

52. The official US views on The War and Human Freedom were developed by the US Secretary of State (C. Hull) in a radio address on 23 July 1942. He stated *inter alia* that all processes of international co-operation presupposed respect for law and obligations and that one of the institutions that needed to be established and be given vitality was an international Court of Justice.[50] In this context it may also be mentioned that between 1942 and 1944 ideas for a Central European Union were discussed in the US (*see* American debates on Central European Union, Documents of the American State Department, Euroclio – studies and documents, by Jozef Laptos and Mariusz Misztal, Peter Lang Publishers, 2002).

53. Lord Gladwyn also notes[51] that Churchill was quite allergic to any proposals for post-war action he had not himself engendered or at least discussed personally with the President of the US. When writing in October 1942 to his Foreign Minister, Anthony Eden, Churchill expressed the hope 'that the European family may act unitedly as one under a Council of Europe. I look forward to a United States of Europe with reduced barriers to trade and movement and where the economy of Europe could be studied as a whole'. The note ended with the words 'Unfortunately the war has prior claims on your and my attention.'[52] A further question was whether or not the UK was to be a part of a Council of Europe.

54. Churchill has been criticized by Lipgens[53] for having failed to discuss in 1942, which was a decisive year, with the US and the Soviet Union any definite plans for the post-war world. His broadcast speech of March 1943 (mentioned below) came, in the view of Lipgens, too late. It is interesting to note that already on 28 December 1942, US Vice-President Wallace spoke of a 'world-wide new democracy on which we hope to build on'.

---

48. *Ibid.*, 113.
49. *See* Simpson, pp. 222–223.
50. *See* Documents on American Foreign Relations, vol. V (July 1942–June 1943), 1–12.
51. Lord Gladwyn, Memoirs, 118.
52. Salmon & Nicoll, 26 and Lipgens, 6.
53. *See* Lipgens, 6, 11.

55. On 15 January 1942, Greece and Yugoslavia concluded in London an agreement concerning the constitution of a Balkan Union, open to other Balkan states. An interesting fact is that the agreement provides for co-operation between parliaments:

> The Governments of the Balkan Union will facilitate regular meetings between parliamentary delegations of the states of the Union, allowing these delegations to proceed to exchanges of views and of expressions of their wishes in the form of questions of common interest which would be submitted to them by competent organs.[54]

On 23 January 1942, an Agreement for a Polish-Czechoslovak Confederation was concluded in London which provides in its Article 12 that the constitutions of these individual states will guarantee to the citizens of these states about a dozen of fundamental rights.

§4. The Situation in 1943: Churchill's and Eden's Proposals for a Council of Europe

56. Because of the important victories of the Allies in Stalingrad and North Africa and the need to examine the consequences for war strategies and post-war settlement, major meetings of the Allies took place in 1943 in Moscow (meeting of Ministers of Foreign Affairs) and in Tehran (Summit of the Big Three). In this situation Churchill considered it necessary to outline his position on the creation of a European Organization. According to political scientists this was aimed at signalling both to the US and Russia that Britain was ready to take the lead in reorganizing Europe, as a counterpoise to the US and Russia.[55] Furthermore, Churchill was aware that after Stalingrad the UK was facing a Europe that could be dominated militarily and possibly politically, by the Soviet Union after the war.[56]

57. In a radio broadcast on 21 March 1943 Churchill said:

> One can imagine that under a world institution embodying or representing the United Nations and some day all nations, there should come into being a Council of Europe and a Council of Asia. As according to the forecast I am outlining the war against Japan will still be raging it is on the creation of the Council of Europe and the settlement of Europe that the first practical task will be centred […]. In Europe lie most of the causes which have led to the two world

54. Text in: Documents on American Foreign Relations (July 1941–June 1942), 273–278.
55. Wilhelm Cornides, 'Das Problem der europäischen Sicherheit auf der Berliner Viermächtekonferenz 1954', *Europa-Archiv* (1954): 6489 et seq.
56. Martin McCauley, 'Yalta, Potsdam and the Emergence of the Cold War: An Overview from the United Kingdom in the Light of the Latest Research', in *Crossroads of European Histories, Multiple Outlooks on Five Key Moments in the History of Europe*, edited by Robert Stradling (Strasbourg: Council of Europe Publishing, December 2006), 251–259, 258.

wars. In Europe dwell the historic parent races from whom our western civilisation has been so largely derived. [...] I hope that we shall not lightly cast aside all the immense work which was accomplished by the creation of the League of Nations. Certainly we must take as our foundation the lofty conception of freedom, law and morality which was the spirit of the League.

We must try – I am speaking of course only for ourselves – to make the Council of Europe, or whatever it may be called, into a really effective League with all the strongest forces concerned woven into its texture, with a High Court to adjust disputes and with armed forces national or international or both, held ready to enforce these decisions and prevent renewed aggression and the preparation of future wars. Anyone can see that this Council when created must eventually embrace the whole of Europe and that all the main branches of the European family must some day be partners in it. [...] Side by side with the Great Powers there should be a number of groupings of States or confederations which would express themselves through their own chosen representatives, the whole making a Council of great States and groups of States. It is my earnest hope [...] that we can achieve the largest common measure of the integrated life of Europe that is possible without destroying the individual characteristics and traditions of its many ancient and historic races. All this will, I believe, be found to harmonise with the high permanent interests of Britain, America and Russia. It certainly cannot be accomplished without their cordial and concerted agreement and participation. [...] Nothing could be more foolish at this stage than to plunge into details and try to describe the exact groupings of States or lay down precise machinery for their co-operation or still more to argue about frontiers [...]. This does not mean that many tentative discussions are not taking place between the three great nations concerned or that the whole vast problem of European destiny is not the subject of ceaseless heart-searchings.[57]

58. One may note that, unlike from 1940 to 1942, there is no more discussion on taking a remodelled League of Nations as the basis of regional (European and Asian) Organizations. However Churchill referred to the League's lofty ideals. Furthermore the question, if a COE should be established in advance of world machinery, would be settled by a negative reply.[58]

59. Following the war, events at the beginning and in spring 1943 convinced the US that the future peace settlement would depend above all on American-Soviet co-operation. Important circles in the US feared that an effective new World organization might be weakened if it was constructed on the basis of regional/ continental unions.[59] The opposition of the Soviet Union to continental/regional unions allowed the US to do likewise.

---

57. Full text of the speech in Keesing's Contemporary Archives, March 1943.
58. Lord Gladwyn's Memoirs, 130, and Moscow meeting (October 1943) of the Allies.
59. Lipgens, 11.

60. Real progress in post-war planning was made at the Conference of Foreign Affairs Ministers of the Allies in Moscow in October 1943. Anthony Eden had in his files a plan for a Council of Europe.[60] However, this did not materialize as the Allies gave a clear priority to the creation of the UN.

61. It is known that US President Roosevelt did not particularly like the idea of a Council of Europe. While he accepted the idea of a security commission of Britain, the US and Russia 'to police the peace of Europe until the political reorganization of the Continent is completed', he feared Churchill's European Council as 'a device for tying the USA down in Europe'. He was very emphatic that the US could not join any independent regional body such as a European Council. Furthermore a European Council to which the US did not belong presented a different set of problems. It might resist US influence or evolve into an anti-Soviet combination.[61] Roosevelt feared in particular that any proposals for a federal organization of Europe would prejudice the understanding between the US and the Soviet Union.

62. Finally, Eden proposed a draft declaration according to which the Big Three would promise to assist other European States to form any associations designed to increase mutual welfare and the general prosperity of the continent. This was opposed by both the US and the Soviet delegations. Molotov said that this proposal reminded him of the policy of the 'cordon sanitaire' directed in earlier years against the Soviet Union.[62] Eden withdrew his draft declaration and the Conference finally called for a general international organization, based on the principle of the sovereign equality of all peace-loving states, while making the Big Four (the Three and China) responsible for security pending the establishment of such a body and for organizing agreement on the regulation of armaments in the post-war period.[63] During the Tehran Summit of Roosevelt, Stalin and Churchill held at the end of November 1943, the Soviet support for a new League of Nations on the basis of the 'Big Four' hegemony was confirmed. An important decision taken at the Moscow conference was to establish a European Advisory Commission tasked to advise the Governments of the USA, Russia and the UK in reaching a joint policy on European political problems. It attempted to achieve this purpose by studying questions as they came up and making joint recommendations to the three governments.

---

60. Churchill, *The Second World War*, vols I–VI, esp. vol. V (Boston: Houghton Mifflin Company, 1948–1954), 251; 'We (Great Britain) hold strong to a system of a League of Nations which will include a Council of Europe, with an International Court and an armed power capable of enforcing its decisions.'
61. John Lamberton Harper, *American Visions of Europe* (Cambridge: STET University Press, 1996), 96.
62. Lipgens, 13.
63. Foreign Relations of the United States, *Diplomatic Papers*, 1943, vol. 1 (Washington: Government Printing Office, 1963), 624 et seq.

§5. NON-GOVERNMENTAL ACTIVITIES

I. The Churches

63. As already mentioned, the major Churches worked already before 1940 for the respect of European values and for the respect of human dignity and human rights in general. The Pope's Christmas broadcast of 1942 is particularly important as he then expounded his five fundamental points for the order and pacification of human society. These five milestones were: the dignity and right of the human person, the sense of social unity and especially of the family, the dignity and prerogatives of labour, the rehabilitation of juridical order and the conception of the State according to the Christian spirit. In his speech, the Pope developed the contents of these fundamental points.[64] They are, according to certain authors, the spiritual basis for the human rights declarations of the UN and the CoE (ECHR).

II. Proposals from Dissidents, Resistance Movements and Other Major Private Contributions

64. It is not possible to mention even roughly, the many private initiatives which are completely described by Lipgens in his numerous works.[65] Therefore only three special features are evoked.

III. Officials of the League of Nations

65. Some senior officials of the League of Nations, among which the former Secretary General of the League, Joseph Avenol, made already in March 1944 a very complete proposal for European co-operation, including a Council of Europe.[66] Avenol proposed *inter alia* that a fundamental charter should be elaborated by the Council and that each Member State of the Council would have to undertake to practise the Four Freedoms proclaimed by President Roosevelt. Furthermore, each CoE Member State would declare its resolve to join in resisting a threat of aggression against any other member of the Community and undertake to carry out programmes for European economic and social reconstruction decided by the Council. It would be formed at top level by heads of Government who laid down principles and main lines of policy. Unlike the Council of the League of Nations the main function of the CoE would not be to conciliate and arbitrate disputes but to coordinate, decide and take action. There would be a Council of Europe Court of Justice.

64. Text in Keesing's Contemporary Archives, 1943, 5531.
65. *See* his bibliography in Lipgens, 827, 828.
66. Lipgens, 322,323.

IV. Coudenhove-Kalergi

66. In particular with respect to the idea of a European Assembly, the action taken by Coudenhove-Kalergi was important. Already in an article published in October 1941[67] Coudenhove-Kalergi referred to a European Federation with a Federal Parliament and a Federal Bill of Rights. During Coudenhove-Kalergi's exile in the US a draft constitution of the United States of Europe was elaborated in March 1944 at the New York University, which had created a 'Study Centre for a European Federation after the War'. It provided for a two-chamber European Assembly. This study was prepared, *inter alia*, by Professor Zurcher[68] at the instigation of and in co-operation with Coudenhove-Kalergi. He sent this draft constitution to Anthony Eden and Winston Churchill and invited the latter to take it 'into account for his Council of Europe project'.[69] In his memoirs[70] Lord Gladwyn confirms that this draft constitution had been on Churchill's desk in May 1944 and mentions in particular that members of the CoE (its Assembly) would be elected for four years. In internal notes however, Lord Gladwyn heavily criticized the draft constitution.[71]

V. Resistance Movements

67. A famous contribution of a resistance movement for the building of European Union is the Ventotene manifesto (August 1941) prepared by the dissidents of the Fascist government of Italy. This manifesto and complementary documents of 1942[72] call *inter alia* for the abolition of the division of Europe into sovereign national states, the establishment of a federal regime, with a federal legislature and organs of control based on the direct participation of citizens, not merely representatives of the federated states. Another major contribution is the book 'A l'échelle humaine' of Léon Blum who also calls for a European Federation. He insists on the need to limit the sovereignty of national States and is convinced of the interdependence of the peoples in Europe.[73] It is also appropriate to mention the French resistance group 'Liberté' composed of Catholic law professors, including P.H. Teitgen, who was in 1949 the CoE Assembly's rapporteur on a draft European Convention on Human Rights. This resistance group produced a declaration on 'Les droits des personnes et des collectivités'.[74]

---

67. Lipgens, 793; *see also* the interesting article on Coudenhove-Kalergi in Diario de Noticias (Lisbon) of 29 Apr. 2008 by Professor Adriano Moreira.
68. Arnold J. Zurcher, *The Struggle to Unite Europe, 1940–58* (New York, 1958).
69. Lipgens, 395.
70. Lord Gladwyn, Memoirs, 197.
71. Lipgens, 812.
72. Trevor Salmon & William Nicoll, *Building European Union*, 17–20.
73. Details are to be found in Marie-Thérèse Bitsch, *Histoire de la construction européenne de 1945 à nos jours*, 2nd edn (Bruxelles: Éditions Complexe, 1999), 24–25.
74. *See* Simpson, 215–216.

§6. ACTION FROM 1944 UNTIL THE POTSDAM CONFERENCE (JULY/AUGUST 1945)

68. In short, the US activities were centred on the preparatory work for the future World Organization. It is noteworthy that a private Commission to study the organization of peace prepared in May 1944 a report including a detailed discussion entitled International Safeguards of Human Rights.[75]

69. Great Britain hoped that after the war an arrangement could be found for a peace settlement with Germany and Austria in order to avoid the development of two distinct state blocks in Europe. It always had in mind the wider Europe including Russia. Already in 1944 these matters were the subject of negotiations with the Soviet Union, and at that time Great Britain had defined as its priority the creation of a world organization. Furthermore, it proposed a British-Soviet alliance as an assurance against Germany.[76]

70. According to Lord Gladwyn,[77] the UK also favoured rather artificial confederations in Eastern Europe. Furthermore, Churchill's Council of Europe idea would still be opposed by the Soviet Union and support by the US was not certain. Another UK analysis of 17 April 1944 indicated that Moscow was busy constructing a *cordon sanitaire* along its western frontier. The aim was a group of smaller States tied to the Soviet Union by treaties, if possible. A European Organization or Federation would make it more difficult to influence these smaller States.[78] Another important UK project at that time was to promote an economic reorganization of Europe and to create several specialized European Organizations to this end (for coal, for transport including maritime and air transport …) under the umbrella of a European Economic Commission (*see* Diplomates en guerre. *La seconde guerre mondiale racontée à travers les archives du Quai d'Orsay, par Pierre – Jean Rémy*. Paris: Éditions Lattès, 2007, 13–915). In this connection it is to be recalled that the Benelux Treaty on economic co-operation was signed in London in 1944. Following a proposal made at an international conference in London in July 1946 and reported to the UN Economic and Social Council, a United Nations Economic Commission for Europe (UNECE) was set up in March 1947. According to some sources, this Commission might have been used as a basis for initiating closer European co-operation in other fields. Another important UK project at that time was to promote an economic reorganization of Europe and to create several specialized European Organizations to this end (for coal, for transport, including maritime and air transport, et al.) under the umbrella of a European Economic Commission.[79]

---

75. *See* Simpson, 195.
76. Wilhelm Cornides & Herrmann Volle, 'Die Vorgeschichte des Brüsseler Fünfmächte-Pakts', *Europa-Archiv* (1949): 1755–1767 and speech by Ernest Bevin before the House of Commons of 22 Jan. 1948.
77. Lord Gladwyn, Memoirs, 138, 139.
78. Martin McCauley, 255.
79. Diplomates en guerre, *La seconde guerre mondiale racontée à travers les archives du Quai d'Orsay, par Pierre-Jean Remy* (Paris: Éditions Lattès, 2007), 913–915.

71. Churchill spoke in May 1944 before the House of Commons of the need to have a united Europe, however, this speech remained quite unnoticed and the US did not react.[80] It is to be noted that at least before 1947 he did not refer to a European Assembly. In particular, his Zurich Speech of September 1946 on the creation of a kind of United States of Europe and of a Council of Europe did not mention a European Parliament or Assembly.

72. In 1944, the idea of a Western Bloc again got a certain importance in the work of the UK War Cabinet. In May and November 1944, it discussed two different projects:

- forming a bloc as an ideological counter to USSR communism;
- Churchill's idea of three regional Councils (for Europe, Asia and the Americas) consistent with the proposals for and the principles of the future UN.

The problem was not to antagonize the USSR by giving the appearance of building up the Western Bloc against her.[81]

73. After a year of campaigning by the UK, the European Advisory Commission, agreed to at the Moscow Conference of the Allied Foreign Ministers in 1943, was established in 1944. After June 1944, which saw 'D-Day', an acceleration of decisive events took place in Europe and there was a need for major Allied Conferences in Dumbarton Oaks (August 1944, concerning the UN), Yalta (February 1945) and Potsdam (July/August 1945). Based on a US proposal, the Yalta Conference adopted a declaration on liberated Europe. It reaffirmed the faith of the Allies in the principles of the Atlantic Charter and their pledge in the Declaration by the UN of January 1942. The declaration dealt *inter alia* with the establishment of order in Europe, the creation of democratic institutions of their own choice by the liberated nations and the joint assistance by the Big Three to people in liberated States to facilitate the holding of free elections. No implementation mechanism was foreseen for the declaration. The main Western aims for the Yalta Conference were winning the war, and organizing the peace in a way that would not lead to an imminent conflict between the wartime alliance but would rather bring Russia into some form of co-operation with the rest of Europe and with the US.[82]

74. Before the restoration of France at the end of August 1944, the Government in exile and particularly Monnet and de Gaulle had presented proposals for European Organization.[83] At the Potsdam Conference, the Allies established a Council of Foreign Ministers to prepare the peace settlement and in particular peace treaties with Italy, Romania, Bulgaria, Hungary and Finland and to propose settlements of

80. Coudenhove-Kalergi, *Kampf um Europa* (Zürich: Atlantis Verlag, 1949), 243.
81. *See* Simpson, 232–233.
82. Martin McCauley, 250.
83. Charles Melchior de Molènes, *L'Europe de Strasbourg une première expérience de parlementarisme international* (Paris: Rondil, 1971), 140–142; *see also* Diplomates en guerre, 750, 751.

pending territorial matters. At a later stage the Council was also supposed to propose a settlement for peace with Germany. This 'Permanent' Council which had a secretariat in London held its first meeting in that city in September 1945, after the unconditional surrender of Japan. Within the Permanent Council the US, France and the UK deployed – between September 1945 and March 1947 – all their efforts to secure international co-operation with the Soviet Union and the reorganization of Europe. This system has been described as a World 'Directoire'[84] (as compared with the European 'Directoire' in 1815). The basis for the Permanent Council had already been established at the Conference of Foreign Ministers in Moscow in October 1943 (*see* above). At that occasion a declaration was adopted according to which in order to maintain international peace and security, pending the re-establishment of the rule of law and order and the creation of a general security system, the Allies would consult each other and, if appropriate, other members of the 'UN' with a view to a common action on behalf of the 'UN'.

§7. Initiatives Between August 1945 and the End of 1947

I. By the Allies

75. Between August 1945 and February/March 1947 no relevant European Treaty was concluded. This had several reasons. The Allies had focused their action within the aforementioned Permanent Council (Council of Foreign Ministers) in London and on launching the UN and making it function. Before 1947, one did not dare envisage officially a European Organization or Federation. It was feared that this could trouble the Soviet Union and thus threaten the efficiency of collective security at world level.

76. This dilemma became evident in the policy of UK Foreign Secretary Bevin. In May 1946, it was considered that the UK should not act independently but continue to attempt to negotiate a solution to the German problem through the Council of Foreign Ministers. A breach with the USSR should be avoided and no ideological alternative to communism be established. Work should rather focus on building up democratic institutions in Germany. Another position could only be taken when the hope of reaching an agreement with the USSR over a peace settlement with Germany would have been abandoned and the division of Germany into an eastern and a western part had become unavoidable. Only then the time would be ripe to pursue the Western Bloc plan.[85]

77. The growing disagreement of the Allies on the terms of a quadripartite European order is best illustrated by Churchill's Fulton (March 1946) speech. Also the Zürich speech (September 1946) is an expression of the Allies' differences. At Fulton, Churchill referred to the iron curtain, which had descended from Stettin to Trieste across the continent. He described the situation on the continent 'which

84. Roger Céré, *Entre la guerre et la paix 1944–49* (Paris: Presses Universitaires de France, 1949), 11.
85. *See* Simpson, 554–555.

certainly was not the liberated Europe for which we fought to build up. Nor is it one which contains the essentials of permanent peace. The safety of the world requires a new unity in Europe from which no nation should be permanently outcast. We should work with conscious purpose for a grand pacification of Europe within the structure of the United Nations and in accordance with its Charter'.[86] In this connection it might be recalled that the League of Nations had ceased to exist as of 20 April 1946.

78. Churchill knew well the opposition of the Soviet Union to concrete projects for Europe. Nevertheless, after having given his warning and referred to the 'tragedy of Europe', Churchill outlined in Zürich his concept for Europe as follows:[87] Under and within the UN Organization:

> the European family must be recreated in a regional structure called – it may be – the United States of Europe and the first practical step will be to form a Council of Europe. If at first all the States of Europe are not willing or able to join a union, we must nevertheless proceed to assemble and combine those who will and those who can. […] In all this urgent work France and Germany must take the lead together. Great Britain, the British Commonwealth of Nations, mighty America and, I trust, Soviet Russia – for then, indeed, all would be well – must be the friends and sponsors of the new Europe and must champion its right to live and shine.

79. It will be noted that Churchill did not infer that Britain should be part of such a United States of Europe. He rather observed that Great Britain, the British Commonwealth of Nations must be the friends and sponsors of the new Europe. Churchill referred to the Pan-European Union, to Aristide Briand and, interestingly, to the 'Grand Design' (*see* above). Furthermore he explicitly mentioned President Truman's interest and sympathy with the project.

80. One sensational feature of the speech was that less than twenty months after WW II, Churchill invited France and Germany to take the lead together. Roughly, Churchill's project is in line with his prior – above-mentioned – statements on a CoE but less precise and, perhaps, ambitious. Some political writers consider the Zürich speech as a political project to oppose to the Soviet Union an important Western Bloc.[88]

81. A positive aspect concerning future European co-operation was that, since 1946, the US was in favour of a regional Organization of Europe.

---

86. In Randolph S. Churchill, *The Sinews of Peace, Post-War Speeches by Winston S. Churchill* (London: Cassell, 1948).
87. *Ibid.*
88. For example, Journal de Genève, 20 Sep. 1946.

82. According to Lord Gladwyn,[89] at the beginning of 1947, the whole idea of Great Power co-operation was in grave danger of collapse. The first turning point was the breakdown of the negotiations at the Moscow meeting of the Council of Foreign Ministers in March and April 1947. On 4 March 1947, France and the UK concluded in Dunkirk a treaty of alliance and mutual assistance, which also had an economic dimension, that is the strengthening of the economic relations between the two countries to their mutual advantage and in the interests of general prosperity. An important clause obliged the two countries to give themselves all the military and other support and power in case of a renewed involvement in hostilities with Germany.[90] It is interesting that Britain and France, which had taken the last joint initiative of a European character in June 1940 (*see* above), resumed their European ambition also with a joint action.

83. Only one week later, on 12 March 1947, the US adopted the Truman doctrine which expanded the US's role in checking the spread of communism. The doctrine was linked to the granting of important US loans to Greece and Turkey to help both countries to survive. The Truman Doctrine led directly to the Marshall Plan. Both the Dunkirk Treaty and the Truman Doctrine increased tensions with Moscow.

84. The Peace Treaties of the Allies with Bulgaria, Finland, Hungary, Italy and Romania, signed in February 1947 in Paris, all include references to commitments entered into by these countries to ensure the respect of human rights and fundamental freedoms. In this connection it is to be noted also that the renowned Institute of International Law, at its Lausanne session on 8 August 1947, had at the centre of its deliberations a report by Charles de Visscher on the Human Rights as basis of a restoration of International Law. According to de Visscher, more than thirty years of disorder and violence had compromised international law.[91] Both aspects are important because of the role played by the CoE for the protection of human rights.

II. The Marshall Plan

85. A milestone for the building of Europe was the Marshall Plan contained in the speech of the US Secretary of State George C. Marshall at Harvard University on 5 June 1947. His project aimed at addressing the disastrous economic situation and at placing Europe on its feet economically. The US was ready to offer up to USD 20 billion for recovery. Leading European politicians, such as Ernest Bevin,[92] warmly welcomed the plan. In the parts of Europe where the plan was allowed to be established, it was an unprecedented success.

89. Lord Gladwyn, Memoirs, 197.
90. For details *see* Wilhelm Cornides & Herrmann Volle, 'Die Vorgeschichte des Brüsseler Fünfmächte-Pakts', *Europa-Archiv* (1949): 1755–1767.
91. Annuaire de l'Institut de Droit International, session de Lausanne, 1947, 152, 153.
92. Alan Bullock, *Ernest Bevin – Foreign Secretary 1945–51* (London: 1983), 517.

86. A condition for US aid was that there had to be some agreement among the countries of Europe as to the requirements of the situation and the part those countries themselves would take in order to give proper effect to whatever action might be undertaken by the US. Thus the initiative had to come from the Europeans. The programme was to be a joint one agreed to by a number of, if not all European nations. As the Marshall Plan thus obliged the Europeans to act for the first time as a single economic unit, the Plan was the starting point for an economic Europe. In a debate in the House of Commons on 19 June 1947,[93] Anthony Eden said in this respect:

> This offer [...] can mean that European countries are going to be stimulated to agree upon common economic measures for their joint salvation. Such indeed is the first step towards that United Europe which my Right Hon. Friend the Leader of the Opposition (Winston Churchill) has so much at heart.

87. Indeed less than one year after the Harvard speech, the OEEC Treaty was signed. The Marshall Plan also had two further important consequences. First, there was a link between post-war rehabilitation of economic structures and political and social conditions in which free institutions can exist. Second, as the programme was offered to the whole of Europe, the Soviet Union and other Central and East European countries were obliged to indirectly take a position on possible European economic integration. Stalin finally denounced the programme as a trick and did not allow the satellite States behind the iron curtain to participate in it. This did not fail to increase existing tensions with the Western Allies. By the end of 1947, the whole projected post-war settlement of the Allies had collapsed.[94] Fortunately, 1948 was the year in which an alternative settlement was constructed.

III. The Work of the Pan-European Union for a European Assembly from 1946 to Summer 1947

88. After his return to Europe in 1946, Coudenhove-Kalergi continued his action for European Union. As he was sceptical about the capacity and readiness of governments to renounce parts of national sovereignty for the sake of European unity, he considered that a European Union could only be achieved by mobilizing parliamentarians in European countries. In November 1946, the pan-European Union sent a questionnaire to more than 4,400 members of most of the national parliaments in Western Europe asking them if they were in favour of the creation of a European federation in the framework of the UN. More than 90% of almost 1,800 parliamentarians replied with 'yes'. The pan-European Union invited *inter alia* those parliamentarians favouring a European Federation to create in their parliaments 'committees for European Federation'. On 12 February 1947, Coudenhove-Kalergi prepared a memorandum on the Organization of a parliament for Europe, which outlined the various steps to be taken to this end. He proposed to hold a Congress on

93. Hansard, col. 2238.
94. Lord Gladwyn's memoirs, 208.

this issue in Gstaad, Switzerland in September 1947, and to invite to it members of already existing national parliamentary committees for European Federation and members of the European Parliamentary Union which was set up in July 1947.

89. Coudenhove-Kalergi considered that the Congress should constitute itself as a permanent body, meeting periodically and representing a kind of preliminary parliament for Europe. A Council of Europe composed of leaders from various European nations and parties should constitute the continent's supreme moral authority and lead Europe towards a new era of peace, prosperity and liberty. The Resolution adopted by the Gstaad Congress contained the following proposals:

- To create a European regional grouping in the sense of Article 52 of the Charter of the UN.
- To create, with the support of the European States interested, a permanent community under the name of the United States of Europe.
- To convene a European Constituent Assembly whose members should be elected by national parliaments or the peoples themselves, with the task of elaborating a European Constitution. The draft constitution should be presented to the European States for approval or rejection.

90. It is to be noted that former statesmen from Romania, Yugoslavia and Hungary, who lived in exile, had attended the Gstaad Congress as observers. Following the Congress, a draft constitution for a European Federation was prepared and submitted to a conference in Interlaken in September 1948.

IV. Initiatives Taken by Other Private Political 'Movements for Europe'

91. In addition to the pan-European Union, other political movements, created since 1946, worked for 'more Europe' to use a word which could serve as a common denominator. The son-in-law of Sir Winston Churchill, Sandys (Lord Duncan-Sandys) created in January 1947 the United Europe Movement. It disseminated *inter alia* the main political subjects raised by Sir Winston Churchill. However, the creation of a European Assembly was no immediate concern of the United Europe Movement.

92. Furthermore, a European Union of Federalists (EUF/UEF) – (Spinelli, Marc, Frenay), an independent League for Economic Co-operation (van Zeeland) and other groupings were created. One of them was the Labour Europe Group set up in 1947 by Ronald W.G. Mackay, which was transformed afterwards into an All-Party Group. Mackay became later, like Duncan-Sandys, a member of the Parliamentary Assembly of the CoE.[95] The UEF held a major Congress in Montreux in August

95. Further details can be found in the fundamental studies carried out by Walter Lipgens (*see* Documents on the History of European Integration, vol. 2 (Dublin, New York, 1986) and in Lubor Jilek, 'Projets d'Assemblée européenne en 1946–48, rôle des associations militantes', in *Jalons pour une histoire du Conseil de l'Europe*, actes du colloque de Strasbourg (8–10 Jun. 1995), 17–37 et seq.

1947. The political resolution adopted on that occasion asked *inter alia* for a government of the European Federation which should not be answerable to the federated States, but to the peoples, a Supreme Court to settle disputes between the federated States and a common police force.

§8. The Situation in the Autumn of 1947 and the Response of the Western Allies

93. In autumn 1947, and limited to Western Europe, where European Economic co-operation had been launched by the Marshall Plan, the initiatives for a more political Europe were left mainly in the hands of private movements, which, however, had different priorities. In particular, the pan-European Union promoted a European Assembly. The United Europe Movement worked, *inter alia*, for an intergovernmental European Council (Council of Europe) and Ronald W.G. Mackay tried to find a compromise between these two trends. Duncan-Sandys managed finally in December 1947 to set up an international Coordination Committee of Movements for European unity. It planned already at that moment the holding of a Congress of Europe in The Hague, essentially for propagating the idea of a European Council, but still without the prospect of an Assembly.[96]

I. The Divide among the Allies on a Post-War Order in 1947 and the Promotion of a 'Western Bloc'

94. Whereas in the spring of 1943, Roosevelt had proposed to the Russians that they take part in the construction of a new political order in Europe,[97] the year 1947 saw the rupture between the four Allies after the failure of the Foreign Affairs Ministers' Conference in London in December 1947. They were incapable of finding a four-power framework for Europe as a whole.[98] This made visible the growing divide between the three Western Allies and the Soviet Union concerning a European peace order and peace in the World. The situation had worsened *inter alia* because of the iron curtain, the conclusion of a system of bilateral co-operation and assistance Treaties between the countries behind the iron curtain and their alignment on the Soviet economic system. These measures constituted preparatory work for framing an Eastern Bloc.

95. In that situation there was agreement among the Foreign Ministers of the UK (Bevin), the US (Marshall) and France (Bidault) that Western Europe needed to rise

---

and in a doctoral thesis by Martin Posselt on Richard Coudenhove-Kalergi und die Europäische Parlamentarier-Union, 1946–52 (University of Graz, 1984).

96. Lubor Jilek, 78, 28, interestingly this happened at about the same moment when the Foreign Ministers of the four Big Powers had adjourned *sine die* their London session.

97. Harper, American Visions of Europe, 88.

98. Robert Schuman, speech on the occasion of the tenth anniversary of the Council of Europe, 20 Apr. 1959, Council of Europe document A.46.544, 34–37; he spoke of the rupture provoked by Russia in December 1947 concerning a peace treaty with Germany.

above the destructive effects of the war and had to restore a healthy society. The policy, initiated with the Marshall Plan, of making Western plans for the future outside the communist sphere was to be pursued. Bidault accepted that Bevin should prepare a project. It was clear to Bevin and Bidault that spring 1948 was a dangerous period. There had been an open breach with the Soviet Union and at the same time nothing had been done in practice to provide for either the recovery or the security of Western Europe.[99]

II. Alternative Settlement

96. Bevin found an alternative solution to a four-power solution. His ideas then centred around a Western Union, a sort of spiritual federation of the West. The underlying idea was that it was impossible to promote economic recovery without a political and moral mobilization. Furthermore, it should be made clear to the Soviet Union that having gone so far they could not advance any further. In early January 1948, he presented the following proposals to the UK Cabinet:

> With the backing of the US and the dominions we should seek to form a Western democratic system (civil liberties and fundamental rights). The moment is ripe for a consolidation of Western Europe. This need not take the shape of a formal alliance, though we have an alliance with France and may conclude one with other countries. It does however mean close consultation with each of the Western European countries, beginning with economic questions.

The Cabinet urged Bevin not to lay too much emphasis on the anti-Soviet aspects of his proposals.

97. The US reactions to the prospect of a Western European Union were warm: 'Only such a union holds out […] any hope of restoring the balance of power in Europe without permitting Germany to become again the dominant power.' But the US administration also asked for some clarifications, and that it envisaged the creation of a European third force which was not merely the extension of US influence but a real European Organization strong enough to say no both to the Soviet Union and to the US.[100] Although this was not specified by Bevin, there was agreement between France and the UK that action should focus on the enlargement of the Dunkirk Treaty. The Benelux countries should be integrated in the security and defence system created by the Dunkirk Treaty, which thus would get a multilateral and European dimension.[101]

98. In a further step a political institution could be created, the CoE, in which five other powers would be added to the Five Power Brussels nucleus, so to create

99. Bullock, 498.
100. Bullock, 517.
101. Wilhelm Cornides & Herrmann Volle, 1755–1765.

a greater nucleus still. In this, the UK and France acted on the principle of geographical propinquity, but they imagined, that the CoE when formed, would include other States.

§9. The Bevin Speech, the Conclusion of the Brussels Treaty and the Creation of the OEEC (OECD) and NATO

99. On 22 January 1948, Bevin held his great speech in the House of Commons which is generally considered as the starting point of the governmental efforts to create the above-mentioned quartet of four International Organizations: the WEU, the OEEC, NATO and the CoE. He put forward his general broad conception of WEU as a whole. This concept led to the conclusion of the Brussels Treaty, which was largely defensive but partly also covered economic, social and cultural matters.

100. The main themes of Bevin's speech were Soviet policy since WW II, and the means by which Western Europe could and should defend its independence. Bevin said that all the developments described pointed to the conclusion that the free nations of Western Europe must draw together and that the time is ripe for consolidation. He hoped that treaties would be signed with the near neighbours, the Benelux countries making with the UK treaty with France (Dunkirk Treaty) an important nucleus in Western Europe. 'We have then to go beyond the circle of our immediate neighbours. We shall have to consider the question of associating other historic members of European civilisation, including the new Italy, in this great conception […] Britain cannot stand outside Europe and regard her problems as quite separate from those of her European neighbours.' Finally, Mr Bevin said that 'if one wanted to have an Organism in the West it should be a spiritual union[102] which is constructed on the fundamental freedoms and ethical principles which all are common to us. It should be based on total equality and contain all elements of liberty which we share'.[103]

101. Already one day before Bevin's speech, France and the UK had proposed to the Benelux countries to study the conclusion of a political pact on the basis of a draft prepared by the Foreign Office. The draft was submitted on 19 February

102. The idea of a spiritual reconstruction was already present in the 1940 work of the post-war aims committee in the UK of which Bevin had been a member and had been developed mainly by Lord Halifax; *see* Simpson, 578–579.
103. Hansard of 22 Jan. 1948. In February 1948, the Council of the UK Royal Institute of International Affairs convened a meeting of members to advise on a study of the implications of European Co-operation and of what Mr Bevin termed 'Western Union'. Ralph George Hawtrey, *Western European Union, Implications for the UK* (London and New York: Royal Institute of International Affairs, printed at the Welwyn Garden City, Hertfordshire: Broadwater Press, 1949).

1948. The three countries then insisted that the pact should be conceived as a multilateral treaty. In addition to a military entente, also political and economic activities should be foreseen. Finally, the pact should not mention a specific country but refer to an armed aggression.[104]

102. From 4–12 March, negotiations took place in Brussels, and already on 17 March 1948, the Brussels Treaty was signed by France, the UK and the Benelux countries. US President Truman declared in the US Congress on the same day that the Treaty was an act whose significance went far beyond the actual terms of the agreement itself and one which deserved 'our full support'. 'I am sure that the determination of the free countries of Europe to protect themselves will be matched by an equal determination on our part to help them do so.'[105] Some authors, particularly Prof. Bitch from the Robert Schuman University in Strasbourg[106] consider that the Brussels Treaty and OEEC were mainly wished by the US to contribute to limit the advancement of communism in Europe, to convince the Americans of the need of their assistance programmes for Europe and to facilitate the adoption of the respective laws in the US Congress.

103. 1948 then saw the creation of the OEEC with the main task of contributing to the European Recovery Programme (Marshall Plan) and the preparatory work for the NATO Treaty,[107] which was signed in April 1949. Despite these impressive achievements it should be noted that the Americans would have liked to see a stronger OEEC and particularly a commitment to European federation, but this was not yet possible in 1948. Furthermore, it is admitted that in that year there was no one except the British capable of organizing a European response to the existing challenges.[108]

§10. The Preparatory Work for a CoE

I. The Congress of the Hague (May 1948)

104. The idea of a greater unity in Europe was pursued by the Movements for European unity.[109110] This allowed involving a wider public, differently from the processes which led to the creation of the League of Nations or the preparation of the Briand Plan. Churchill and his son-in-law, Duncan-Sandys, were also aware of

104. Bert Zeeman, 'Der Brüsseler Pakt', in *Vom Marshallplan zur EWG*, edited by Herbst, Bührer & Sowade (München: Oldenbourg Verlag, 1990), 402.
105. Bullock, 537.
106. *Histoire de la construction européenne*, 5th edn (Paris: Éditions Complexe, 2008), 43.
107. For more details *see* Lord Gladwyn's memoirs, 208–227.
108. Bullock, 539, 540.
109. For the details *see* Simpson, 597–648 and – regarding the European Convention on Human Rights – 649 et seq.; Ugo Leone, Le origine diplomatiche del Consiglio d'Europa, Giuffre, Mailano, 1966 and Bitsch, *supra*.
110. Details are given in: European Movement and the Council of Europe (London, New York, Melbourne, Sydney, Cape Town: European Movement by Hutchinson & Co. Ltd, 1949), 33–34.

the need to mobilize a larger public. They managed to group together the different branches of the private Movements for European Unity under an International (Coordination) Committee. This Committee announced in January 1948 the organization of a Congress of Europe in The Hague from 7–10 May 1948.

105. About 780 persons from almost every European nationality attended the Congress. There were observers from the US, the Commonwealth, the Holy See and some Eastern European countries. Those present included former Prime Ministers and Ministers, MPs of all political shade, industrialists, trade unionists, lawyers, professors. They could as a gathering claim to represent almost every important aspect in the life and opinions of Europe.

106. Winston Churchill was the President of Honour of the Congress. He underlined that one of the main tasks would be the elaboration of the European Convention on Human Rights, and to guarantee the rights which were enshrined in it by a European Court of Human Rights.

107. One of the main matters dealt with by the Congress was the creation of an Assembly for Europe. During the closing sitting of the Congress, Denis de Rougemont read a 'Message to the Europeans' which included the following passage: 'We want a European Assembly where the active forces of all our nations are represented.' Therefore, in the views of the majority of the participants at the Congress in The Hague, the building of political Europe had to start with an autonomous European Assembly.

108. The Congress also:

- asked for the creation of an economic and political union to ensure security and social progress;
- underlined the need for European nations to transfer and merge some portion of their sovereign rights so as to secure common political and economic action for the integration and proper development of their common resources;
- considered that any Union or Federation of Europe should be designed to protect the security of its constituent people; and
- stated that such Union or Federation should be free from outside control and should not be directed against any other nation.

109. With respect to the European Assembly, the Congress:

- asked for the Assembly's urgent convening;
- proposed that parliaments of the participating nations should appoint representatives to the European Assembly from among their members or others;
- asked that the Assembly should advise upon measures destined to progressively bring about the necessary economic and political union of Europe; and
- proposed that the Assembly should examine the juridical and constitutional implications arising out of the creation of such a Union or Federation and their economic and social consequences.

110. The resolutions adopted in The Hague had a significant effect on thought in political circles and served the furtherance of the supranational idea. In addition, it formed the basis for submitting to the European Governments the project of a European Assembly.

111. In this connection it may also be noted that in the period of late 1948 and 1949 the support (and the financial aid) of the American Committee for a United Europe, officially set up on 5 January 1949, was important for the creation of the CoE.

II. Governmental Action since 1948 in Favour of a European Assembly and a CoE

112. The International Committee of the movements for European Unity (which in October 1948 became the European Movement) was tasked by the Congress of The Hague to ensure follow-up action to the resolutions adopted. They were forwarded to the European Governments. Furthermore, the International Committee of the Movements for European Unity prepared a memorandum on the convening, the participating countries, financing and tasks of the European Assembly.

113. Following the adoption of the Brussels Treaty and the Congress of The Hague, motions were tabled by Assembly members in several national parliaments. The most important was probably that by Mr Bonnefous, of 19 March 1948 tabled in the French National Assembly on the convening of a democratic European Constituent Assembly, composed of members of national parliaments. This motion led to the preparation of the report of 23/24 July 1948 outlining the tasks of such an Assembly, that was to:

- prepare a declaration on human rights;
- coordinate the customs systems; and
- propose a general plan for economic organization.[111]

114. It was thanks to an initiative by the then French Foreign Minister Georges Bidault that the process of the building of Europe was brought to the intergovernmental level. At a meeting of the Consultative Council of the Brussels Treaty Organisation (WEU) on 19 July 1948 he proposed for urgent consideration:

- the creation of a European Assembly with representatives of the parliaments of the five Member States of the Brussels Treaty and of other European States wishing to participate; and
- the creation of an Economic and Customs Union.

111. Edouard Bonnefous, *La construction de l'Europe par l'un de ses initiateurs* (Paris: 2002), 22.

115. These proposals were referred for study to the Standing Committee of the Brussels Treaty. On 18 August 1948, the aforementioned memorandum by the International Committee on the European Assembly was ready. On the same day, the French Council of Ministers supported the memorandum and decided to take all appropriate initiatives.[112] On 2 September 1948, France and Belgium submitted to the Standing Committee a draft concerning the convening of a preparatory conference for the creation of an Assembly composed of representatives of the parliaments of the Brussels Treaty.

III. The Debate on the Creation of a European Assembly and a CoE in the Organs of the Brussels Treaty and the Convening of a 'Study Commission'

116. The subsequent debate in the organs of the Brussels Treaty on the European Assembly was soon transformed into a Franco-British dialogue showing major differences in the attitudes of both countries. This was further complicated by the fact that the UK proposed in the discussions to create an intergovernmental CoE, which was at least partly based on ideas concerning such an organization advanced by Churchill.

117. On 21 October 1948, the Standing Committee presented a short report on the question of a European Assembly. Some days later, the matter was discussed by the Foreign Ministers in the Paris meeting of the Consultative Council of the Brussels Treaty (25 and 26 October 1948). Bevin reiterated his criticism of the planned European Assembly. Schuman said that France and other countries attached importance to the Assembly which would also make it easier to associate Germany. Furthermore, France had to take such an initiative because of public opinion in the US. Bevin, however, favoured the idea that in January every year the Western European Prime Ministers should meet as a Council of Western Europe with the power to consider reports and take initiatives. For Bevin, the solution was to create a sense of security against the greatest fear of all, that of repeating the experience of war and occupation and that could only come into being through a North Atlantic, not purely European, defence pact. Schuman and Spaak felt that it was essential to merge national sovereignties into a European Community.[113] At the end of the meeting a committee was set up composed of five members each for France and the UK, three members each for Belgium and the Netherlands and two members for Luxembourg. Its main task was to propose to the Governments the measures to be taken with a

112. Some of the reasons for the very active role of France are given by Marie-Thérèse Bitsch, 48–50, and by Raymond Poidevin, 'Die europapolitischen Initiativen Frankreichs des Jahres 1950 – aus einer Zwangslage geboren?', in *Vom Marshallplan zur EWG*, edited by Herbst, Bührer & Sowade (München: Oldenbourg Verlag, 1990), 257–278.

113. Bullock, 617–618.

view to achieving a greater unity among European States. To this end the Committee would take into consideration all proposals of Governments or private Organizations, including those made by Belgium and France concerning a European Assembly, and the proposal by Mr Bevin for a European Council composed of Ministers of the interested States.[114]

118. It has already been mentioned that the Committee had almost the same name as that instituted within the League of Nations in 1930 to follow-up the Briand Plan, namely Study Commission for European Union. In November the new Committee, chaired by Edouard Herriot, started its preparatory work for the elaboration of the Statute of a new European Institution to take either the name of European Union or Council of Europe. On 26 November 1948, the UK presented a memorandum on the proposal for a CoE.

119. The work of the Committee was not easy and marked by differing views. On the one side, the French and Belgian representatives wished to integrate into the new organization a genuine parliamentary Assembly with a wide competence and constituted by representatives, which were independent from Governments. On the other side, the UK representatives wished an intergovernmental organization, the CoE with a CM as the executive body and an Assembly with limited competences and without a genuine parliamentary character.[115]

120. Finally, in January 1949, a compromise was found between the two positions during two meetings between Schuman and Bevin which gave shape to a CoE with a CM as executive organ but an Assembly composed in principle of members of national parliaments. Furthermore the British and the French Governments reached a compromise on the structures of the European Organization to be created. Robert Schuman wished that a really efficient organization be established in Strasbourg with wider possibilities and powers for the Assembly. Realizing that he could not obtain more from the other governments, he said that 'l'essentiel est de commencer … Il faut laisser les idées se frayer leur chemin en leur proposant une ambiance, un commencement d'exécution, quelque timide qu'il soit. Il faut procéder par étapes … '.[116] This concluded the work of the Study Commission for European Union. The important contribution of the European Movement to this work should be underlined. It submitted two memoranda to the Study Commission and a delegation of the European Movement was heard by it.

IV. Finalization of the Draft Statute of the CoE

121. On 4 March 1949, at the meeting of the Consultative Council of the Brussels Treaty, a declaration of the principles on which the future CoE would be based,

114. Ugo Leone, *Le origine diplomatiche del Consiglio d'Europa* (Milano: 1966), 60.
115. The Memoirs of Lord Gladwyn, 222, 223; for the details *see* Leone.
116. Raymond Poidevin & Robert Schuman, *homme d'Etat (1886–1963)* (Paris: Imprimerie nationale, 1986), 233.

was agreed. The draft Statute was finalized on 5 March–14 April 1949 in a Conference of Ambassadors at which Representatives of Denmark, Ireland, Italy, Norway and Sweden had been invited to participate, and afterwards in the Conference of Foreign Ministers of the ten powers.

122. At the first meeting of the Conference of Ambassadors, on 5 March 1949, the chairperson, Sir Gladwyn Webb, outlined the scheme for the CoE:

> 'The COE as we conceive it is a machine primarily designed to bring ever closer together those European States who to a large extent, share a common historical background and a common way of life sometimes referred to as a civilisation. It is purposely not designed to deal with any matters relating to defence and it cannot therefore be said to be directed against anybody. Nevertheless, there are certain traditions, principles and standards which are associated with our respective countries and which in the world of today are increasingly threatened. The Council of Europe will, we hope, be chiefly engaged in preserving these principles in the world. And thus in making the voice of Europe heard in the world. It will be seen that, if this is to be achieved, there must be some means whereby we can all of us try to formulate our common principles and ideals, whether they relate to things of the spirit – and by this world I would include cultural activities, the rule of law and human rights – or whether they relate to material things such as economic and social advancement and political co-operation.' [...]. 'The body whose establishment we are suggesting is of an entirely novel type. It is partly – perhaps chiefly – governmental, but to a considerable extent it is also non-governmental. Its successful functioning will hence demand not only great enthusiasm, great organisational ability and grand fertility in adapting old procedures and inventing new ones [...].'

The European Movement presented a major memorandum to the ambassadors, including, in particular, very precise proposals on the functions and structure of the proposed Assembly of the CoE. It sincerely hoped that it would develop into a kind of European Parliament. It should also be recalled that in 1949 the European Movement worked hard on a European Convention on Human Rights (including democratic liberties) together with a statute of the European Court of Human Rights. A draft was submitted to the Signatory States of the CoE's Statute in July 1949. This draft had been prepared in particular by Pierre-Henri Teitgen, Sir David Maxwell-Fyfe and Fernand Dehousse, who all took over later important functions in the Assembly of the CoE. About a third of the European Movement's members in 1949 also became Assembly members.

123. The Conference of Ambassadors could not solve all questions related to the Statute, such as the name of the future organization, the majorities required for decisions of the CM, the accession of new Member States, etc. These were left to the Conference of Ministers of Foreign Affairs, held on 14 April–5 May 1949. The Statute (Treaty of London) with a CM and a Consultative (since 1974: Parliamentary)

Assembly as its main organs, was adopted and signed on 5 May 1949 by the Ministers of ten European Powers: the five States of the Brussels Treaty and Denmark, Ireland, Italy, Norway and Sweden.

§11. Some Special Features of the CoE

124. The main particularities of the new organization were:

- its marked moral and spiritual outreach in the preamble of the Statute; Robert Schuman spoke in this connection of a spiritual unity which had been inscribed in the preamble;[117]
- the pronounced commitment of the COE to human rights and their development;
- its clear aim (although not explicitly mentioned) of reintegrating Germany into the European family (special provision of Article 5 of the Statute); and
- its Assembly with explicit possibilities for its evolution built into the Statute; this was in particular to the credit of France which would also have preferred the title of European Union for the organization to underline its dynamic character.

125. Between 1949 and the end of 1951, the CoE was without competition in Europe and all evolutions were still possible, for example towards a European Union. The Assembly dealt then with the fundamental questions of European unification and the CoE had a genuine political programme.[118] When, for instance, in October 1951, Robert Schuman envisaged launching a new initiative in favour of a European Political Authority, the Parliamentary Assembly was the appropriate forum to be chosen. However, as in December 1951 the Assembly could not find a majority to agree on convening a European Conference to elaborate a draft treaty for a European Political Community, this major project was then followed up at the level of the six Member States of the European Coal and Steel Community (ECSC).

126. Thanks to the French delegation and Robert Schuman, the Statute of the CoE contains several provisions which subject to a corresponding political will of the governments and the Assembly would have permitted a considerable evolution of the Assembly:

- Article 38d (budgetary powers of the Assembly).
- Articles 23–35 (Assembly).
- Article 41d (simplified procedure of modification of the Statute).

127. At a given moment it was also envisaged to allow a change of Article 11 of the Statute on the seat of the CoE by consent between the CM and the Assembly.

117. Robert Schuman, 'L'Europe est une Communauté spirituelle et culturelle', in *European Yearbook*, vol. I (The Hague: Council of Europe, Martinus Nijhoff, 1955), 18–24.
118. For the details *see* articles in Europa-Archiv, 1950, 3227 and 3342.

§12. Final Remarks

128. According to the protagonists of European Union the creation of the CoE and its Assembly were major innovations and generated a new hope in Europe. Both allowed a first institutional experience in Europe. Their experimental nature was clearly expressed by two Foreign Ministers when signing the Statute of the Organization in London. Due to its outstanding composition in the early years the Assembly was exceptionally brilliant.

129. Harold Macmillan said during a debate in the House of Commons on 21 July 1949, that the Assembly was a European Parliament *in embryo*. In any case, the Assembly always behaved like a genuine parliament and most of its members wished that this would materialize.

130. The CoE and its Statute only marked the beginnings of European integration.[119] However, the CoE clearly had the possibility of becoming a kind of European Community/European Union in its first two years of existence. Due to their great flexibility the Council and its Assembly were always able to adapt rapidly to changing conditions and situations in Europe.

131. Despite the limits fixed by the Statute, the CoE has major achievements among its assets. Until 1989, it managed to have all Western European States among its members.[120] It was in the Parliamentary Assembly that Mikhail Gorbachev presented his great European speech in July 1989, a few months before the Berlin Wall collapsed. As soon as this was allowed by the political situation, the Assembly was ready to enlarge membership to East European countries which fulfilled the requirements, thereby stabilizing them. Today, with the exception of Belarus, all European countries are Member States. By means of its manifold organs and institutions the CoE and its Member States actively promote a wider Europe without dividing lines and democratic stability in this area.[121]

---

119. Coudenhove-Kalergi, *Kampf um Europa* (Zürich: Atlantis Verlag, 1949), 294.

120. The only exceptions then were the mini-States Andorra and Monaco.

121. More details are to be found in Bruno Haller, *An Assembly for Europe – The Council of Europe's Parliamentary Assembly 1949–1989* (Strasbourg: Council of Europe Publishing, 2006), (…) and in Denis Huber, *A Decade that Made History – The Council of Europe 1989–1999* (Council of Europe Publishing, 1999) and, more recently, in Jean Petaux, *Democracy and Human Rights for Europe – The Council of Europe's Contribution* (Council of Europe Publishing, 2009). For further details *see also* Birte Wassenberg, *Histoire du Conseil de l'Europe (1949–2009)*, Peter Lang, 2012 and, by the same author, *Histoire du Conseil de l'Europe*, Council of Europe Publishing, 2013.

Part II. The CoE's Institutional Structure

Chapter 1. Overview

Tanja E. J. Kleinsorge

132. When the CoE was established in 1949, its institutional structure was the result of a compromise between those countries (and European movements) favouring a revolutionary model of an international organization dominated by independent members (mainly of parliament) and those countries (in particular, the UK) attached to the tried-and-tested model of an intergovernmental organization.[122] Thus, the Statute of the CoE knows only two organs:[123] the CM (vested with most decision-making powers) and the (Consultative, later Parliamentary) Assembly, composed of members of national parliaments with full voting freedom. These two organs were thus entrusted with achieving the CoE's ambitious aims of achieving 'a greater unity between its members for the purpose of safeguarding and realizing the ideals and principles which are their common heritage and facilitating their economic and social progress' (Article 1a of the Statute) 'by discussion of questions of common concern and by agreements and common action in economic, social, cultural, scientific, legal and administrative matters and in the maintenance and further realisation of human rights and fundamental freedoms' (Article 1b of the Organization's Statute).

133. They are served by a Secretariat of – by now – roughly 2,000 staff members headed by a Secretary General elected by the Parliamentary Assembly. The seat of the organization is in the historically important, symbolic city of Strasbourg, France, and its membership has in the meantime grown to forty-seven countries (as of 1 January 2019), with five observers.[124] This means that the CM now has forty-seven members (the Ministers of Foreign Affairs of those forty-seven member countries), permanently represented by their Deputies (most of which have the rank of

---

122. *See* Mario Heinrich's contribution on the process that led to the creation of the Council of Europe and its Assembly in this volume, as well as the Council of Europe's website: www.coe.int, Chapter 'A Short History of the Council of Europe'.

123. Statute of the Council of Europe, Preamble: '[...] Have in consequence decided to set up a Council of Europe consisting of a committee of representatives of governments and of a consultative assembly, and have for this purpose adopted the following Statute.' (Adopted in London on 5 May 1949). *See also* Art. 10 of the Statute.

124. Forty-seven Member States (with the dates of accession in brackets): Albania (13 Jul. 1995), Andorra (10 Nov. 1994), Armenia (25 Jan. 2001), Austria (16 Apr. 1956), Azerbaijan (25 Jan.

Ambassador) in Strasbourg. The PACE now has 648 members (324 representatives and 324 substitutes) from the forty-seven national parliaments, plus thirty observers and thirty partners for democracy (who do not hold voting rights).

134. The ECHR, arguably the CoE's most important treaty, is already foreshadowed in Article 3 of the Statute:

> Every member of the Council of Europe must accept the principles of the rule of law and of the enjoyment by all persons within its jurisdiction of human rights and fundamental freedoms, and collaborate sincerely and effectively in the realisation of the aim of the Council as specified in Chapter I.

It is tempting to describe the ECtHR, the treaty body charged with adjudicating on the ECHR, as the 'third' CoE organ, but *stricto sensu* this is not correct, even though the Court has been entrusted with more powers over time.[125] The CoE thus does not mirror the classic national model of checks and balances, with a legislative, an executive and a judicial body. It is the CM which exercises both legislative and executive functions, and ensures that the judgments of the ECtHR are abided by. The CM, not the Court, decides whether a Member State which has violated Article 3 of the Statute should be suspended from the organization,[126] it is the CM which drafts the treaties upon which the CoE has built the European treaty-infrastructure, and which makes recommendations to Member States – and the Court has no possibility to invalidate any of these or parts thereof.

2001), Belgium (5 May 1949), Bosnia and Herzegovina (24 Apr. 2002), Bulgaria (7 May 1992), Croatia (6 Nov. 1996), Cyprus (24 May 1961), Czech Republic (30 Jun. 1993), Denmark (5 May 1949), Estonia (14 May 1993), Finland (5 May 1989), France (5 May 1949), Georgia (27 Apr. 1999), Germany (13 Jul. 1950), Greece (9 Aug. 1949), Hungary (6 Nov. 1990), Iceland (7 Mar. 1950), Ireland (5 May 1949), Italy (5 May 1949), Latvia (10 Feb. 1995), Liechtenstein (23 Nov. 1978), Lithuania (14 May 1993), Luxembourg (5 May 1949), Malta (29 Apr. 1965), Moldova (13 Jul. 1995), Monaco (5 Oct. 2004), Montenegro (11 May 2007), Netherlands (5 May 1949), Norway (5 May 1949), Poland (26 Nov. 1991), Portugal (22 Sep. 1976), Romania (7 Oct. 1993), Russian Federation (28 Feb. 1996), San Marino (16 Nov. 1988), Serbia (3 Apr. 2003), Slovakia (30 Jun. 1993), Slovenia (14 May 1993), Spain (24 Nov. 1977), Sweden (5 May 1949), Switzerland (6 May 1963), 'The Former Yugoslav Republic of Macedonia' (9 Nov. 1995), Turkey (9 Aug. 1949), Ukraine (9 Nov. 1995), United Kingdom (5 May 1949). Five observers: Canada (29 May 1996), Holy *See* (7 Mar. 1970), Japan (20 Nov. 1996), Mexico (1 Dec. 1999), United States of America (10 Jan. 1996).

125. Thus, for example, Protocol 11 to the ECHR created a 'single', full-time Court by merging the European Commission and the European Court of Human Rights, and abolishing the possibility for states to opt out of allowing individual petitions to the Court.

126. The Committee of Ministers only came close to using this prerogative once, in 1969, after the Greek colonels had overthrown the legally elected government and installed an authoritarian regime which openly contravened the democratic principles defended by the organization. On 12 Dec. 1969, just a few hours before a decision would have been taken to exclude Greece, the colonels' regime anticipated matters by denouncing the European Convention on Human Rights and withdrawing from the Council of Europe. *See* the Council of Europe's website: www.coe.int, cha pter 'a short history of the Council of Europe'.

135. The Parliamentary Assembly, though entrusted with few decision-making powers (besides elections),[127] has used its power of making recommendations to the CM to become the motor and the conscience of the organization. The idea for nearly all CoE treaties originated in the Assembly, and the Assembly has often managed to convince the CM – even 'at the last moment', shortly before a treaty was opened for signature – to strengthen its content or control-machinery, in keeping with Article 1b of the Statute. However, the relationship between the two organs has at times been fraught with some tension – though they both jealously guard their prerogatives, especially in relation to 'newcomers', that is other bodies which would aspire to being the 'third pillar' of the CoE, such as the ECtHR or the Congress of Local and Regional Authorities,[128] the Commissioner for Human Rights[129] or the Conference of INGOs.[130]

136. The Statute foresees the possibility for both organs of the CoE to establish Committees or Commissions (Articles 17 and 24), and both have used this right. The Parliamentary Assembly currently[131] has a Bureau and nine Committees:

- Political affairs.
- Legal affairs and human rights.
- Social affairs, health and sustainable development.
- Migration, refugees and displaced persons.
- Culture, science, education and media.
- Equality and non-discrimination.
- Honouring of obligations and commitments by Member States of the CoE (monitoring).
- Rules of procedure, immunities and institutional affairs.
- Election of judges to the ECtHR.

137. Most of the Committees have, furthermore, set up Sub-Committees to deal with important specific matters (e.g., the Sub-Committee on Human Rights of the Committee on Legal Affairs and Human Rights, or the Sub-Committee on Gender Equality of the Committee on Equality and Non-Discrimination). As a political body, the Assembly's six political groups[132] are, however, practically as important as the Committees when it comes to decision-making (i.e., voting), though the drafting process is done in Committee.[133]

---

127. Of, for example, the Secretary General and Deputy Secretary General of the Council of Europe, the judges on the European Court of Human Rights, and the Human Rights Commissioner.
128. *See* the contribution on the Congress in this volume, as well as the Congress website (on the Council of Europe's website): www.coe.int/T/Congress.
129. *See* the contribution on the Commissioner in this volume, as well as the Commissioner's website (on the Council of Europe's website): www.coe.int/commissioner.
130. *See* the contribution on the Council of Europe's place in Europe and the world in this volume, as well as the Conference's website (on the Council of Europe's website): www.coe.int/T/NGO.
131. The structure of the Assembly and the number of Committees has varied over time.
132. At present the Assembly counts six political groups: the Socialist Group (SOC); the Group of the European People's Party (EPP/CD); Alliance of Liberals and Democrats for Europe (ALDE); the European Conservatives Group (EC), the Group of the Unified European Left (UEL) and the Free Democrats Group (FDG). Members of the Assembly are entirely free to choose the Group they

138. The CM Deputies have set up a Bureau and a number of subsidiary bodies which have changed over time.[134]

139. The CM has also set up a number of Steering Committees, which direct the CoE's activities. While all members of the Assembly's Committees and political groups are members of the Assembly (i.e., parliamentarians), and all members of the 'Rapporteur groups' of the CM' Deputies are members of the former (i.e., Permanent Representatives/Ambassadors), members of the Steering Committees are usually government-appointed experts.

140. However, in the end it is the responsibility of the CoE's two organs, the Parliamentary Assembly and the CM, to ensure that the organization's aims are fully reached: that is, first and foremost, to protect human rights, pluralist democracy and the rule of law; but also to promote awareness and encourage the development of Europe's cultural identity and diversity, to find common solutions to the challenges facing European society: such as discrimination against minorities, xenophobia, intolerance, bioethical challenges, terrorism, trafficking in human beings and in organs, organized crime and corruption, cybercrime, violence against women and children; and to consolidate democratic stability in Europe by backing political, legislative and constitutional reform.

wish to join (provided the Group accepts them). The President of the Assembly and the leaders of the groups form the Presidential Committee of the Assembly.

133. For more information on the Assembly and its structure, please *see* my own contribution and the Assembly's website (on the Council of Europe's website): http://assembly.coe.int.

134. *See* the contribution on the Committee of Ministers in this volume, as well as the Committee of Ministers' website (on the Council of Europe's website): http://www.coe.int/T/CM/WCD/Groups_en.asp.

Chapter 2. The Parliamentary Assembly: Europe's Motor and Conscience

Tanja E.J. Kleinsorge

§1. Introduction

I. An Assembly at the Service of the 'Greatest Achievements of Human Civilization'

141. On 10 August 1949, the first session of the Consultative Assembly[135] of the CoE took place in Strasbourg, two days after the first meeting of the new organization's CM. The session was opened by the Honorary President, Edouard Herriot, who declared that the Assembly members' statute 'mandates you to give body and expression to the aspirations of the people of Europe and to furnish the means to governments to constantly keep in contact with European public opinion. […] We simply want to come together to defend the two greatest achievements of human civilisation: freedom and law'.[136]

142. The Assembly, as the CoE's forum of the elected representatives of the people of Europe, has been at the service of these ideals ever since. Over the years, the Assembly has turned out to be both the motor and the conscience of the organization,[137] as well as its democratic underpinning. Its strength lies in its composition, as well as in its powers: The Statute defines it as the 'deliberative organ of the Council of Europe', which 'shall debate matters within its competence under this Statute and present its conclusions, in the form of recommendations, to the Committee of Ministers'.[138] The Assembly has always attracted the continent's great personalities.[139] It consists exclusively of members of national parliaments.[140] Being

---

135. It was only in the 1970s that the Assembly changed its name from 'Consultative Assembly' to 'Parliamentary Assembly'; the new title was officially recognized by the Committee of Ministers in February 1994. *See* Bruno Haller, *Une Assemblée au service de l'Europe, L'Assemblée parlementaire du Conseil de l'Europe 1949–1989* (Strasbourg: Editions du Conseil de l'Europe, janvier 2006), 10.

136. Cited *ibid.*, 25 (author's translation): *Votre statut vous confie le mandat de donner corps et expression aux aspirations des peuples de l'Europe et de fournir aux gouvernements le moyen de rentrer constamment en contact avec l'opinion publique européenne. […] Nous voulons simplement nous associer pour défendre les deux plus grandes acquisitions de la civilisation humaine: la liberté et le droit.*

137. It was German Chancellor Konrad Adenauer who termed the Assembly the 'conscience' of Europe in a speech before the Assembly in 1951.

138. Statute of the Council of Europe, Art. 22.

139. There is hardly a famous European politician who has not, at one time, been a member of the Assembly, from Winston Churchill over Pierre Pflimlin and Helmut Kohl to Tarja Halonen and Mikhail Saakashvili (for a full list of former members, please *see* http://assembly.coe.int). If they were not members of the Assembly, they held speeches before the Assembly, for example Konrad Adenauer (1951, 1954), Robert Schumann (1951), Willy Brandt (1958), Mário Soares (1974, 197 7), Robert Badinter (1981), Hans-Dietrich Genscher (1984), Pope John-Paul II (1988), François Mit terrand (1989), Lech Walesa (1989), Mikhail Gorbachev (1989), Jacques Delors (1989), Helmut

thus legitimated as representatives of the people, the Assembly has used its independence and its freedom of speech to push for what it believes in, regardless of governments' possible hesitations linked to '*Realpolitik*'. It has never delegated its powers to diplomatic 'deputies', as the CM has done. Meeting in Plenary Session four times a year (so-called part-sessions), and in Standing Committee in between these part-sessions, the Assembly also has every possibility to swiftly react to developments on the continent,[141] including via urgent and/or current affairs debates.[142]

II. The Assembly's Composition and Functioning

143. The composition of the Assembly's 324 members[143] reflects the realities on the continent[144] well, composed as it is of national delegations of different size in accordance with a carefully crafted formula, which takes both population size and budgetary contributions into account.[145] Each national delegation must include a member of each sex, and be representative of the political make-up of the national parliament. Each member is paired with a Substitute, also a member of a national parliament elected/appointed in the same manner, who replaces the Assembly member when he/she is unable to attend. When it comes to voting, there is no need for unanimity[146] – draft recommendations and draft opinions require two-thirds' majorities, while draft resolutions require only simple majorities. It is thus rare that the

Kohl (1993 and 1995), Jean-Claude Juncker (2002), Viktor Yushenko (2005), Franco Frattini (20 06), Angela Merkel (2008), Mahmoud Abbas (2011), David Cameron (2012), Joachim Gauck (20 13), Petro Poroshenko (2014 and 2017) and Pope Francis (2014).

140. *See* Art. 25a of the Council of Europe's Statute: 'The Consultative Assembly shall consist of representatives of each member, elected by its parliament from among the members thereof, or appointed from among the members of that parliament, in such manner as it shall decide … […] Each representative must be a national of the member whom he represents, but shall not at the same time be a member of the Committee of Ministers.'
141. The Committee of Ministers, at ministerial level, has recently limited itself to one (carefully prepared) meeting a year.
142. During each part-session, in accordance with the Assembly's rules of procedure, one current affairs debate and/or one or several urgent debates can be held, the difference being that there is no vote on a draft text at the end of a current affairs debate.
143. There are also thirty observers all in all, from the Israeli Knesset (since 1957), the Parliament of Canada (since 1997) and the Parliament of Mexico (since 1999). They have the right to speak, but not to vote.
144. Arguably, the Assembly's system reflects the realities better than the Committee of Ministers' system, where each Member State has only one vote, and, the voice of micro-states such as Andorra, Liechtenstein, Monaco and San Marino thus counts as much as that of the five main contributors to the budget, France, Germany, Italy, Russia and the UK.
145. The current composition is as follows: Albania (4), Andorra (2), Armenia (4), Austria (6), Azerbaijan (6), Belgium (7), Bosnia and Herzegovina (5), Bulgaria (6), Croatia (5), Cyprus (3), Czech Republic (7), Denmark (5), Estonia (3), Finland (5), France (18), Georgia (5), Germany (18), Greece (7), Hungary (7), Iceland (3), Ireland (4), Italy (18), Latvia (3), Liechtenstein (2), Lithuania (4), Luxembourg (3), Malta (3), Moldova (5), Monaco (2), Montenegro (3), Netherlands (7), Norway (5), Poland (12), Portugal (7), Romania (10), Russia (18), San Marino (2), Serbia (7), Slovak Republic (5), Slovenia (3), Spain (12), Sweden (6), Switzerland (6), 'the former Yugoslav Republic of Macedonia' (3), Turkey (18), Ukraine (12), United Kingdom of Great Britain and Northern Ireland (18).
146. The Committee of Ministers' Deputies prefer to take decisions by consensus whenever possible.

Assembly is not able to take a position, even on divisive subjects such as abortion,[147] prostitution,[148] creationism,[149] etc.

144. The Assembly deals with all subjects – with the exception of defence[150] – but concentrates its energies on defending the core principles of the CoE: pluralist democracy, human rights and the rule of law. However, it is also very active in the social and cultural fields. The Assembly also provides a forum for international organizations such as the OECD, the European Bank for Reconstruction and Development (EBRD) and several of the UN specialized agencies, and reviews their activities. It also has external relations and a good working relationship with other parliamentary bodies, in particular the IPU and the EP.

145. To start dealing with a given subject, twenty or more members of the Assembly belonging to at least five national delegations draw up a motion for a recommendation or resolution. This motion is tabled, examined by the Bureau of the Assembly, and then referred to the appropriate committee for report (and possibly to other committees for opinion, if the subject concerns two or more committees). The reporting committee then appoints a rapporteur who draws up a report on the subject within the two-year deadline (sometimes after having been on a fact-finding visit), which is divided into two parts: the operational draft resolution, recommendation or opinion and the explanatory memorandum. Committees often organize hearings, or consult experts, before discussing the report in committee, and voting on the operational part. Once a report has been adopted in the committee, it is tabled for discussion by the Assembly either at a part-session or at a meeting of the Standing Committee, where the operational part is voted upon.

146. Another possibility for Assembly members to give formal expression to their views on matters of European interest are written declarations, which must be quite short,[151] and signed by at least twenty representatives or substitutes of four nationalities and two political groups. If judged by the President to be in order, the written declaration is printed as an Assembly document and distributed.[152]

147. *See* Res. 1607(2008) on access to safe and legal abortion in Europe.
148. *See* Res. 1579(2007) and Recommendation 1815(2007) on prostitution – which stance to take?
149. *See* Res. 1580(2007) on the dangers of creationism in education.
150. In the early days, the Assembly also debated issues linked to defence.
151. They may not exceed 200 words.
152. If a written declaration receives new signatures before the opening of the next part-session, it is redistributed.

§2. The Achievements of the Assembly

I. Standard-Setting

A. The ECHR, the European Social Charter and the European Cultural Convention

147. The Assembly has always played an important role when it comes to CoE standard-setting, that is, treaty-making. Many of the CoE's more than 200 multilateral treaties were drafted at the initiative of the Assembly. Indeed, it was during the Assembly's first session, in August 1949, that it recommended the elaboration of three treaties which were to become the organization's historic achievements: the ECHR, the European Social Charter and the European Cultural Convention.[153] Thus, one of the particularities of the ECHR, that it applies to 'everyone' within the jurisdiction of the High Contracting Parties (rather than just their nationals),[154] goes back to the Assembly's Recommendation 38(1949), in which it:

> Recommends the Committee of Ministers to cause a draft Convention to be drawn up as early as possible, providing a collective guarantee, and designed to ensure the effective enjoyment of all persons residing within their territories of the rights and fundamental freedoms referred to in the Universal Declaration of Human Rights ... (Article 1).

In fact, the ECHR was rapidly elaborated and adopted: it was opened for signature in Rome on 4 November 1950, just fifteen months after the Assembly's recommendation. The Assembly recognized the paramount importance of this treaty, and considered from the outset that the willingness to ratify it should become a *sine qua non* condition for membership for states wishing to join the CoE.[155] From the date of the adoption of the treaty, the Assembly lobbied in favour of extending the rights enshrined therein, which led to the adoption of a number of additional protocols to the ECHR, guaranteeing *inter alia* the right to free and secret elections, to individual property, and to be free of discrimination.

B. The Outlawing of Torture

148. One of the perpetual worries of the Assembly has been torture. The right to be free of torture and inhuman or degrading treatment or punishment was already included in the ECHR in a very prominent place (Article 3) at the behest of the Assembly. But that was not the end of it: The subject came up again in the 1970s, when the UN and NGOs such as Amnesty International campaigned against the

153. Bruno Haller, *Une Assemblée au service de l'Europe*, 8.
154. Article 1 of the ECHR – Obligation to respect human rights: 'The High Contracting Parties shall secure to everyone within their jurisdiction the rights and freedoms defined in Section I of this Convention.'
155. Bruno Haller, *Une Assemblée au service de l'Europe*, 68.

practice,[156] unfortunately somewhat popular again at the time, in particular with military and dictatorial regimes. In 1975, the Assembly held a debate on the matter, during which the idea of creating a mechanism to prevent torture came up.[157] But it was not until 1983 that the Assembly adopted Recommendation 971(1983) on the protection of detainees from torture and from cruel, inhuman or degrading treatment or punishment, to which it appended a draft convention on the matter. Moving swiftly, the intergovernmental side negotiated a new treaty on this basis, which was opened for signature in November 1987. Again, this Convention proved a milestone for the CoE,[158] and the Assembly rapidly made its ratification by new Member States a condition for membership in the CoE.[159]

149. The question of the treatment of detainees made a comeback onto the political agenda following the attack on the World Trade Center in New York on 11 September 2001, which involved the US in a 'war on terror' during which the definition of torture was bent to suit the US's perceived needs. The effects were felt in Europe, as well, when it came to light that a number of European states had assisted the US in the 'rendition' of terror suspects for possible torture, or illegal secret detentions. It appears that the Assembly was able to put a stop to these practices by Member States of the CoE through the publicity and media attention received on the two reports on the matter drawn up by the rapporteur of the Committee on Legal Affairs and Human Rights, the Swiss lawyer and parliamentarian Dick Marty in 2005–2007.[160]

C. The Abolition of the Death Penalty

150. The abolition of the death penalty is one of the Assembly's greatest achievements. The death penalty was originally written into the ECHR in 1950,[161] when it was still legal in most of the CoE's founding states, and applied in some of them.[162] But public opinion evolved over the years, and already in the 1970s the Assembly counted among its members a number of convinced and courageous abolitionists, who tried to change the Assembly's position on capital punishment – at first, sadly, without success.[163] However, by 1980, the abolitionists had succeeded,

156. *Ibid.*, 80.
157. *Ibid.*
158. For more information on the Convention and its body, the CPT, please *see* Hugh Chetwynd's contribution in this volume.
159. Bruno Haller, *Une Assemblée au service de l'Europe*, 81–82.
160. Document 10957 on Alleged secret detentions and unlawful inter-state transfers of detainees involving Council of Europe Member States, which led to the adoption of Res. 1507(2006) and Recommendation 1754, and Doc. 11302 on Secret detentions and illegal transfers of detainees involving Council of Europe Member States: second report, which led to the adoption of Res. 1562(2007) and Recommendation 1801(2007).
161. *See* Art. 2 of the ECHR.
162. Bruno Haller, *Une Assemblée au service de l'Europe*, 91.
163. For details of the struggle, please *see ibid.*, 91–99.

and the Assembly, considering the death penalty 'inhuman',[164] appealed 'to the parliaments of those Member States of the CoE which have retained capital punishment for crimes committed in times of peace, to abolish it from their penal systems', and recommended that the CM draw up a Protocol to the ECHR to abolish the death penalty. The CM concurred, and Protocol No. 6 to the ECHR, abolishing the death penalty in times of peace, was opened for signature on 28 April 1983 in Strasbourg.

151. While most Member States ratified Protocol No. 6 in the 1980s, the Assembly soon realized that the enlargement of the organization to the East, following the fall of the Berlin Wall, was undermining its position on the death penalty, since most of the states of the former Warsaw Pact had held onto it. It was in these circumstances that the Assembly took up the matter again, debating the abolition of capital punishment in October 1994 on the basis of a report by the Swedish parliamentarian Hans Göran Franck.[165] The Assembly ended up taking the courageous – and unprecedented – step to impose its will on these candidate states, via the following provision in Resolution 1044(1994) on the abolition of capital punishment: 'The adequate implementation of the additional protocol to the ECHR should be a matter of continuous concern to the Assembly and the willingness to ratify the protocol be made a prerequisite for membership of the Council of Europe' (paragraph 6). The Assembly from then on negotiated with candidate states in the accession process to ensure that a moratorium on executions was put into place upon accession to the CoE, and the death penalty formally abolished within a certain time frame. The success of the new policy was not immediate: In January 1997, the Assembly had to forcefully remind two Member States (Russia and Ukraine) that it meant what it said, and would hold Member States to their commitments under the threat of sanctions.[166]

152. But by October 1997, the CoE's Second Summit of Heads of State and Government had made the Assembly's position on the abolition of the death penalty its own, which helped to guarantee that Europe would remain a death-penalty-free zone. The Summit also cleared the way for another Protocol to the ECHR, Protocol No. 13, which in 2002 abolished the death penalty in all circumstances (i.e., also in wartime) – again, a wish the Parliamentary Assembly had formulated already in 1994. The Assembly – and its rapporteurs on the death penalty, formerly parliamentarian Renate Wohlwend from Liechtenstein and now Marietta Karamanli from France – is still trying to export this success, in particular to the two CoE

164. *See* Res. 727(1980) on the abolition of capital punishment and Recommendation 891(1980) on the European Convention on Human Rights – the abolition of capital punishment.
165. The debate was quite tumultuous, and even included a roll-call vote (a rare event in the Assembly at the time, which then voted by show of hands as a general rule).
166. *See* Res. 1111(1997) on the honouring of the commitment entered into by Russia upon accession to the Council of Europe to put into place a moratorium on executions and Res. 1112(1997) on the honouring of the commitment entered into by Ukraine upon accession to the Council of Europe to put into place a moratorium on executions.

observer states which still execute prisoners, Japan and the US,[167] but also world-wide, by supporting the UN's initiative in favour of a moratorium on executions.

D. Codifying the Rights of National Minorities

153. The Assembly started dealing with the complex subject matter of the rights of national minorities in the 1950s and 1960s,[168] and had asked that an article on the protection of national minorities be included in the Second Protocol to the ECHR[169] already in 1961. But with the enlargement to the East in the early 1990s, the Assembly once more considered the time ripe to push for a codification of the rights of national minorities. In 1990, it adopted Recommendation 1,134 on the rights of minorities, in which it enunciated the main principles it considered important, and once again recommended that the CM draw up an Additional Protocol to the ECHR on the question – or, draw up a separate, special CoE Convention.[170] It took the CM nearly nine years to reply to this recommendation[171] – no doubt reflecting the fact that this particular topic proved rather divisive in the CM. In fact, some Member States, including certain EC Member States, blocked all attempts at codifying minority rights at the time.[172]

154. Pressure exerted both by the then Secretary General of the CoE, Catherine Lalumière, and the Assembly, resulted in a first success in 1992:[173] the opening for signature of the European Charter for Regional or Minority Languages on 5 November 1992.

---

167. *See* Renate Wohlwend's reports on the abolition of the death penalty in Council of Europe observer states of 2001 (Doc. 9115) and 2003 (Doc. 9908) and her 2006 report on the position of the Parliamentary Assembly as regards the Council of Europe member and observer states which have not abolished the death penalty (Doc. 10911), as well as the Resolutions and Recommendations adopted by the Assembly on this basis.
168. *See*, for example, Res. 136(1957) on the position of national minorities in Europe, Recommendation 213(1959) on the same question, and Recommendation 285(1961) on rights of national minorities.
169. Labelled as follows: *Persons belonging to a national minority shall not be denied the right, in community with the other members of their group, and as far as compatible with public order, to enjoy their own culture, to use their own language, to establish their own schools and receive teaching in the language of their choice or to profess and practise their own religion*, Recommendation 285(1961) on rights of national minorities.
170. Recommendation 1134(1990) on the rights of minorities, para. 17.
171. The Committee of Ministers made a 'grouped reply' to several recommendations on 26 Jan. 1999, Doc. 8306.
172. Walter Schwimmer, an Austrian member of parliament who became Secretary General of the Council of Europe in 1999, detailed the problems in an essay published in 2000: 'Der Einfluss der Parlamentarischen Versammlung auf die Konventionen des Europarats', in *Law in Greater Europe – Towards a Common Legal Area*, edited by Bruno Haller, Hans Christian Krüger & Herbert Petzold (The Hague/London: Kluwer Law International, 2000), 377–406.
173. *Ibid.*, 377–406, 395–396.

155. However, it took the First Summit of the organization, held in Vienna in October 1993, to give the necessary impetus for the codification of national minority rights in general. To the regret of the Assembly – and that of the then President-in-Office of the CM, Austrian Foreign Minister Alois Mock – the suggestion of the Assembly that this codification take the form of an Additional Protocol to the ECHR,[174] was discarded in favour of the (weaker) solution of a 'Framework Convention'.[175] The Assembly's own draft Additional Protocol, included in Recommendation 1201(1993), had obviously been too ambitious for some governments. The rapid elaboration of the Framework Convention for the Protection of National Minorities, which was opened for signature on 1 February 1995, was thus no compensation for the Assembly at the time – it was 'weakly worded' and 'vague' in the eyes of the Assembly.[176] Luckily, both the Convention itself and its control mechanism, the Advisory Committee, proved to have more teeth than originally feared.[177]

E. Protecting Human Rights in the Field of Bioethics

156. Keeping pace with medical and scientific progress, the Assembly started looking into the compatibility of human rights and human dignity with developing medical and scientific procedures in the 1980s. In 1982, it adopted a Recommendation on genetic engineering;[178] in 1986 on the use of human embryos and foetuses for diagnostic, therapeutic, scientific, industrial and commercial purposes;[179] and in 1989 on the use of human embryos and foetuses in scientific research.[180] In these Recommendations, the Assembly elaborated the main principles it felt should be respected in the field, and asked the CM to 'provide a framework of principles from which national laws or regulations can be developed in as universal and uniform a manner as possible'.[181] In 1990, the meeting of the CoE Ministers of Justice recommended to the organization's CM (also in light of the Assembly's recommendations) to ask the organization's expert Committee on Bioethics to study the feasibility of drawing up a Framework Convention.[182] The Assembly welcomed this decision in its Recommendation 1160(1991) on the preparation of a convention on bioethics. It agreed that the convention 'should provide a flexible formula with regard to its form', but warned that it 'must not constitute the lowest common denominator as to its content', and insisted on the inclusion of human rights aspects.[183]

---

174. In fact, the Summit did suggest the elaboration of an Additional Protocol to the ECHR on cultural rights, including those of members of national minorities, but it never saw the light of day.
175. *Ibid.*, 396–398.
176. Recommendation 1255(1995) on the protection of national minorities, para. 7.
177. For more information on the Council of Europe's work on national minorities, please *see* the relevant contribution in this volume.
178. Recommendation 934(1982).
179. Recommendation 1046(1986).
180. Recommendation 1100(1989).
181. *Ibid.*, para. 9A.
182. Walter Schwimmer, *Der Einfluss der Parlamentarischen Versammlung auf die Konventionen des Europarats*, 382–383.
183. Recommendation 1160(1991) on the preparation of a convention on bioethics, para. 7i.

157. Thus started one of the biggest fights within the Parliamentary Assembly in the standard-setting field, pitting several Committees and their rapporteurs against each other.[184] Following several debates in Committees, the Assembly, and other fora, the majority in the Assembly voted in favour of Opinion 184(1995) on the draft bioethics convention (draft convention for the protection of human rights and dignity of the human being with regard to the application of biology and medicine) – an Opinion which basically sent the CM back to the drawing board, so many amendments did it suggest to the draft convention submitted by the latter. However, the Assembly's constructive criticism bore fruit, and in June 1996, the CM presented the Assembly with a new draft convention. In Opinion 198(1996) on that draft, the Assembly this time considered the text 'coherent and balanced',[185] and suggested only a few amendments. As a result, the first legally binding international instrument in the field of bioethics was opened for signature in 1997: the Convention for the protection of Human Rights and dignity of the human being with regard to the application of biology and medicine – Convention on Human Rights and Biomedicine, which twenty-nine states have ratified so far.[186] With the active involvement of the Assembly, this landmark text was completed over the following years by several additional protocols: on the Prohibition of Cloning Human Beings (1998), concerning Transplantation of Organs and Tissues of Human Origin (2002), concerning Biomedical Research (2005), and concerning Genetic Testing for Health Purposes (2008). However, the Assembly opposed the drafting of an Additional Protocol aimed at protecting the human rights and fundamental freedoms of people with mental disorder with regard to the use of involuntary placement and involuntary treatment[187] as discriminatory and a violation of the UN Convention on the Rights of Persons with Disabilities.

II. Enlargement of the CoE

A. Early Days

158. The first two new members of the CoE, Greece and Turkey, were admitted on 9 August 1949 by the CM, one day before the Assembly met for its very first session (in which the parliamentary representatives of the two new Member States were already allowed to participate).[188] This type of accession, however, quickly turned out to be an exception to the rule: It was the Assembly which suggested that Germany be invited to become a member, and which welcomed its representatives

184. For details, please *see* Walter Schwimmer, *Der Einfluss der Parlamentarischen Versammlung auf die Konventionen des Europarats*, 383–389, and Bruno Haller, *Une Assemblée au service de l'Europe*, 82–86.
185. Opinion 198(1996) on the draft Convention on Human Rights and Biomedicine, para. 4.
186. As of 1 May 2015.
187. Recommendation 2091 (2016) on the case against a Council of Europe legal instrument on involuntary measures in psychiatry.
188. Bruno Haller: *Une Assemblée au service de l'Europe*, 27–28.

in its midst when Germany became an associate member on 13 July 1950.[189] Similarly, it was the Assembly which took the initiative to recommend to the CM to admit Austria, as well – and which welcomed Austrian parliamentary observers from 1952 until 16 April 1956, when Austria became the fifteenth Member State of the CoE and the members of the Austrian parliament thus became full members of the Assembly.[190] In May 1959, the Assembly invited the federal chambers of the Swiss parliament to send observers to its debates, in particular its economic ones; an invitation which was accepted in March 1961, and an experience which turned out to be so convincing as to persuade Switzerland to ask for membership of the CoE in December 1962. On 6 May 1963, Switzerland acceded to the organization.[191]

B. Completing the Map to the West

159. Also in the 1960s, two newly independent states became members of the CoE: Cyprus (1961) and Malta (1965). (N.B.: The Cypriot question and the fraught relationship between Greece and Turkey – as well as political crises in those states, became some of the most-debated subjects by the Assembly over the years.) With the fall of their dictatorships, Portugal and Spain joined the CoE in the late 1970s, followed by Liechtenstein (in 1978), San Marino (in 1988), Finland (in 1989) and Andorra (in 1994).

C. Expansion to the East and Southeast

160. However, it was the expansion to the East following the fall of the Berlin Wall which made the name of the Assembly in the enlargement process. The Assembly played an important role in the enlargement process of the CoE – perhaps the most important role, because it rose to the occasion when it was necessary to define the frontiers of Europe, update the conditions for membership and negotiate to a large extent the conditions for accession. Through its debates, its action in the field, the observation of elections, its invention of the 'special guest status' (to allow MPs from candidate states to participate in the work of the Assembly, albeit without the right to vote), its programmes of parliamentary co-operation, the Assembly made a major contribution to stabilizing and deepening democracy in the candidate and new Member States, and thus made the enlargement process of the organization possible and viable.

161. Having obtained the commitment by the CM already in 1951 that it would be consulted before any new Member State was admitted to the organization, the Assembly slowly, but surely, built a solid procedure which all candidate states had

189. Germany became a full member on 2 May 1951. At the July session of the Assembly in 1950, Iceland and the Saar were also represented in the Assembly. *Ibid.*, 29–30.
190. *Ibid.*, 31–33.
191. *Ibid.*, 34–36.

to submit to. This procedure was, of course, built upon the statutory requirements – Article 4 in combination with Article 3,[192] but added a political evaluation of whether the candidate state was 'willing and able' to guarantee the rule of law and the enjoyment of human rights for all on its territory. Over the years, the Assembly thus developed precise conditions for membership: some which needed to be fulfilled before membership (e.g., the holding of free and fair elections),[193] some which had to be fulfilled the day of the accession (e.g., putting into place a moratorium on executions),[194] and some which the state had to commit itself to fulfil within a certain time frame (e.g., the signature and ratification of certain Conventions, in particular, of course, the ECHR and its most important Protocols).[195]

162. As the Assembly gained experience, it honed both the procedural aspects of the accession procedure and the details of the commitments and obligations the candidate states had to be willing to enter into. The Opinions on the accession of states – and the list of commitments and obligations – became longer and longer with each accession. Of course, this reflected not only the Assembly's increasing attention to detail, but also the fact that, the farther East and southeast the Assembly moved the borders of Europe with each new accession, the more difficult the geopolitical situation became: Large countries such as Ukraine and Russia, which had no democratic tradition to speak of and which had been under the yoke of brutal dictatorships for decades, obviously found it more difficult to rapidly reform their political and legal systems to fulfil the CoE's conditions for membership than smaller countries with a pre-war tradition of democracy and the rule of law, and a sizeable opposition to Communist rule (e.g., Poland, Czechoslovakia and Hungary). The Assembly was also wary of being too hasty in taking in new members with important unresolved conflicts: conscious of the experience with Greece and Turkey, the Assembly moved with caution when it came to the question of admitting Armenia and Azerbaijan, for example, two countries which had just fought a vicious war over Nagorno-Karabakh.

---

192. Article 3: *Every member of the Council of Europe must accept the principles of the rule of law and of the enjoyment by all persons within its jurisdiction of human rights and fundamental freedoms, and collaborate sincerely and effectively in the realisation of the aim of the Council as specified in Chapter I.* Article 4: *Any European State which is deemed to be able and willing to fulfil the provisions of Article 3 may be invited to become a member of the Council of Europe by the Committee of Ministers. Any State so invited shall become a member on the deposit on its behalf with the Secretary General of an instrument of accession to the present Statute.*
193. This was the case with Poland, for example, which was not allowed to accede before it had held free and fair elections to the Polish Sejm.
194. From 1994 onwards.
195. From 1993 onwards. In 1994, the Assembly set a deadline:

> The Assembly recalls in this connection that accession to the Council of Europe must go together with becoming a party to the European Convention on Human Rights. It therefore considers that the ratification procedure should normally be completed within one year after accession to the Statute and signature of the Convention.

See Res. 1031(1994) on the honouring of commitments entered into by Member States when joining the Council of Europe, para. 9.

D. The Accession Procedure

163. The borders of Europe were defined in 1994[196] by the Assembly on the basis of a report drawn up by German Christian-Democrat Gerhard Reddemann.[197] The Assembly stipulated that: 'Membership of the Council of Europe is in principle open only to states whose national territory lies wholly or partly in Europe and whose culture is closely linked with the European culture' (paragraph 2 of the Recommendation) and then enumerated which states should have the right to become members – including Russia. The CM accepted this definition.[198] By 1994, the Assembly had already put into place its procedure for reviewing requests for membership, which involved, first, the granting of 'special guest status'[199] to a parliamentary delegation from the country concerned if certain minimum conditions were met.[200] Then came an assessment by eminent lawyers (usually members of the European Commission of Human Rights or the ECtHR)[201] – following a fact-finding visit – on whether a candidate state fulfilled the conditions of being a state based on the rule of law and respectful of human rights. The report of the eminent lawyers was followed by one – or several – fact-finding visits of the rapporteurs of the three competent Committees: the Political Affairs Committee (seized for report), the Committee on Legal Affairs and Human Rights (seized for opinion)[202] and the Committee on Relations with European Non-member Countries (seized for opinion).[203] In some cases (e.g., Russia), a letter signed by the Prime Minister, the President of the country, and the Speakers of both Chambers of Parliament was sent to the Assembly acknowledging the willingness of the country concerned to accept the commitments and obligations enumerated by the Assembly (and negotiated with the country beforehand on the basis of a 'checklist-questionnaire').[204] Following a debate in plenary session, the Assembly then adopted an Opinion addressed to the CM (with a two-thirds majority required). The CM then usually rapidly decided to follow the Assembly's Opinion (which was expressly cited in the CM decisions as from 1993 with the case of Estonia, giving it formal legal value[205]) and invited the state concerned to accede.

---

196. Recommendation 1247(1994) on the enlargement of the Council of Europe.
197. Assembly Document 7103 on the enlargement of the Council of Europe.
198. *See* the Reply of the Committee of Ministers of 3 Mar. 1995, published as Assembly Document 7263.
199. This status was created in 1989. *See* Bruno Haller, 'L'Assemblée parlementaire et les conditions d'adhésion au Conseil de l'Europe', in *Law in Greater Europe – Towards a Common Legal Area*, edited by B. Haller, H.C. Krüger & H. Petzold (The Hague/London: Kluwer Law International, 2000), 35.
200. Following the dissolution of the elected parliament by President Lukashenka of Belarus, the special guest status granted to that parliament was suspended – and has not been 'unfrozen' since.
201. Systematically used since September 1991, starting with the accession procedures of the three Baltic states. *See* Bruno Haller, *L'Assemblée parlementaire et les conditions d'adhésion au Conseil de l'Europe*, 35.
202. From 1990, *ibid.*, 35.
203. Until its dissolution in April 1997, *ibid.*, 35.
204. From 1993 onwards, *ibid.*, 36–37.
205. *Ibid.*, 28.

E. Political Decisions

164. Not all accession procedures went smoothly, of course, and some procedures were quite lengthy. Thus, for example, the Assembly suspended the accession procedure for Russia during the first Chechen war, effectively blocking Russia's accession until the Assembly was confident that Russia was 'committed to finding a political solution to the conflict', and that 'alleged and documented human rights violations were being investigated'.[206] In fact, the decision to allow Russia to accede in early 1996 was a political one: Russia was perhaps the only European country which would have had the alternative of orienting itself to the East, or creating its own club.[207] From a purely legal point of view, Russia was not ready for membership when it was admitted.[208] For the first time, in the Opinion on Russia's request for membership, the Assembly thus used the formula: 'On the basis of these assurances and of the following considerations and commitments, the Assembly believes that Russia – in the sense of Article 4 of the Statute – is clearly willing *and will be able in the near future* to fulfil the provisions for membership of the Council of Europe as set forth in Article 3 [...]' (emphasis added)[209] – instead of deeming Russia 'willing and able' as the Statute demands. The accession Opinions of Armenia and Azerbaijan a few years later (in the summer of 2000) were also quite disputed, though in these cases the Assembly went for the following formula:

> The Assembly considers that [Armenia/Azerbaijan] is moving towards a democratic, pluralist society in which human rights and the rule of law are respected, and, in accordance with Article 4 of the Statute of the Council of Europe, is able and willing to continue the democratic reforms initiated in order to bring its entire legislation and practice into conformity with the principles and standards of the Council of Europe.[210]

III. Monitoring Procedures

A. The 'Halonen-Order'

165. In 1993, when the CoE held its first Summit in Vienna, which sealed the organization's political decision to continue its enlargement process to the East and the southeast, the Assembly adopted Order 488(1993) on the honouring of commitments entered into by new Member States. This Order became known as the

---

206. Opinion 193(1996) on Russia's request for membership in the Council of Europe.
207. Which it did, creating the Commonwealth of Independent States, the CIS.
208. *See* Assembly Document 7463, the Opinion of the Committee on Legal Affairs and Human Rights on Russia's application for membership of the Council of Europe (Rapporteur: Mr Rudolf Bindig, Germany, Socialist Group).
209. Opinion 193(1996) on Russia's request for membership in the Council of Europe, para. 7.
210. Paragraph 6 of Opinion 221(2000) on Armenia's request of membership of the Council of Europe and of Opinion 222(2000) on Azerbaijan's application for membership of the Council of Europe.

'Halonen-Order' after the mover of the motion on which it was based: then Finnish parliamentarian (and later Finnish President) Tarja Halonen. The text is short enough to merit being cited *in extenso*:

(1) Recent Assembly opinions on applications for membership of the CoE refer to specific commitments entered into by the authorities of the candidate states on issues related to the basic principles of the organization.
(2) The Assembly considers that the honouring of these commitments is a condition for full participation of parliamentary delegations of new Member States in its work.
(3) The Assembly therefore instructs its Political Affairs Committee and Committee on Legal Affairs and Human Rights to monitor closely the honouring of commitments entered into by the authorities of new Member States and to report to the Bureau at regular six monthly intervals until all undertakings have been honoured.

166. Thus the Assembly invented the CoE's first 'monitoring procedure'. The motivation of the Assembly was to avoid situations where new Member States, after having become members of the organization, stalled in their reform efforts – in effect thus making the solemn commitments they had entered into more or less meaningless. The 'Halonen-Order' already brandished the threat of punishment within the Assembly for the parliamentary delegations of those new Member States not living up to their commitments. This threat was made more explicit in Resolution 1031(1994) on the honouring of commitments entered into by Member States when joining the CoE.[211] However, the procedure chosen – reports to the Assembly's Bureau – was not a public one, and thus not entirely transparent.[212] In addition, it inspired a certain rivalry between the two Committees seized (on equal terms) with the task of reporting to the Bureau, the Political Affairs Committee and the Committee on Legal Affairs and Human Rights.[213]

B. Order 508(1995)

167. In 1995, the Committee on Legal Affairs and Human Rights was given the lead role in the Assembly's monitoring procedure, and the procedure became public and more rigorous, thanks to the adoption of Order 508(1995) on the honouring of obligations and commitments by Member States of the CoE. The new Order also made clear that 'old' Member States could be tackled if they did not respect their obligations under the Statute, the ECHR and all other conventions to which they

211. 'Persistent failure to honour commitments freely entered into will have consequences however. For this purpose, the Assembly could use the relevant provisions of the Council of Europe's Statute and of its own Rules of Procedure, as well as paragraph 2 of Order No. 488 (1993).', para. 7.
212. In 1994, the first of these reports were submitted to the Assembly (and thus, public scrutiny) as part of the Bureau's report to the Assembly.
213. Independently, Order 485(1993) had already instructed the Committee on Legal Affairs and Human Rights 'to report to it [the Assembly] when problems arise on the situation of human rights in Member States, including their compliance with judgments by the European Court of Human Rights'.

were parties.[214] The Order added the requirement to respect Assembly Recommendation 1201(1993) on the protection of national minorities in Europe, as well.[215] The Committee's reports were to concern one single country and include a draft resolution in which clear proposals were made for the improvement of the situation in the country under consideration – in the case of persistent failure to honour commitments or obligations, or a lack of co-operation with the Assembly's monitoring procedure, sanctions were (again) threatened.[216] This was an important clarification of the Assembly's monitoring procedure, which underlined the differences with the CM's newly installed monitoring procedure, based on the 'Declaration on compliance with commitments accepted by Member States of the Council of Europe' of 10 November 1994. The CM' approach was confidential and thematic, covering all CoE Member States, while the Assembly's approach was country-specific and public.[217] The first – and last – two reports presented to the Assembly under Order 508(1995) concerned the honouring of obligations and commitments by Albania[218] and by Estonia,[219] both of which were presented to the Assembly during the January 1997 part-session. The monitoring procedure on Estonia was the first one to be 'closed' by the Assembly on 30 January 1997.

C. The Assembly's 'Monitoring Committee'

168. By the January 1997 part-session, it had become clear that the two Committees seized with the reporting under Order 508(1995) were being forced to spend an inappropriate amount of time on the various monitoring procedures, and that 'normal' Committee business was suffering. The Assembly thus decided to create a Committee dedicated to the monitoring procedure during that part-session, via Resolution 1115(1997). Unlike the Assembly's general committees,[220] the members of the Monitoring Committee are nominated by the Assembly's political groups and appointed by the Bureau. Again unlike in the Assembly's general committees, the Monitoring Committee appoints two co-rapporteurs[221] for each file (of different nationality and political affiliation). Thus the Assembly furnished itself with a specialized Committee, which has ensured that the Assembly's monitoring procedure has been of utmost professionalism, as well as clearly visible. The Monitoring Committee is still active, even though the organization's enlargement process has been practically completed. Its reports have had considerable influence in the countries

214. Order 508(1995), para. 3.
215. *Ibid.*, para. 7.
216. *Ibid.*, paras 8–10.
217. It also turned out to be more effective in the end, thus leading the Committee of Ministers to abandon the thematic approach after a number of years.
218. Assembly Documents 7716 and 7738, Res. 1114(1997) and Recommendation 1312(1997).
219. Assembly Documents 7715 and 7730, Res. 1117(1997) and Recommendation 1313(1997). *See also* Rudolf Bindig & Tanja E.J. Kleinsorge, 'Monitoring the Compliance of Member States with Obligations and Commitments: The Case of Estonia', in *Law in Greater Europe – Towards a Common Legal Area*, edited by B. Haller, H.C. Krüger & H. Petzold (The Hague/London: Kluwer Law International, 2000), 102–130.
220. Members of general committees are nominated by the national delegations.
221. The general committees appoint only one rapporteur for each file.

concerned over the years: in the last decade, developments in Armenia, Azerbaijan, Bosnia-Herzegovina, Georgia, Moldova, Russia, Turkey and Ukraine, to name but a few,[222] can certainly be proven to have been influenced by the Assembly's monitoring procedure, in particular the public debates in the Assembly (but, to a lesser extent perhaps, also by the confidential high-level meetings the co-rapporteurs have with the authorities of the countries concerned during their – often multiple – fact-finding visits). In its first ten years of existence, the Monitoring Committee monitored twenty countries. Many monitoring procedures were closed over the years by the Assembly. The decision to close a procedure was often of a political nature, taken when countries had fulfilled most of their commitments and obligations, if not all. The Assembly thus soon felt the need to continue monitoring a country's progress even after the stringent and intensive monitoring procedure itself had been closed: Thus the 'post-monitoring dialogue' was born. In January 2019,[223] thirteen countries were still under a monitoring procedure or engaged in post-monitoring dialogue.

169. However, democracy, the rule of law and respect for human rights are never achieved once and for all, so that the other Member States of the CoE also need to be reminded of the need to respect their statutory obligations as Member States of this organization from time to time. The Monitoring Committee therefore took the initiative in 2006 with a view to monitoring also the record of Member States not placed under the Assembly's monitoring or post-monitoring procedure, by appending to its annual progress report to the Assembly periodic reports on groups of states containing summaries of the findings of other CoE bodies and institutions. These reports were first debated in the framework of the Assembly's annual debates on the state of human rights and democracy in Europe (instituted in 2007 and ended in 2012), and continue to be debated annually in a different format. More recently, the Monitoring Committee was also entrusted with the – rather political – task of preparing the Assembly's position on the consequences of the war between Georgia and Russia[224] (which took place in the summer of 2008), as well as on the reconsideration of previously ratified credentials of the Russian delegation on substantial grounds in this context.[225] On the basis of these reports, the Assembly ratified the credentials of the Russian delegation[226] (while leaving open the option of returning to the matter), and adopted a strongly worded Resolution on the consequences of

---

222. In alphabetical order.
223. The last progress report of the Monitoring Committee was debated during the fourth part-session 2014 of the Assembly.
224. Assembly Document 11724.
225. Assembly Document 11726.
226. Resolution 1631(2008) on the reconsideration of previously ratified credentials of the Russian delegation on substantial grounds. The credentials of the Russian delegation had been challenged once before, in the context of the second Chechen war in April 2000. At the time, the Assembly decided to ratify the credentials of the Russian delegation, but deprive its members of their voting rights (*see* AS (2000) PV 15 of 6 Apr. 2000: 'The Assembly agreed to ratify the credentials of the Russian delegation, but to deprive the members of the delegation of their voting rights in the Assembly and its bodies in accordance with Rule 8.5.c of the Rules of Procedure'). These rights were only restored in January 2001.

the war.[227] It is important to note in this context that the Assembly considered 'that the recent war between Russia and Georgia, two Member States of the organization, constitutes in itself a serious violation of the Statute of the Council of Europe and of their obligations and commitments as Member States of the Council of Europe'.[228]

170. More recently, during the April 2014 part-session of the Assembly, the Monitoring Committee had to prepare a report on the 'Reconsideration on substantive grounds of the previously ratified credentials of the Russian delegation' due to the events in Ukraine. In its Resolution 1990(2014), the Assembly 'in order to mark its condemnation and disapproval of the Russian Federation's actions with regard to Ukraine' resolved to suspend the following rights of the delegation of the Russian Federation until the end of the 2014 session: '15. 1. voting rights; 15.2. right to be represented in the Bureau of the Assembly, the Presidential Committee and the Standing Committee; 15.3. right to participate in election observation missions', thus taking the strongest sanctions against the Russian delegation since Russia's accession to the CoE. The Assembly also reserved the right to annul the credentials of the Russian delegation, 'if the Russian Federation does not de-escalate the situation and reverse the annexation of Crimea'.

171. On 26 January 2015, the still unratified credentials of the Russian delegation were challenged on the basis of Rules 8.1 and 8.2 of the Rules of Procedure of the Parliamentary Assembly on the grounds that the role and participation of the Russian Federation in the conflict in eastern Ukraine, as well as its continued illegal annexation of Crimea was in violation of the Statute of the Council of Europe (ETS No. 1) as well as its accession commitments to the Council of Europe, which, in general, brought into question the 'commitment of the Russian delegation to the principles and membership obligations of the Council of Europe'(paragraph 1 of Resolution 2034(2015)). In order to foster dialogue with the Russian Federation, the Assembly resolved to ratify the credentials of the Russian delegation two days later. But, at the same time, as a clear expression of its condemnation of the continuing grave violations of international law in respect of Ukraine by the Russian Federation, the Assembly resolved to suspend the following rights of the Russian delegation for the duration of the 2015 session of the Assembly: the right to be appointed rapporteur; the right to be a member of an ad hoc committee on observation of elections; and the right to represent the Assembly in CoE bodies as well as external institutions and organizations, both institutionally and on an occasional basis. In addition, the Assembly resolved to suspend the voting rights and the right to be represented in the Bureau of the Assembly, the Presidential Committee and the Standing Committee of the Russian delegation to the Assembly, but resolved to return to this issue, with a view to reinstating these two rights at its April 2015 part-session if Russia made marked and measurable progress towards implementing the demands of the Assembly (which it did not). Finally, the Assembly brandished the threat to

227. Resolution 1633(2008) and Recommendation 1846(2008) on the consequences of the war between Georgia and Russia.
228. Paragraph 2 of Res. 1631(2008).

annul the credentials of the Russian delegation at its June 2015 part-session if no progress was made with regard to the implementation of the Minsk Protocol and Memorandum as well as the demands and recommendations of the Assembly as expressed in Resolution 2034(2015), in particular with regard to the immediate withdrawal of Russian military troops from eastern Ukraine. However, the Assembly's call on the Russian delegation to re-establish dialogue with the Assembly without further delay in its Resolution 2063 (2015) adopted in June 2015 did not lead to a return of the Russian delegation: the Russian parliament no longer submitted credentials to the Assembly in January 2016–2019. The Russian Federation decided to suspend its payments to the budget of the CoE as of July 2017, causing budgetary uncertainty.

IV. Campaigning and Prizes

172. The Assembly is relatively new to the 'campaigning' business *stricto sensu*, though some of its prizes have been awarded for decades (such as the Europe Prize, the highest distinction that can be bestowed on a European town for its actions in the European domain since 1955,[229] or the Museum Prize, awarded since 1977). The Václav Havel Human Rights Prize, which aims to reward outstanding civil society action in the defence of human rights in Europe and beyond, has been awarded since 2013.[230]

173. Over the years, the Assembly has taken an active part in various CoE campaigns, for example, the successful '*all different – all equal*' – campaign the organization ran against racism, xenophobia and intolerance in the early 1990s. It was only in 2006, however, that the Assembly itself jumped head-first into campaigning, by organizing the parliamentary dimension of the Council's campaign to stop violence against women, including domestic violence. The Assembly had asked for such a campaign to be organized for a long time, and faced with a certain reluctance on behalf of the CM, had got to the point where it decided to run the campaign itself, inviting the CM to join in.[231] The Assembly's determination prodded the CM into action, and a joint campaign with the slogan 'Stop domestic violence against women!' was thus launched in Madrid in November 2006, uniting a parliamentary, intergovernmental, and regional/local dimension. The Assembly set up a network of contact parliamentarians tasked with running the campaign in national parliaments, published a handbook of good practices, and held several meetings and seminars (at times in conjunction with the national focal points active on the intergovernmental side). The campaign was a resounding success (measured in terms of

229. The Europe Prize rewards municipalities for their active promotion of the European ideal (through twinnings, European events, exchange visits, etc.), via four awards: the European Diploma, the Flag of Honour, the Plaque of Honour and the Europe Prize. For more information, please *see* http://website-pace.net/web/apce/the-europe-prize.

230. The winners of the Prize have been: 2018 – Oyub Titiev, 2017 – Murat Arslan, 2016 – Nadia Murad, 2015 – Ludmilla Alexeeva, 2014 – Anar Mammadli, 2013 – Ales Bialiatski.

231. Recommendation 1712(2005) on the follow-up to the Third Summit, para. 13.

the number of countries reaching certain minimum benchmarks as outlined in Resolution 1582(2007) on 'Parliaments united in combating domestic violence against women' – mid-term assessment of the campaign). The campaign certainly also enabled the Assembly to strengthen its relations with national parliaments in the gender equality field and contributed to the drafting of a Convention to combat violence against women and domestic violence, the 'Istanbul Convention', which entered into force on 1 August 2014. Indeed, the network of contact parliamentarians is still active (now under the slogan 'Women Free from Violence') and continues to meet several times a year.

174. The CoE ran a new five-year campaign from November 2010 under the slogan 'ONE in FIVE' – the CoE Campaign to stop sexual violence against children.[232] From January 2011, the Parliamentary Assembly built up its parliamentary dimension, constituting a new network of contact parliamentarians (under the authority of its Committee on Social Affairs, Health and Sustainable Development), which met at least five times a year until its dissolution in January 2017, when most of its tasks were transferred to the newly created Sub-Committee on Children (of the Committee on Social Affairs, Health and Sustainable Development). The ONE in FIVE campaign had two main goals: (1) to achieve further signature, ratification and implementation of the CoE Convention on the Protection of Children against Sexual Exploitation and Sexual Abuse (short: 'Lanzarote Convention'); (2) to equip children, their families/carers and societies at large with the knowledge and tools to prevent and report sexual violence against children, thereby raising awareness of its extent. The Assembly concentrated on the first goal and contributed to the signature by all Member States and its ratification by forty-four of them (as of 1 January 2019). Since 2015, the Assembly has also been campaigning to end immigration detention of children.

§3. Towards an Institutional Balance with the CM

I. Finding a Balance of Powers Between the Two Organs of the CoE

175. While the CM may have had 'the upper hand' within the CoE in the first post-war years of the organization's existence, when the beginning of the cold war seemed to make strong government a necessity – and, incidentally, governments' foreign policy was closely prescribed by parliaments – the Assembly's importance soon increased, despite its apparent lack of formal powers. In fact, the Assembly has never been quite content with the scope of its powers as fixed in the CoE's statute. The first President of the Assembly, the Belgian Paul-Henri Spaak, already declared on 11 August 1949, during the Assembly's first session, that he considered the

---

232. Available data suggest that about one in five children in Europe are victims of some form of sexual violence. *See* the campaign's website: www.coe.int/oneinfive and its Facebook page (under the same name) for more information.

Assembly 'without doubt the most important organ' in the CoE,[233] and pushed for a strong and independent Assembly with more powers (such as being consulted before the CM admitted new members, a power which was conferred upon the Assembly in 1951).[234]

II. Co-decision Making and Budgetary Powers

176. The fight for more powers has continued over the years: as late as October 2006, the former President of the Assembly, Austrian Peter Schieder, presented a report to the Assembly on 'The institutional balance at the Council of Europe'.[235] This report came hard on the heels of the Assembly's Recommendation 1756(2006) on the implementation of the decisions of the third Summit of the CoE, in which the Assembly called on the Secretary General and the CM to continue efforts aimed at the strengthening of the CoE's institutional system. The Assembly had insisted at the time that a set of measures be taken by the CM to reinforce the Parliamentary Assembly, in particular in the standard-setting and budgetary fields and to provide it with the right of legislative initiative. Mr Schieder's report led to the adoption of Recommendation 1763(2006) on the institutional balance at the CoE, in which the Assembly invited the CM to reach an agreement with it on strengthening the Assembly's involvement concerning the elaboration, adoption and implementation of the conventions and other legal instruments of the organization; improving interaction with the Assembly in the decision-making process of the organization; and strengthening the Assembly's role concerning the adoption of the budget of the CoE and of its own budgetary appropriations, as well as concerning supervisory functions over CoE activities.

177. It took the CM some time to reply to these proposals, but on 21 March 2007, the Ministers' Deputies adopted a joint reply[236] to Recommendation 1728(2005) on the budgetary powers of the PACE and Recommendation 1763(2006) on the institutional balance at the CoE. In this reply, the CM recognized 'that the Parliamentary Assembly contributes fully to the promotion of fundamental European values thus opening the way for a Europe without dividing

233. Cited in Bruno Haller, *Une Assemblée au service de l'Europe*, 27 (author's translation): *Cette Assemblée la voici réunie. Elle est, dans le Conseil de l'Europe, l'organisme sans doute le plus important.*

234. *Ibid.*, 27. This particular demand can probably seen in connection with the fact that the Committee of Ministers had, on 9 Aug. 1949, admitted Greece and Turkey as new Member States, and had extended an invitation to Iceland to join, as well.

235. Assembly Document No. 11017, available in English and French from the Assembly's website: htt p://assembly.coe.int.

236. Assembly Document No. 11122, available *ibid.*

lines',[237] and declared itself 'prepared to consider with the Assembly how the various forms of consultation and the quality of the information supplied can be substantially improved'.[238] However, it drew the line at reapportioning responsibilities (in particular in budgetary matters) or codifying existing practice in writing.[239]

178. National parliaments vote national budgets (including the budgetary contributions to the CoE), and it is national parliaments which generally ratify CoE treaties. The Assembly will thus probably continue to develop its current practice of putting pressure on the CM and the Secretary General in budgetary matters via its annual Opinions on the budget of the CoE and its own expenditure.[240]

III. Treaty-Making

179. In some cases, the Assembly already appends its own draft treaty-texts to its recommendations and opinions: Thus, for example, Assembly Recommendation 1201(1993) on the protection of national minorities in Europe included a draft Additional Protocol to the ECHR, and was directly quoted as a standard in the Treaty between Hungary and Slovakia and in the appendix to the Treaty between Hungary and Romania. However, it is not always feasible for a parliamentary body like the Assembly to try and draft treaty-texts in addition to its core business, especially since it usually takes years (and many meetings of drafting committees) for such treaties to be drafted on the intergovernmental side. It is thus probably better for the Assembly to continue its traditional approach of initiating new treaties, while strengthening its supervisory role in the drafting and treaty-adoption phase. This approach was successfully used by the Assembly, for example, as regards the CoE Convention on Action against trafficking in human beings, which the Assembly first asked for in Recommendation 1325(1997) on traffic in women and forced prostitution in CoE Member States. The Assembly and its representatives were closely involved in the drafting phase, but it took both an Opinion (No. 253 of 2005) and a Recommendation (No. 1695 of the same year, adopted following an urgent debate in the Standing Committee) on the draft Convention for the CM to accept the most important amendments proposed by the Assembly, designed to protect the victims of trafficking in human beings. In fact, the drafting phase of this Convention showed quite clearly that the main danger to meaningful treaty-making and standard-setting within the CoE is not intra-institutional rivalry, but rather the inter-institutional sort: It was the European Commission, negotiating on behalf of twenty-two states of the EC, which at first blocked the most important provisions.[241] This led the Assembly

237. *Ibid.*, para. 2.
238. *Ibid.*, para. 3.
239. *Ibid.*, paras 3 and 10.
240. The most recent adopted texts are Opinion 284(2013) on Budgets and priorities of the Council of Europe for the biennium 2014–2015, and Res. 1935(2013) on the Expenditure of the Parliamentary Assembly for the biennium 2014–2015, available on the Assembly's website.
241. *See* Recommendation 1695(2005) on the Draft Council of Europe convention on action against trafficking in human beings, paras 3 and 4.

to declare that questions regarding the competences and procedures of CoE treaty-making had been raised, and that it was necessary to engage the EC and its Member States in this matter.[242] Following the entry into force of the Lisbon Treaty in December 2009, this question is more acute than ever.

§4. Conclusion

180. It is no wonder that the Assembly is widely recognized as the motor and conscience of the CoE. From the outset, the Assembly has taken a wide range of initiatives: it has set new standards by initiating new treaties, created new forms of co-operation with national parliaments and Member States by setting-up accession and monitoring procedures, and constantly redefined itself and its activities to meet the challenges of an ever-changing Europe. The PACE has thus successfully carved itself an important place in the institutional landscape of Europe.

242. *Ibid.*, para. 9. For more information on treaty-making in the Council of Europe, please *see* the contribution of Christina Olsen in this volume.

Chapter 3. The Committee of Ministers

Simon Palmer, updated by Christophe Poirel and Elise Cornu

§1. The Organic Role of the CM

> The Committee of Ministers is the organ which acts on behalf of the Council of Europe […] (Article 13 of the Statute of the Council of Europe).[243]

181. The CM is the executive organ of the CoE. However, this definition should not lead to the assumption that the Council, in conformity with conventional constitutional doctrine, also has a legislative branch – even in the evident presence of a Parliamentary Assembly. For insofar as any organ legislates in the CoE, it is the CM, which also makes law, as Article 15 of the Statute empowers it to do.

---

243. Chapter IV of the Statute concerning the Committee of Ministers provides as follows:

Article 13

The Committee of Ministers is the organ which acts on behalf of the Council of Europe in accordance with Articles 15 and 16.

Article 14

Each member shall be entitled to one representative on the Committee of Ministers, and each representative shall be entitled to one vote. Representatives on the Committee shall be the Ministers for Foreign Affairs. When a Minister for Foreign Affairs is unable to be present or in other circumstances where it may be desirable, an alternate may be nominated to act for him, who shall, whenever possible, be a member of his government.

Article 15

a. On the recommendation of the Consultative Assembly or on its own initiative, the Committee of Ministers shall consider the action required to further the aim of the Council of Europe, including the conclusion of conventions or agreements and the adoption by governments of a common policy with regard to particular matters. Its conclusions shall be communicated to members by the Secretary General.
b. In appropriate cases, the conclusions of the Committee may take the form of recommendations to the governments of members, and the Committee may request the governments of members to inform it of the action taken by them with regard to such recommendations.

Article 16

The Committee of Ministers shall, subject to the provisions of Articles 24, 28, 30, 32, 33 and 35, relating to the powers of the Consultative Assembly, decide with binding effect all matters relating to the internal organisation and arrangements of the Council of Europe. For this purpose the Committee of Ministers shall adopt such financial and administrative arrangements as may be necessary.

Article 17

The Committee of Ministers may set up advisory and technical committees or commissions for such specific purposes as it may deem desirable.

182. The role of the Committee cannot be analysed in isolation from that of the Parliamentary Assembly. The drafters of the Statute did not foresee an organic structure based on that of a state, but rather a dynamic partnership between parliamentary and governmental representatives; a structure specifically adapted to an international organization operating in the context of co-operative reconstruction following a prolonged, catastrophic passage of history.

183. Thus, even though some of the Statutory provisions concerning the collaboration between the two organs have fallen into misuse (*see* in particular Article 21, paragraph c: 'The Committee shall meet before and during the beginning of every session of the Consultative Assembly and at such other times as it may decide'), their relationship remains a central statutory and political reality in the life of the organization. In particular, the obligations to report regularly to the Assembly and to reply in a timely and constructive way to its Recommendations provide a minimum of control by the representatives of Parliaments over the representatives of governments. The ways in which these minima may be developed and exceeded are discussed elsewhere.

§2. The CM in Practice

> Each member shall be entitled to one representative on the Committee of Ministers, and each representative shall be entitled to one vote (Article 14).

184. The Conference of The Hague from which the organization emerged was a conference of Ministers for Foreign Affairs. It is therefore natural that the governing body of the CoE should be composed of Foreign Ministers. However, only three years into its life the Ministers concluded that it would be necessary for them to be represented by Deputies. As the scope of the Organization's activities became more and more extensive and complex, the need became evident to supervise them closely and in continuity. The Ministers' Deputies (i.e., accredited, diplomatic representatives of the Member States sitting in Committee with full powers) progressively became the backbone of the executive function within the Council.

185. The Ministers themselves continue to meet in regular formal Session once a year.[244] These Sessions provide a forum for regular assessment at political level of progress in the work of the organization and for setting political orientations to these activities. They are also an occasion of heightened solemnity for the adoption of texts of particular importance. Examples of this latter role have been the adoption of Protocol No. 14 to the ECHR at the 114th Session (May 2004), of Protocol

244. Throughout most of the history of the Council of Europe, the Committee has met at ministerial level twice a year, in May and November, to coincide with the transfer of the semestrial Chairmanship. However in recent years, due to the poor attendance referred to, Sessions have become annual as an experiment.

No. 15 to the Convention at the 123rd Session (May 2013) and more recently of the Amending Protocol to the Data Protection Convention at the 128th Session (May 2018).

186. Efforts have been made in recent years to make Sessions more politically relevant and more attractive to Ministers. One important change has been the decision to hold at each Session an informal discussion among Ministers on a highly topical issue. These informal discussions, limited to Ministers, allow them to freely exchange views on sensitive political or other matters of particular importance on the pan-European scene. The most recent example was the informal working session devoted to the future of the CoE at the Ministerial Session in May 2018.

187. Summits of Heads of State and Government also play a similar 'milestone' role: all three Summits held so far (Vienna 1993, Strasbourg 1997 and Warsaw 2005) have launched important initiatives (e.g., the European Commission against Racism and Intolerance (ECRI), the Framework Convention for the Protection of National Minorities, the Europe-wide consensus on the abolition of the death penalty, the Convention on Action against trafficking in human beings, etc.). However, it should be noted that Summits exist outside the statutory framework, and it is the task of the CM to implement their conclusions.

§3. The Ministers' Deputies

188. Thus the Ministers' Deputies occupy the role of 'Board of Directors' of the CoE. As such, they oversee the strategy and execution of all intergovernmental activity within the organization, they determine the programme of activities and they fix the resources devoted to its implementation and the infrastructures required in support. They adopt the annual budget. They follow and discuss political developments of relevance to the values and mandate of the organization and manage the Council's key relationships within the European and global institutional architecture.

189. They also adopt (and if necessary negotiate) international legal texts (conventions, protocols), approve CoE strategies (e.g., on counter-terrorism, gender equality, or the rights of the child) and draw up and adopt replies to the Recommendations adopted by the Parliamentary Assembly and the written questions addressed to the Committee by its members.

190. They are responsible for monitoring Member States' compliance with their commitments under the legal *acquis* of the CoE[245] as well as the specific monitoring and other tasks given to them by the main human rights instruments (in this context, the ECHR, the European Social Charter, the European Convention for the Prevention of Torture and Inhuman or Degrading Treatment or Punishment and the

245. *See* the Declaration adopted by the Committee of Ministers at its ninety-fifth Session, November 1994.

Framework Convention for the Protection of National Minorities) and its duties arising out the work of other institutions such as the CoE Commissioner for Human Rights and the ECRI.

191. The breadth and complexity of these functions imply intense and extensive activity. The calendar of the Deputies' plenary meetings has progressed in the past two decades from monthly meetings (alternately 'A' – and 'B'-levels – i.e., permanent representatives and deputy permanent representatives with a two-month break in the summer) to weekly meetings. Plenary meetings held for the purposes of the supervision of the execution of the judgments of the European Court under Article 46, paragraph 1, of the ECHR are additional to this schedule.

192. The effectiveness of the schedule depends to a considerable extent on the ability of subsidiary bodies to prepare the Deputies' decisions effectively so that they can in principle be adopted in plenary without excessive or time-consuming debate.

§4. Subsidiary Bodies

> The Committee of Ministers may set up advisory and technical committees or commissions for such specific purposes as it may deem desirable. (Article 17 of the Statute).

193. Subsidiary bodies set up by the CM may be divided into two distinct groups: on the one hand, the expert technical bodies (steering committees, expert and ad hoc groups which are established in the context of the intergovernmental activity programme) and on the other, the permanent monitoring structures set up under many of the standard-setting instruments adopted within the CoE. These bodies, whose creation was provided by Article 17 of the Statute, are described elsewhere.

194. The purpose of this section is to describe another group of subsidiary bodies, that is, those set up by the CM among its own members in order to ensure as far as possible the effective preparation of their decisions, in line with the need expressed at the end of the last section of this chapter. Informal, non-statutory subsidiary committees called 'rapporteur groups' were set up as long ago as 1985. These groups, whose membership was originally restricted on a voluntary basis, have been given areas of competence equivalent to the major domains of competence of the organization: the so-called operative areas: legal co-operation, human rights, social and health affairs, education, culture, youth, sport and environment; as well as the over-arching subjects such as programme, budget and administration, democracy and external relations. Rapporteur groups may be supplemented by so-called Ad hoc Working Parties tasked with studying and making recommendations on specific topics, normally within a defined time frame. One such example was the working party established by the CM to steer the work on the reform of the ECHR.

195. At a time when the number of Member States was twenty-one, the Ministers' Deputies were under considerably less pressure than they are in the first decades of the twenty-first century, with forty-seven Member States and a political agenda vastly more controversial than that of twenty years before. However, the basic structure remains very similar today. Rapporteur groups are now open to all delegations, their meetings are scheduled and their agendas and procedures determined by rules. However, the essence of their non-statutory character is maintained: they are not empowered to take decisions, they may only recommend. Thus any votes taken are purely indicative and the statutory rules on majorities[246] do not apply. Under the working methods adopted by the Deputies in 2005, there is a presumption that an understanding reached in a rapporteur group should not be breached when the matter is submitted to decision in a plenary meeting.

196. Rapporteur groups may be supplemented by individual Deputies who accept the role of thematic coordinator for specific matters (there is currently one thematic coordinator, on Information Policy). Thematic coordinators act as individual rapporteurs: they may convene meetings to assist them in achieving a task set by the Deputies, but are not obliged to do so. It is open to them to submit advice under their personal responsibility if they see fit.

197. The non-statutory nature of rapporteur groups has not prevented the Deputies from delegating to them the detailed preparation of statutory tasks. The best example of this is the Deputies' formal decision to instruct their Rapporteur Group on Human Rights (GR-H) to prepare their decisions concerning the follow-up to be given to the Opinions issued by the Advisory Committee set up under the Framework Convention for the Protection of National Minorities. This practice, which has now been in force for several years, demonstrates how it is possible to give adequate scope for debates which are highly technical and which may also be politically extremely controversial, without excessively taxing the Deputies' limited meeting time.

198. The proper functioning of the system of rapporteur groups depends on the willingness of individual Deputies to accept a charge which involves stepping outside the limits of mere national interests so as to exercise a function related to the collective responsibility of the Deputies as a whole and most often also to the individual qualifications and commitment of the Deputy concerned. This is a feature of the workings of the CM which mitigates the fact – certainly unavoidable – that the decisions of the Committee are the result of different and even sometimes opposed national interests.

---

246. *See* Art. 20 of the Statute and Art. 10 of the Rules of Procedure of the Ministers' Deputies.

§5. Consensus and Majorities

199. There is a popular expectation that an organization – even an intergovernmental organization – should act as if it were the expression of a single, individual will. This chapter was originally drafted shortly after the fiftieth anniversary of the Hungarian uprising and the Suez crisis of 1956. Both events gave rise to strident expressions of outrage at the fact that the UN had not taken action to react, respectively, to the Soviet and the Franco-British interventions in the dramatic events concerned. In more recent times, the same was said of many situations where in particular serious human rights violations have taken place, including for some in Europe. The press and the popular opinion which expressed these points of view failed to understand a fact which still seems reserved to those who have direct experience of the workings of international organizations: the capacity of an organization to act or to take a firm position on a fact of international politics depends on the attitudes of the Member States.

200. Given the mandate of the CoE, related to respect for human rights, the promotion of democracy and the rule of law, and given also the diversity of situations and sensitivities among Member States regarding these matters, not all issues which are on the agenda of the CM can be settled on the basis of consensus. However, the commitment of Member States to the fundamental values of the organization implies that certain positions should be accepted unequivocally. This has led to the idea that, although the rules of procedure of the CM provide for the adoption of most decisions by a qualified majority, unanimity should be the 'normal' basis for decisions. But that is a fallacy if the aim of the collectivity is to draw conclusions concerning one of its numbers, who may not agree. A standard-setting and standard-monitoring body can evidently not accept such a limitation.

§6. Replies to the Parliamentary Assembly

201. An obvious illustration of the Committee's inability to achieve a collegial position on all occasions is the difficulty it has on occasions to adopt meaningful replies to the Recommendations addressed to it by the Parliamentary Assembly. As the attitude of the Committee as a body is seldom unequivocal because of greater or lesser divergences of view between the Member States, the Committee indeed equivocates. The result may sometimes be replies, the drafting of which is either impenetrably complex or – worse still – with limited substance when it comes to their content.

202. It is nonetheless clear that the statutory obligation of the Committee to reply to the Assembly's Recommendations is one of the most important aspects of the accountability of the intergovernmental organ before the inter-parliamentary one. This is the reason why the CM has always maintained a commitment to answering the Assembly's Recommendations as substantially and swiftly as possible. Some may consider that the Ministers' Deputies, being diplomats, try to be too diplomatic in responding to the Assembly. Healthier, more transparent communication might be achieved if the Deputies, faced with a Recommendation, which they consider irrelevant or ill-conceived, would actually say so to the Assembly.

203. Recommendations are not the only communications calling for replies by the CM: the same applies to written questions submitted by members of the Assembly in their individual capacity. In this case, while making every effort to provide substantial responses to questions related, for example to the Committee's policies, the Deputies have from time to time been obliged to declare themselves unable to agree on a consensual reply to questions which concern sensitive political or societal issues, often in circumstances opposing one Member State to another. Under these circumstances, the Chairperson of the Deputies writes to the President of the Assembly explaining that it is impossible to reply.

§7. Role of the CM as Supervisory Body under Article 46 of the ECHR

> The final judgment of the Court shall be transmitted to the Committee of Ministers, which shall supervise its execution. (Article 46, paragraph 2, of the ECHR as amended by Protocol No. 11).

204. The sole statutory text establishing and governing the role of the CM in supervising the execution of the Court's judgments resides in the nineteen words quoted above. Accordingly the Committee has, since the first case was referred to it under the then Article 32 by the European Commission of Human Rights, constantly developed its practice and procedures. In 1959, such supervision was an occasional and relatively rare task: it has now attained an enormous scale, but in refining its working methods, the Committee has constantly remained faithful to a number of basic principles. First, it places total reliance on the fact that all High Contracting Parties have committed themselves to accepting the compulsory jurisdiction of the Court.

205. Second, there is the collective nature of the CoE's machinery for the protection of human rights, which means that all States are equally responsible for ensuring a satisfactory outcome to the cases which are submitted to it. Cases are not a matter for respondent States alone.

206. Third, the Committee has enshrined in its procedures the doctrine that, in carrying out its function, it cannot preside over any kind of adversarial procedure – it cannot, in other words, substitute itself for the Court. The supervision of execution is a collegial, and not an accusatory process.

207. Today, the Ministers' Deputies devote four three-day meetings a year to the examination of the cases on their roll. Wherever the Court has found a violation, the Committee must assure itself that any just satisfaction awarded has been paid, that the respondent State has taken all individual measures needed to put an end to the violation and, to the extent possible, erase its consequences for the applicant (*restitution in integrum*) and that adequate general measures have been taken to ensure that similar violations will not occur in the future.

208. As the Court develops its capacity to keep pace with the almost overwhelming demand it faces, its output – and thus the volume of judgments to supervise – increases. The Committee must thus keep its working methods constantly under review in order to keep pace. Much insistence has been placed, not least by the Warsaw Summit in May 2005 and more recently in the Copenhagen Declaration of April 2018, on the absolute need to optimize the efficiency of the supervision of execution, in the interest of the credibility of the system and so as not excessively to prolong the time needed for applicants to obtain justice. It is against this background that the CM has developed since 2010 a twin-track approach whereby most cases are handled under a simplified supervision procedure while those requiring urgent action or raising complex problems are the subject of an enhanced procedure leading to closer scrutiny.

209. Except in cases where the obstacles to execution may be seen to be political in nature, the main difficulties in the execution process arise from different factors: the complexity of the measures to be taken by the respondent States to implement the Court judgments, the sometimes important financial and other resources which States must put in place to this end, as well as in some instances the difficulty of ensuring that all the relevant information can be effectively placed before the CM.

210. The response of the Committee has been to keep its working methods constantly under review, not only in terms of streamlining procedures and documentation, but also in grouping similar cases, for example, or avoiding duplication of effort in cases where the necessary measures have already been taken. The Committee has also made use of the infringement procedure provided for by Article 46(4) of the Convention, referring the Ilgar Mammadov case to the Court in late 2017 for a ruling on Azerbaijan's compliance with the Court's original judgment. However, the ultimate answer to the problem of case-load growth (and thus the salvation of the European human rights protection system) is the same as for the Court. States must, to an ever-greater extent, take measures to ensure that the rights protected in the Convention are automatically respected at home or, if they are violated, that redress may be obtained within the national system.[247]

---

247. *See* the package of texts adopted by the Committee of Ministers at their 114th Session in May 2004 on the occasion of the adoption of Protocol No. 14 to the European Convention on Human Rights, including:

- Recommendation Rec(2004)4 on the European Convention on Human Rights in university education and professional training.

§8. Institutional Relationships: The CM and the Parliamentary Assembly

211. As mentioned above, the key institutional relationship in the CoE is that of the CM with the Parliamentary Assembly. The aim of the drafters of the Statute appears to have been to set up a creative relationship between governmental and parliamentary interests in post-war Europe. It may be imagined that the largely parietary relationship proposed in 1949 between the CM and the then 'Consultative' Assembly was born in part from a willing suspension of the usual hostility between the legislative and executive branches in the face of recent, potentially more destructive hostilities.

212. This truce evidently did not last long, because the relationship between the Committee and the Assembly is, and has for years been structurally adversarial. This antagonism can, if properly managed, be a creative tension, the spur to effective political action by the CoE.

213. If the Parliamentary Assembly represents the authentic expression of electoral opinion in the Member States and the CM represents that of the governments, a constructive dialogue and interaction between them can only lead to positive results, as demonstrated in recent years by their joint efforts to promote the rights of minorities, combat domestic violence or sexual abuse of children, or protect the right to privacy with regard to the automatic processing of personal data, to mention only a few examples.

- Recommendation Rec(2004)5 on the verification of the compatibility of draft laws, existing laws and administrative practice with the standards laid down in the European Convention on Human Rights.
- Recommendation Rec(2004)6 on the improvement of domestic remedies.
- Resolution Rec(2004)3 on judgments revealing an underlying systemic problem.

Part III. The CoE's Activities

Chapter 1. General Overview

Tanja E.J. Kleinsorge

§1. Introduction

214. The CoE's structure and activities have evolved significantly since its creation in 1949. The organization's Statute created a 'bipolar' organization with only two organs:[248] the CM and the (Consultative, later Parliamentary) Assembly. The organization has become increasingly 'multipolar' over the years, adding a sometimes seemingly bewildering array of institutions, committees and various bodies to the two original organs, in order to fulfil its mandate – to bring Europe closer together 'by discussion of questions of common concern and by agreements and common action in economic, social, cultural, scientific, legal and administrative matters and in the maintenance and further realization of human rights and fundamental freedoms'.[249]

215. To enable the CoE to fulfil its function, Article 40 of the Statute foresees that:

> The Council of Europe, representatives of members and the Secretariat shall enjoy in the territories of its members such privileges and immunities as are reasonably necessary for the fulfilment of their functions. These immunities shall include immunity for all representatives to the Consultative Assembly from arrest and all legal proceedings in the territories of all members, in respect of words spoken and votes cast in the debates of the Assembly or its committees or commissions.

This provision was given concrete form in the organization's second treaty, the General Agreement on Privileges and Immunities of the CoE, which was opened for

248. Statute of the Council of Europe, Preamble: 'Have in consequence decided to set up a Council of Europe consisting of a committee of representatives of governments and of a consultative assembly, and have for this purpose adopted the following Statute.' (Adopted in London on 5 May 1949). *See also* Art. 10 of the Statute.
249. Article 1b of the Organization's Statute.

signature on 2 September 1949 and entered into force on 10 September 1952. In accordance with this treaty, the CoE has judicial personality (with the Secretary General acting on behalf of the organization in such matters as concluding contracts, acquiring property or instituting legal proceedings).[250] The buildings, premises and archives of the CoE are inviolable.[251] The representatives of the members of the CM, the representatives to the Assembly, and the officials of the CoE are all accorded a number of important privileges and immunities in the discharge of their duties, similar to those usually granted to national parliamentarians and/or diplomatic envoys.

§2. The European Court of Human Rights

216. First, and arguably most importantly, the ECHR, opened for signature in Rome on 4 November 1950, created a mechanism for the enforcement of the obligations entered into by Contracting States under the Convention. The ECHR is a classic human rights treaty, inspired by the 1948 Universal Declaration of Human Rights, guaranteeing a wide range of civil and political rights. It is constantly updated by the means of additional protocols, adding new rights. Today, the body entrusted with adjudicating cases under the Convention is the ECtHR – with one of the two original organs of the CoE, the CM, enforcing its decisions. Originally, however, three institutions were entrusted with this responsibility: the European Commission of Human Rights (set up in 1954), the ECtHR (set up in 1959) and the CM itself.

217. Under the Convention in its original version (when it entered into force in September 1953), complaints could be brought against Contracting States either by other Contracting States or by individual applicants.[252] The complaints were first the subject of a preliminary examination by the Commission, which determined their admissibility. Where an application was declared admissible, the Commission placed itself at the parties' disposal with a view to brokering a friendly settlement. If no settlement was forthcoming, it drew up a report establishing the facts and expressing an opinion on the merits of the case. The report was transmitted to the CM.[253]

218. Where the respondent State had accepted the compulsory jurisdiction of the Court, the Commission and/or any Contracting State concerned had a period of three months following the transmission of the Commission's report to the CM within which to bring the case before the Court for a final, binding adjudication.[254] If a case was not referred to the Court, the CM decided whether there had been a

250. General Agreement on Privileges and Immunities of the Council of Europe, Art. 1.
251. *Ibid.*, Arts 4 and 5.
252. However, recognition of the right of individual application was optional and it could therefore be exercised only against those States which had accepted it.
253. *See* the Court's website: www.echr.coe.int, Chapter 'Historical background'.
254. Individuals were not entitled to bring their cases before the Court. *Ibid.*

violation of the Convention and, if appropriate, awarded 'just satisfaction' to the victim. As is the case today, the CM also had responsibility for supervising the execution of the Court's judgments.

219. The 1980s and the 1990s saw an unprecedented increase in the case-load of the Commission and the Court (and, in view of their finite resources, in the length of proceedings). A rather lengthy debate on the necessity of a reform of the ECHR's supervisory bodies ensued. In the end, the debate resulted in the adoption of Protocol No. 11 to the Convention, which simplified the structure of the ECHR's supervisory bodies with a view to shortening the length of proceedings and thus enabling the supervisory machinery to deal with the ever-increasing case-load in a Europe where, sadly, violations of human rights were no longer so exceptional. Protocol No. 11 strengthened the judicial character of the system by replacing the existing, part-time Court and Commission with a single, full-time Court, making the Convention and the acceptance of the supervisory machinery fully compulsory (including the right of individual application) and abolishing the CM' adjudicative role. This Protocol, which transformed the human rights system in Europe, came into force on 1 November 1998.

220. The Court is thus now composed of forty-seven full-time judges, who are elected by the Parliamentary Assembly from a list of three candidates proposed by the government concerned.[255] Judges enjoy complete independence in the performance of their duties and do not represent the states which proposed them. The Court's final judgments are binding on the state concerned. They cover a wide range of issues: disappearances and unlawful killings; torture and ill-treatment of detainees; arbitrary loss of liberty; lack of access to a court; lack of a fair trial within a reasonable time; telephone tapping; deportation and extradition; discrimination against homosexuals; freedom of the press; rights of parents of children taken into care; interference with property rights and dissolution of political parties, to name but a few.[256]

221. Sadly, the number of cases before the Court has increased exponentially in the last decades, so that the CoE has been obliged to further reform – Protocol No. 14 to the Convention entered into force on 1 June 2010. This Protocol further strengthens the Court (and, indeed, also its Registry) and streamlines procedure. Thus, for example, a single judge (assisted by Court officials) – instead of a committee of three judges – is now able to declare certain applications inadmissible.[257] However, the procedure before the Court's Chambers and Grand Chamber have not changed much, though the role of the CoE's Commissioner for Human Rights was

255. A dispute between the Parliamentary Assembly and the Committee of Ministers on whether that list of candidates must always include a member of the under-represented sex on the Court took some time to be solved in the last decade. For more information, please *see* the first ever Advisory Opinion of the European Court of Human Rights, spring 2008 and PACE Res. 1627 (2008).

256. The issues and their order are taken from the brochure 'The Council of Europe – 800 million Europeans,' edited by the Directorate of Communication – Public Relations Service, July 2006, 29.

257. Court information document issued by the Registrar of the European Court of Human Rights, available on the Court's website: www.echr.coe.int.

strengthened,[258] and the notion of 'significant disadvantage' was introduced, allowing the Court to reject cases if the applicant has not suffered such a disadvantage and the complaint has been duly examined by a domestic tribunal. Protocol No. 16 to the Convention – which came into force on 1 August 2018 – introduced a new procedure, allowing the highest courts and tribunals of a High Contracting Party, as specified by the latter, to request the ECtHR to give advisory opinions on questions of principle relating to the interpretation or application of the rights and freedoms defined in the Convention or the protocols thereto. [259]

§3. The Commissioner for Human Rights

222. The institution of the Commissioner for Human Rights is, though much younger than the venerable ECtHR, the other key institution in the CoE's web of human rights protection. Created by the CM in 1999 as a non-judicial institution 'to promote education in, awareness of and respect for human rights, as embodied in the human rights instruments of the Council of Europe',[260] the Commissioner fills the void previously felt in the CoE regarding human rights education – and thus prevention of human rights violations. While the Commissioner – currently the first female Commissioner, Dunja Mijatović – cannot take up individual complaints, she enjoys an otherwise rather broad mandate. The current Commissioner pays particular attention to the human rights of disadvantaged and vulnerable groups; gender equality and women's rights; children's rights; migration; transitional justice; and the situation of human rights defenders. She has continued with her predecessor's particular emphasis on a renewed commitment to human rights principles in the face of inequality, terrorism and uncertainty.[261]

§4. The European Committee of Social Rights

223. The European Social Charter is the natural complement to the ECHR. Adopted in 1961 and revised in 1996, the Charter sets out rights and freedoms in the social and economic sphere and establishes a supervisory mechanism – the European Committee of Social Rights (ECSR) – guaranteeing their respect by the States' Parties. The rights guaranteed concern housing, health, education, employment, legal and social protection, movement of persons and non-discrimination.[262]

224. The ECSR ascertains whether countries have honoured the undertakings set out in the Charter. Its fifteen independent, impartial members are elected by the CoE

258. *See* the contribution on the Commissioner in this volume.
259. The first such request to issue an advisory opinion came from France's Court of Cassation in October 2018, on the question of surrogacy.
260. Committee of Ministers' Res. No. (99)50, Art. 1.1.
261. *See* the contribution on the Commissioner in this volume, as well as the Commissioner's website (on the Council of Europe's website): www.commissioner.coe.int.
262. For a full list of the rights protected, please *see* the European Social Charter itself (text available on the Council of Europe's website via the treaty office).

CM for a period of six years, renewable once. The Committee determines whether or not national law and practice in the States Parties are in conformity with the Charter,[263] based on national reports submitted annually by the States Parties. Each report concerns some of the accepted provisions of the Charter and is then examined by the Committee, which publishes its decisions, known as 'conclusions', every year.

225. If a state takes no action on a Committee decision to the effect that it does not comply with the Charter, the CM addresses a recommendation to that state, asking it to change the situation in law and/or in practice. The CM' work is prepared by a Governmental Committee comprising representatives of the governments of the States Parties to the Charter, assisted by observers representing European employers' organizations and trade unions.

226. There is, however, also a complaint procedure. Under a protocol opened for signature in 1995 (which came into force in 1998), complaints of violations of the Charter may be lodged with the ECSR. In the case of all states that have accepted the procedure, there are four types of organizations entitled to lodge complaints with the Committee: first: the European Trade Union Confederation (ETUC), the Union of Industrial and Employers' Confederations of Europe (UNICE) and the International Organization of Employers (IOE); second: NGOs with participative status with the CoE which are on a list drawn up for this purpose by the Governmental Committee; third: Employers' organizations and trade unions in the country concerned; and fourth (in the case of states which have also agreed to this – so far only one, namely Finland): national NGOs.[264]

227. The ECSR examines the complaint and, if the formal requirements have been met, declares it admissible. Once the complaint has been declared admissible, a written procedure is set in motion, with an exchange of memoranda between the parties. The Committee may decide to hold a public hearing. The Committee then takes a decision on the merits of the complaint, which it forwards to the parties concerned and the CM in a report, which is made public within four months of its being forwarded. Finally, the CM adopts a resolution. If appropriate, it may recommend that the state concerned take specific measures to bring the situation into line with the Charter. As a result of this monitoring system, states make changes to their legislation and/or practice in order to bring the situation into line with the Charter.[265] More than a hundred cases of collective complaints had been dealt with by the end of 2018.[266]

263. Article 24 of the Charter, as amended by the 1991 Turin Protocol.
264. *See* the general presentation of the Social Charter on its website: www.coe.int/T/DGHL/Monitoring/SocialCharter.
265. *Ibid.*
266. *See* the document 'Summaries of decisions on the merits', *ibid.*

§5. The Congress of Local and Regional Authorities

228. The CoE has always recognized the crucial importance of democracy at local and regional level. It thus created the Conference of Local Authorities in 1957, which later evolved into the Congress of Local and Regional Authorities.[267] The European Charter of Local Self-Government, opened for signature by CoE Member States on 15 October 1985,[268] obliges the signatory States to recognize the principle of local self-government in domestic legislation. The Congress, which comprises two chambers (the Chamber of Local Authorities and the Chamber of Regions) keeps watch on local democracy in Europe, by producing 'monitoring reports' on the situation in the Member States. In this way, it verifies the effective application of the principles set forth in the European Charter of Local Self-Government, and of the major principles of local democracy. It is also in charge of local and regional election monitoring and of setting the standards for Europe in electoral matters. Finally, it advises the two organs of the CoE, the CM and the Parliamentary Assembly, on all aspects of local and regional policy.[269]

§6. The Conference of INGOs

229. The CoE gave INGOs the possibility to acquire consultative status as early as 1952, thus recognizing the importance of the voluntary sector as a vital component of European society. By virtue of CM Resolution 2003(8), the status of the INGOs recognized by the organization was upgraded from 'consultative' to 'participatory'. There are currently more than 400 INGOs who have been accorded this status.[270] The INGOs with participatory status form the Conference of INGOs, and have set up Committees in the following fields: (1) Democracy, Social Cohesion and Global Challenges, (2) Education and Culture, and (3) Human rights.[271] In practice, practically all CoE committees, be they parliamentary, intergovernmental or part of the Congress of Local and Regional authorities, involve the INGO Conference and relevant NGOs in their work in an advisory capacity, as observers, or to relay information to the general public, for example during campaigns.[272]

267. To be exact, in 1994.
268. It came into force on 9 Sep. 1988.
269. *See* the contribution on the Congress in this volume, as well as the Congress' website (on the Council of Europe's website): www.coe.int/T/Congress.
270. In order to be granted this status, the INGO in question must share the Council of Europe's aims and contribute to its work, be international and representative, both geographically and in its sphere of activity, with permanent headquarters, a structured organization and a secretary general.
271. *See* the Conference's website (on the Council of Europe's website): www.coe.int/T/NGO/default_en.asp.
272. *See* the contribution on the Council of Europe's place in Europe and the world in this volume, as well as the Conference's website.

§7. The Secretariat of the CoE

230. The Secretariat of the CoE is headed by a Secretary General and a Deputy Secretary General, both elected for a period of five years by the Parliamentary Assembly (the Secretariat of the Parliamentary Assembly is headed by a Secretary General with the rank of Deputy Secretary General in the organization). The Secretary General is entrusted with the responsibility of meeting the aim for which the CoE was set up in London on 5 May 1949, namely to achieve greater unity between its members for the purpose of safeguarding and realizing the ideals and principles which are their common heritage and facilitating their economic and social progress. The Secretary General has the overall responsibility for the strategic management of the CoE's work programme and budget and oversees the day-to-day running of the organization and Secretariat. The current Secretary General (re-elected for a second mandate in June 2014) is Thorbjørn Jagland.

231. The Secretariat of the CoE, which comprises roughly 2,000 staff members, is currently structured as follows:

- Private Office of the Secretary General and the Deputy Secretary General.
- Secretariat of the CM.
- Secretariat of the Parliamentary Assembly.
- Directorate of Communication.
- Directorate of Internal Oversight.
- Protocol.
- Directorate of Political Affairs.
- Directorate of External Relations.
- Directorate of Legal Advice and Public International Law.
- Office of the Director General of Programmes.
- Directorate General Human Rights and Rule of Law.
- Directorate General Democracy.
- Directorate General of Administration.
- Secretariat of the Congress of Local and Regional Authorities of the CoE.
- Office of the Commissioner for Human Rights.
- Registry of the ECtHR.

232. The headquarters of the organization are in Strasbourg, France, but the organization also runs external offices in Baku (Azerbaijan), Belgrade (Serbia), Chisinau (Moldova), Kyiv (Ukraine), Moscow (Russian Federation), Sarajevo (Bosnia and Herzegovina), Tbilisi (Georgia), Tirana (Albania) and Yerevan (Armenia). It also has liaison offices in Brussels (Belgium), Geneva (Switzerland), Vienna (Austria) and Warsaw (Poland), and runs two European Youth Centres, one in Strasbourg, the other in Budapest, as international residential training and meeting centres.

§8. THE EUROPEAN COMMISSION AGAINST RACISM AND INTOLERANCE

233. ECRI is a mechanism which was established by the first Summit of Heads of State and Government of the Member States of the CoE via the Vienna Declaration adopted on 9 October 1993. Its role as an independent human rights monitoring body on racism and racial discrimination was consolidated on 13 June 2002, when the CM adopted a new Statute for ECRI. Its task is to combat racism, xenophobia, anti-Semitism and intolerance from the perspective of the protection of human rights. ECRI's action covers all necessary measures to combat violence, discrimination and prejudice faced by persons or groups of persons, notably on grounds of 'race', colour, language, religion, nationality and national or ethnic origin.

234. ECRI's members are independent experts of high moral authority, appointed on the basis of their in-depth knowledge in the field of combating intolerance. Its programme of activities comprises three aspects: a country-by-country approach; work on general themes; and activities in relation with civil society. In the framework of the country-by-country approach, ECRI closely examines the situation in each of the Member States of the CoE, drawing up reports containing its analyses and recommendations as to how each country might deal with the problems identified during a contact visit organized for the ECRI Rapporteurs. ECRI's reports are first transmitted in the form of draft texts to the Member States concerned for a process of confidential dialogue with the national authorities of these countries. The content of the report is reviewed in the light of this dialogue, after which the report is adopted in its final form and transmitted to the government of the Member State concerned, through the intermediary of the CM of the CoE. The report is then made public, unless the government in question is expressly against its publication. The country-by-country approach deals with all Member States of the CoE on an equal footing, based on four/five-year cycles, covering ten/twelve countries per year. ECRI's has also adopted sixteen General Policy Recommendations, which are addressed to the governments of all Member States and provide guidelines which policy-makers are invited to use when drawing up national strategies and policies.[273]

§9. INTERGOVERNMENTAL EXPERT COMMITTEES

235. The CM has created intergovernmental expert committees in most areas of the CoE's work. The most important of these are called Steering Committees; there are also Groups of Specialists, ad hoc Committees and Working Groups. The Steering Committees generally meet once or twice a year to organize the work programme and activities in their relevant area of competence, and organize periodic meetings of European Ministers in their field.[274]

273. More information is available on ECRI's website on the Council of Europe's website.
274. More information is available on the Council of Europe's website by theme.

§10. Bodies Based on Treaties

236. Many of the CoE's Conventions have created bodies. These range from the judicial – the above-mentioned ECtHR – over para-judicial bodies – like the above-mentioned ECSR – to independent expert bodies which monitor compliance – such as the CPT.[275] Some of the CoE's partial agreements have also created bodies, such as the European Commission for Democracy through Law (Venice Commission),[276] the European Centre for Global Interdependence and Solidarity (North-South Centre) and the Council of Europe Development Bank (CEB).

237. The North-South Centre was set up in Lisbon (Portugal) in 1990 as a CoE partial agreement. The North-South Centre was the outcome of a process started in 1984, when the Portuguese Parliament hosted a conference held by the CoE's Parliamentary Assembly on 'North-South: Europe's role'. This conference was followed by a European Campaign on North-South interdependence and solidarity in 1988. The Centre has two objectives: to raise public awareness of North-South interdependence and solidarity and to develop links with governments, local authorities, NGOs, parliamentarians and the media worldwide in order to promote human rights, pluralist democracy and global education.[277] It provides a framework for North-South co-operation to increase public awareness of global interdependence issues and promote policies of solidarity in conformity with the aims and principles of the CoE.

238. The CEB is the oldest international financial institution in Europe and the only one with an exclusively social vocation. Set up in 1956 under a CoE partial agreement, it has forty-one members at present. The CEB is a multilateral development bank which grants loans to Member States facing social problems arising, for example, from the presence of refugees, displaced persons, migrants and victims of natural or ecological disasters. It contributes to the financing of social projects in three major areas: strengthening social integration, responsible management of the environment, and developing human capital.[278]

§11. Other Bodies

239. The European Directorate for the Quality of Medicines and Health Care (EDQM) is a Directorate of the CoE which celebrated its fiftieth Anniversary in 2014. It is responsible for the technical Secretariat of the European Pharmacopoeia Commission, which establishes and provides official standards for the manufacture and quality control of medicines applicable in all the signatory states of the Convention for the elaboration of a European Pharmacopoeia. The EDQM's mission is

275. *See* Hugh Chetwynd's contribution on CPT in this volume.
276. *See* Schnutz Rudolf Dürr's contribution on the Venice Commission in this volume.
277. For more information, please consult the Centre's website: www.coe.int/t/dg4/nscentre.
278. For more information, please consult the most recent PACE report on the Bank, Doc. 13513 and Res. 2007(2014), and the Bank's website: www.coebank.org.

to contribute to the basic human right of access to good-quality medicines and healthcare, and to promote and protect human and animal health.[279]

240. The Pompidou Group is a multidisciplinary co-operation forum to prevent drug abuse and illicit trafficking in drugs, set up in 1971 and incorporated into the CoE in 1980. It is an intergovernmental body which currently comprises thirty-nine states. The Pompidou Group's core mission is to contribute to the development of multidisciplinary, innovative, effective and evidence-based drug policies in its Member States. It seeks to link policy, practice and science and focuses especially on the realities of local implementation of drug programmes.[280]

241. The Group of States Against Corruption (GRECO) was established in 1999 to monitor States' compliance with the organization's anti-corruption standards through capacity-building, the sharing of good practices, mutual evaluation and peer pressure.[281] It currently comprises forty-nine Member States (forty-eight European States and the US).

242. The Committee of Experts on the Evaluation of Anti-money Laundering Measures and the Financing of Terrorism (MONEYVAL) was established in 1997 – and made permanent in 2010 – to monitor compliance with the principal international standards to counter money laundering and the financing of terrorism and the effectiveness of their implementation. It functions similarly to GRECO, but is answerable directly to the CM. In addition to twenty-eight CoE Member States, Israel, The Holy See (including Vatican City State), the UK Crown Dependencies of Guernsey, Jersey and the Isle of Man and the British Overseas Territory of Gibraltar are members.[282]

243. The European Audiovisual Observatory was set up in December 1992 as the only centre of its kind to gather and circulate information on the audiovisual industry in Europe. The Observatory is a European public service body with forty Member States and the EU, represented by the European Commission. It owes its origins to Audiovisual Eureka and operates within the legal framework of the CoE. It works alongside a number of partner organizations, professional organizations from within the industry and a wide network of correspondents with the aim of improving the transfer of information within the audiovisual industry, to promote a clearer view of the market and a greater transparency.[283]

244. Eurimages is the CoE fund for the co-production, distribution and exhibition of European cinematographic works. Set up in 1988 as a Partial Agreement, it currently has thirty-six Member States, and aims to promote the European film industry by encouraging the production and distribution of films, and fostering

279. For more information, please consult the EDQM's website: www.edqm.eu.
280. For more information, please consult the Pompidou Group's website: www.coe.int/t/dg3/pompidou.
281. For more information, please consult GRECO's website: www.coe.int/en/web/greco.
282. For more information, please consult MONEYVAL's website: www.coe.int/en/web/moneyval.
283. For more information, please consult the Observatory's website: www.obs.coe.int.

co-operation between professionals. Eurimages' first objective is cultural, in that it endeavours to support works which reflect the multiple facets of a European society whose common roots are evidence of a single culture. The second one is economic, in that the Fund invests in an industry which, while concerned with commercial success, is interested in demonstrating that cinema is one of the arts and should be treated as such. Bearing this in mind, Eurimages has developed four support schemes: cinema co-production, theatrical distribution, exhibition and digital equipment for cinema theatres. Since it was set up in 1989, Eurimages has supported the co-production of nearly 2,000 full-length feature films and documentaries for a total amount of approximately EUR 582 million. A number of these have received prestigious awards (Oscars, Palme d'Or, Golden Lion etc.).[284]

245. The European Centre for Modern Languages (ECML) was created in 1994 under a partial agreement in Graz, Austria. It is a unique institution whose mission is to encourage excellence and innovation in language teaching and to help Europeans learn languages more efficiently. It currently supports thirty-three Member States (and Canada) in implementing their language education policies. Basing its work on the underlying values of the CoE and its pioneering work in language education, the ECML is ideally equipped to act as a catalyst for reform in the teaching and learning of languages.[285]

§12. CoE Publishing

246. CoE Publishing is the organization's official publishing arm and offers a wide choice of books and electronic products in all the subject areas linked to the co-operation developed between the forty-seven Member States. A leading publisher of reference works in the field of human rights and international law (constitutional law, criminal law, family law, labour law, etc.), CoE Publishing also produces works in other spheres of human and social sciences, including: health, social affairs, bioethics, education, culture, youth, sport, architectural heritage and environment. Its publications include topical debates, comparative studies, monographs, proceedings of colloquies, international legal instruments, official texts, etc. A virtual reading room on the Internet makes it possible to consult excerpts from the main works just published, or the full texts of certain official documents such as conventions, at no cost. The current catalogue presents over 1,200 books and electronic products (CD-ROMs, PDF files, video cassettes, etc.), distributed throughout the world. Some 120 new titles are published each year, in each of the two official languages (English and French). A great many of these works are translated into other European or non-European languages, in partnership with national publishers.[286]

---

284. For more information, please consult the Eurimages' website: www.coe.int/T/DG4/Eurimages.
285. For more information, please consult the Centre's website: www.ecml.at.
286. More information is available on the website: https://book.coe.int/eur/en.

Chapter 2. The Commissioner for Human Rights

Manuel Lezertua & Andrew Forde, updated by Nikolaos Sitaropoulos and Matthieu Birker

247. The Commissioner for Human Rights is an independent, non-judicial institution within the CoE, mandated to promote in all Member States education in, awareness of and effective respect for human rights as embodied in the human rights instruments of the CoE.[287,288] Elected by the Parliamentary Assembly for a non-renewable term of office of six years, the Commissioner is the most recent institution established in 1999 within the CoE. The current Commissioner, Dunja Mijatović, took up her functions in April 2018. She is the fourth Commissioner, succeeding Nils Muižnieks (2012–2018), Thomas Hammarberg (2006–2012) and Álvaro Gil-Robles (1999–2006).

§1. Origin

248. The genesis of the idea for a Commissioner for Human Rights on the European level stems back as far as 1972 within a motion for recommendation to the CM tabled by PACE members Mr Wiklund and others.[289] The aforementioned were of the opinion that there was a need for an Ombudsman or 'Commissioner of Human Rights' on the European level whose primary task would be to assist, free of charge, in receiving and bringing claims before the then European Commission of Human Rights[290] and also to inquire into apparent violations of human rights in States parties to the Convention in order to make complaints before the Commission.

249. The following two decades, practically no progress was made on the original idea. In a speech before the Parliamentary Assembly on 24 January 1996, the then Finnish Minister of Foreign Affairs, Ms Tarja Halonen, herself a former PACE member, put forward the first concrete proposal to create a CoE Commissioner for Human Rights. She echoed the comments on the question of a possible Council Ombudsman made by the then Finnish President, Mr Martti Ahtisaari.

250. In her statement to the CM Deputies on 7 November 1996, Ms Halonen elaborated further the proposal suggesting that the Commissioner could have two main functions (which differ notably from the current functions):

---

287. www.commissioner.coe.int.
288. Resolution (99)50 on the Council of Europe Commissioner for Human Rights, adopted by the Committee of Ministers, at its 104th Session, Budapest, 7 May 1999.
289. Consultative Assembly of CoE, PA Doc. 3092 of 24 Jan. 1972, 'Motion for a recommendation on the need for a Commissioner of Human Rights or equivalent solution at European level.'
290. On 1 Nov. 1998 the Commission was replaced by the new permanent European Court of Human Rights.

- to communicate with citizens who need further information before submitting applications to the (then) European Commission of Human Rights; and
- to deal with human rights grievances under a system which would be lighter than the traditional system of the European Commission of Human Rights.[291]

Importantly, Ms Halonen stressed that the Commissioner's work should be complementary to that of existing mechanisms and not a substitute for them.

251. By 25 June 1997, a third function had been added to the initial Finnish proposal which had asserted the need for a fairly flexibly defined mandate in order to enable the Office of the Commissioner to evolve to meet changing needs over time. Along with 'information and advice' and 'dealing with grievances', the proposal now incorporated the function of 'amicus curiae'.[292] The latter function was described as being 'the centrepiece' of the proposal at the time. However, over time, and through frequent discussion, debate and alternative proposals some common trends became obvious; there was a need for a *non-judicial* means of protecting human rights within Europe which would complement existing mechanisms but maintain a position of non-interference with matters falling within the competence of the ECtHR. Also any institution embarking on accepting individual complaints would face a myriad of obstacles including receiving a large volume of complaints which the office would be ill-resourced to handle, thus the Commissioner could not provide a service to the individual in the same way as national human rights institutions or ombudsmen, for example. The incumbent would have to be highly selective in taking on cases; and of course linguistic obstacles would be inevitable as complainants could not be obliged to express themselves in an official CoE language (English or French). Thus, agreement was eventually reached that the Commissioner would not embark on the examination of any individual complaints whatsoever;[293] despite that, Article 5.1 of the subsequently adopted mandate explicitly entitles the Commissioner to act on any relevant information received from individuals, allowing the scope for the Commissioner to act on such information in a non-judicial manner as he/she sees fit.

252. The initiative for setting-up the institution was finally taken by the CoE Heads of State and Government at their Second Summit in Strasbourg on 10–11 October 1997. For the following two years the CM, the Steering Committee for Human Rights (CDDH) and the Parliamentary Assembly, with the consultative participation of the Court, developed the *travaux préparatoires* of the Commissioner's mandate.

291. Proposal to Create a Council of Europe Commissioner for Human Rights, CoE Doc. CM(97)12, 7 Jan. 1997.

292. Seminar On The Proposal To Create A Council Of Europe Commissioner For Human Rights, CoE Doc. CM(97)109, 25 Jun. 1997.

293. At the beginning of 1998, the German Delegation presented an alternative proposal to the Finnish draft, stating that the 'Commissioner for Human Rights shall not embark on any individual complaints whatsoever.' Appendix 2, Presentation of the alternative proposal by the German Delegation, CoE Doc. GR-H(98)CB1, 4 Mar. 1998, 9.

253. On 7 May 1999, on the occasion of the celebrations of the fiftieth Anniversary of the CoE taking place in Budapest during the Hungarian Chairmanship of the CM, this latter body adopted Resolution (99)50 by which it instituted the Office of the CoE Commissioner for Human Rights.[294]

§2. Election

254. Under Article 9 of Resolution (99)50 the Commissioner is elected by the Parliamentary Assembly by a majority of votes cast, from a list of three candidates drawn up by the CM. Member States may submit candidatures by letter addressed to the Secretary General. Article 11 of Resolution (99)50 provides that the Commissioner is elected for a non-renewable term of office of six years.

255. Candidates for the position must be nationals of a CoE Member State, eminent personalities of a high moral character having recognized expertise in human rights, a public record of attachment to the values of the CoE and the personal authority necessary to carry out the mission effectively.

256. The first Commissioner for Human Rights, Mr Álvaro Gil-Robles, took up office in October 1999. Former Ombudsman of Spain, he shaped the profile of the Office and its role within the European human rights system, establishing international credibility for the institution. His most noteworthy actions included his engagement in the protection of human rights in the aftermath of the second Chechen conflict, advocacy for improving prison conditions, promotion of minority rights and support to national human rights actors, such as Ombudsmen, other national institutions and NGOs.

The second Commissioner, Mr Thomas Hammarberg, took up his function in April 2006. A Swedish national with several decades of experience in promoting the advancement of human rights protection in Europe and worldwide, he further developed the system of country visits and dialogue with national authorities, focusing on effective implementation of human rights standards. He raised the profile of the institution and strengthened its impact. Some of the highlights of his mandate include his humanitarian work following the 2008 conflict in Georgia, the defence of human rights of Roma and migrants, and raising awareness on the human rights of LGBTI persons.

The third Commissioner, Mr Nils Muižnieks, took up his position in April 2012. A Latvian national and former minister who had been working in the field of human rights for the past two decades, he gave emphasis to human rights challenges, such as those arising from the impact of economic crisis and of fiscal austerity measures, from a rapidly evolving information society, from the rise of racist extremism and intolerance in Europe, from the increase in arrivals of migrants and asylum seekers in 2015 and 2016 and the retrogressive trends affecting women's rights and gender

294. *See* Mandate in Appendix below.

equality. The use of social media, along with traditional media intervention including the publication of op-eds in newspaper, significantly increased the visibility of the institution during his tenure.

The fourth, current, Commissioner, Dunja Mijatović, took up her function in April 2018. Whilst building upon her predecessors' achievements, she also tackles new challenges, including the safeguard of human rights in the era of artificial intelligence.

§3. Mandate

257. The fundamental objectives of the Commissioner for Human Rights, as outlined in Resolution 99(50) are to:

- promote education in and awareness of human rights in CoE Member States;
- identify possible shortcomings in the law and practice concerning human rights, promote the effective implementation of the CoE standards and assist Member States in their efforts to remedy such shortcomings;
- facilitate the activities of national ombudsmen and other human rights structures; and
- provide advice and information regarding the protection of human rights and prevention of human rights violations across the region.

258. The Commissioner's work thus focuses on encouraging reform measures to achieve tangible improvement in the area of human rights promotion and protection. Being a non-judicial institution, the Commissioner cannot act upon individual complaints, but he/she can draw conclusions and take wider initiatives on the basis of reliable information regarding human rights violations suffered by individuals.

The Commissioner co-operates with a broad range of international and national institutions as well as human rights monitoring mechanisms. Among the Office's most important intergovernmental partners are the UN and its specialized offices, the EU, and the OSCE. The Office also co-operates closely with leading international human rights NGOs, universities and think tanks.

§4. Main Activities

259. To discharge the functions set out in the mandate, the Commissioner works along three main lines:

- a system of country visits and dialogue with the Governments and other national actors;
- thematic recommendations, opinions and awareness-raising; and
- co-operation with national human rights structures and human rights defenders.

None of the Commissioner's functions are mutually exclusive; quite the contrary, they coexist and many of the activities which may fall under one heading also inevitably support the work within another.

§5. Country Visits

260. Country visits have always been the core of the Commissioner's work. While the first Commissioner's visits aimed at making a comprehensive evaluation of the human rights situation, covering a wide range of human rights issues, the current established practice is to focus on a limited number of issues that are analysed in-depth and provide a concrete basis for a constructive dialogue with Member States. During the visits, the Commissioner meets with the highest representatives of government, parliament, the judiciary, as well as leading members of human rights institutions and the civil society. He/she also visits relevant places, such as prisons, psychiatric hospitals or asylum seekers' reception or detention centres or shelters for women victims of violence, depending on the thematic focus of the visit. After the visits, a report is released containing both an analysis of human rights practices and detailed recommendations about areas for improvement and possible ways to do so. The reports are made public, along with the governments' comments, and widely circulated among policy-makers and NGOs as well as the media.

261. From time to time, the Commissioner also conducts missions to countries or regions in order to take part in human-rights-related events, strengthen relations with the authorities, or examine one or a number of specific areas of concern, without necessarily issuing a report. Following a number of such missions the Commissioner has exchanged letters with Member State governments on various human rights issues.

§6. Thematic Recommendations, Opinions and Awareness-Raising

262. The Commissioner also provides advice and information on the protection of human rights and the prevention of violations. When the Commissioner considers it appropriate he/she may issue recommendations regarding a specific human rights issue concerning a single, or several Member States. Recommendations issued by the Commissioner to date cover various issues, such as the implementation of the right to housing and systematic work for implementing human rights at national level.[295]

263. Either on the request of national bodies or on his own initiative in accordance with Article 3(e) of his mandate, the Commissioner may also offer opinions on draft laws and specific practices. These opinions can be used as important tools for States to remedy shortcomings before they give rise to applications before the ECtHR. Some examples include the Commissioner's opinions on the legislation of

295. *See* list of recommendations at: http://www.coe.int/en/web/commissioner/recommendations.

the Russian Federation on non-commercial organizations in light of CoE standards, and Hungary's media legislation in light of CoE standards on freedom of the media.[296]

264. The successive Commissioners also issued comments on a number of CoE instruments, including the draft Convention on the Prevention of Terrorism (2005) and the interim report of the Group of Wise Persons to the CM (2006).

265. The Commissioner also promotes awareness of human rights in CoE Member States. To this end, the Commissioner regularly publishes Issue Papers[297] that highlight and analyse topical human rights concerns and suggest ways to tackle such problems. They aim to inform the public as well as authorities and members of NGOs working in the field of human rights. Also, Human Rights Comments are published on a regular basis on the Commissioner's blog, in at least three languages: English, French and Russian.[298] In addition, the Commissioner organizes, co-organizes and takes part in seminars and events on various human rights themes. In order to improve public awareness and effective implementation of the CoE human rights standards, the Commissioner engages in a permanent dialogue with governments, civil society organizations and educational institutions in Member States.

§7. Co-operation with National Human Rights Structures and Human Rights Defenders

266. The successive Commissioners considered National Human Rights Structures (i.e., Ombudsmen and National Human Rights Institutions) as key actors for the protection and promotion of human rights and the rule of law. For this reason, they have developed close links with them, in order to foster the effective implementation at the national level of the CoE human rights standards, in accordance with the Commissioner's mandate.

267. While respecting the independence of all those involved, the co-operation consists of a systematic dialogue, notably during the Commissioner's country visits, and of an exchange of relevant information in order to improve reciprocal and common action and to share information about successful practices. Partners of this network are national, regional, local or thematic institutions which comply with the *Paris Principles*. The Commissioner defends his/her partners' independence, facilitates their activities in the field of human rights and supports their empowerment.

268. Lastly, further to a Declaration adopted by the CoE CM on 6 February 2008, the Commissioner has been designated as the main regional mechanism to strengthen the protection of human rights defenders and to promote their activities.

296. *See* list of opinions at: http://www.coe.int/en/web/commissioner/opinions.
297. *See* list of Issue Papers at: http://www.coe.int/en/web/commissioner/issue-papers.
298. http://humanrightscomment.org.

Following this Declaration, the Commissioner has strengthened his/her role and the capacity of the Office in order to provide strong and effective protection for human rights defenders in Europe. The Commissioner has a regular exchange of information with human rights defenders and organizes round tables with them.[299]

§8. Interaction with Other Human Rights Actors in Europe

269. The Commissioner's status as an independent institution within the CoE endows him/her with a unique flexibility to work with other institutions, including human rights monitoring mechanisms and intergovernmental and parliamentary committees. As explained above, the Commissioner co-operates with a broad range of international institutions, most importantly the UN and its specialized offices, the EU, and the OSCE. The Office also co-operates closely with leading international human rights NGOs, universities and think tanks.

I. Third Party Interventions Before the ECtHR

270. The Court's mission is to ensure the observance of the engagements undertaken by the European States Parties to the ECHR. It rules over applications concerning against human rights violations allegedly committed by States Parties, and brought to the Court either by other States Parties or by individuals within the jurisdiction of a contracting Party who claim to be victims of violations of their human rights and fundamental freedoms enshrined in the Convention.

271. The role of the Commissioner in relation to court proceedings has changed following the entry into force in June 2010 of Protocol No. 14 to the ECHR which aimed at further improving the efficiency of the Strasbourg Court. Before 2010, the Commissioner could be involved in the Court's proceedings only upon the Court's invitation. For example, this happened in January 2004, when the Commissioner accepted the Court's request to facilitate 'within the limit of his competencies' the application of Court Rule 39 (interim measures) in order to protect the health of an applicant detained in Tiraspol.[300] Another notable intervention by the Commissioner before the Grand Chamber of the Court occurred in 2010 in the case of *M.S.S. v. Belgium and Greece* (Application No. 30696/09), concerning the transfer of an asylum seeker from Belgium to Greece under the EU 'Dublin Regulation'.

272. Protocol No. 14 has amended Article 36 ECHR and now the Commissioner can take part in the proceedings of the Court on his own initiative, by submitting written comments and participating in hearings. This happened for the first time in the Grand Chamber case of *The Centre for Legal Resources on behalf of*

299. http://www.coe.int/en/web/commissioner/human-rights-defenders.
300. *Ilaşcu, Ivantoc, Lesco and Petrov-Popa v. Moldova and Russia*, Application No. 48787/99. It is interesting to note that the intervention of the Commissioner had been requested by the defendants.

Valentin Câmpeanu v. Romania (Application No. 47848/08), relating to the treatment of a young man of Roma ethnic origin, suffering from a severe learning disability and infected with the HIV virus, who died in a psychiatric hospital. To date, the Commissioner intervened before the ECtHR as a third party on 23 occasions.[301] The observations submitted to the Court do not comment on the merits of the case but address only those aspects of it which concern the Commissioner's particular interests in the matter.

273. Following the entry into force on 1 August 2018 of Protocol No. 16 to the ECHR, the Commissioner also has the right to submit written comments and take part in any hearing in the cases where the Court is requested by the highest courts and tribunals of a Party to the ECHR to give advisory opinions on questions of principle relating to the interpretation or application of the rights and freedoms defined in the Convention or the protocols thereto.

274. In addition, following an amendment to Rule 9 of the Rules of the CM adopted in January 2017, the Commissioner is entitled to submit a communication to the Committee with regard to the execution of all cases examined by it.

II. Co-operation with the EU

275. The Commissioner has developed and established strong links and co-operation with the EU, notably the EP, the European Ombudsman, the Commissioner responsible for enlargement and European neighbourhood policy, the Commissioner for Home Affairs, the Commissioner for Justice, the Commissioner for Employment, Social Affairs and Inclusion, the EU Special Representative for Human Rights, and the EU Agency for Fundamental Rights. This co-operation has facilitated the use of the Commissioner's work as a reference in the context of the EU and the protection of human rights and fundamental freedoms in the EU Member States.

§9. Conclusion

276. In the course of the fifteen years of work the Commissioner has proven to be an institution with an added value due to its independence, impartiality and flexibility that make it possible for it to tackle any topical human rights issue in Europe. The institution has been described as paving the way for democratic stability through enhancing human rights.[302] The Heads of State and Government of the CoE in the 2005 Third Summit Action Plan expressly recognized the institution's effectiveness and undertook to strengthen it.[303] This appreciation is also evident during

301. *See* list of cases at: http://www.coe.int/en/web/commissioner/third-party-interventions.
302. Speech by Finnish Foreign Minister Tuomioja, 114th Session of the Committee of Ministers, Strasbourg, 13 May 2004.
303. *See*: http://www.coe.int/T/CM/Summits_en.asp.

the regular exchanges of views that the Commissioner holds with the CM and with the Parliamentary Assembly to present and discuss his quarterly and/or annual activity reports. All this demonstrates the respect the institution has garnered and therefore the responsibility endowed upon it to fulfil this vastly challenging mandate in a dynamic modern Europe.

APPENDIX

RESOLUTION (99)50

ON THE COUNCIL OF EUROPE COMMISSIONER FOR HUMAN RIGHTS

(adopted by the Committee of Ministers on 7 May 1999 at its 104th Session)

The Committee of Ministers,

Considering that the aim of the Council of Europe is the achievement of greater unity between its Members and that one of the methods by which that aim is to be pursued is the maintenance and further realisation of human rights and fundamental freedoms;

Having regard to the decisions taken by the Heads of State and Government of the Member States of the Council of Europe at their Second Summit (Strasbourg, 10–11 October 1997);

Considering also that the 50th Anniversary of the Council of Europe provides an occasion to enhance further the work undertaken since its creation;

Decides to institute the office of Council of Europe Commissioner for Human Rights ('the Commissioner') with the following terms of reference:

Article 1

1. The Commissioner shall be a non-judicial institution to promote education in, awareness of and respect for human rights, as embodied in the human rights instruments of the Council of Europe.
2. The Commissioner shall respect the competence of, and perform functions other than those fulfilled by, the supervisory bodies set up under the European Convention of Human Rights or under other human rights instruments of the Council of Europe. The Commissioner shall not take up individual complaints.

Article 2

The Commissioner shall function independently and impartially.

Article 3

The Commissioner shall:

a. promote education in and awareness of human rights in the Member States;
b. contribute to the promotion of the effective observance and full enjoyment of human rights in the Member States;
c. provide advice and information on the protection of human rights and prevention of human rights violations. When dealing with the public, the Commissioner shall, wherever possible, make use of and co-operate with human rights structures in the Member States. Where such structures do not exist, the Commissioner will encourage their establishment;

d. facilitate the activities of national ombudsmen or similar institutions in the field of human rights;
e. identify possible shortcomings in the law and practice of Member States concerning the compliance with human rights as embodied in the instruments of the Council of Europe, promote the effective implementation of these standards by Member States and assist them, with their agreement, in their efforts to remedy such shortcomings;
f. address, whenever the Commissioner deems it appropriate, a report concerning a specific matter to the Committee of Ministers or to the Parliamentary Assembly and the Committee of Ministers;
g. respond, in the manner the Commissioner deems appropriate, to requests made by the Committee of Ministers or the Parliamentary Assembly, in the context of their task of ensuring compliance with the human rights standards of the Council of Europe;
h. submit an annual report to the Committee of Ministers and the Parliamentary Assembly;
i. co-operate with other international institutions for the promotion and protection of human rights while avoiding unnecessary duplication of activities.

Article 4

The Commissioner shall take into account views expressed by the Committee of Ministers and the PACE concerning the Commissioner's activities.

Article 5

1. The Commissioner may act on any information relevant to the Commissioner's functions. This will notably include information addressed to the Commissioner by governments, national parliaments, national ombudsmen or similar institutions in the field of human rights, individuals and organisations.
2. The gathering of information relevant to the Commissioner's functions shall not give rise to any general reporting system for Member States.

Article 6

1. Member States shall facilitate the independent and effective performance by the Commissioner of his or her functions. In particular, they shall facilitate the Commissioner's contacts, including travel, in the context of the mission of the Commissioner and provide in good time information requested by the Commissioner.

2. The Commissioner shall be entitled, during the exercise of his or her functions, to the privileges and immunities provided for in Article 40 of the Statute of the Council of Europe and in the agreements made thereunder.

Article 7

The Commissioner may directly contact governments of Member States of the Council of Europe.

Article 8

1. The Commissioner may issue recommendations, opinions and reports.
2. The Committee of Ministers may authorize the publication of any recommendation, opinion or report addressed to it.

Article 9

1. The Commissioner shall be elected by the Parliamentary Assembly by a majority of votes cast from a list of three candidates drawn up by the Committee of Ministers.
2. Member States may submit candidatures by letter addressed to the Secretary General. Candidates must be nationals of a Member State of the Council of Europe.

Article 10

The candidates shall be eminent personalities of a high moral character having recognized expertise in the field of human rights, a public record of attachment to the values of the Council of Europe and the personal authority necessary to discharge the mission of the Commissioner effectively. During his or her term of office, the Commissioner shall not engage in any activity which is incompatible with the demands of a full-time office.

Article 11

The Commissioner shall be elected for a non-renewable term of office of six years.

Article 12

1. An Office of the Commissioner for Human Rights shall be established within the General Secretariat of the Council of Europe.
2. The expenditure on the Commissioner and the Office of the Commissioner shall be borne by the Council of Europe.

Chapter 3. The European Committee for the Prevention of Torture

Hugh Chetwynd

§1. Introduction

277. The European Committee for the Prevention of Torture and Inhuman or Degrading Treatment or Punishment (usually referred to as the CPT) was established in 1989, following the ratification of the European Convention for the Prevention of Torture and Inhuman or Degrading Treatment or Punishment (hereinafter 'the Convention') by seven Member States of the CoE. Today all forty-seven Member States[304] of the CoE are bound by the Convention, and one of the conditions for any new Member State invited to join the CoE is to become a Party to this Convention.

278. The work of the CPT is designed to be an integrated part of the CoE system for the protection of human rights, placing a proactive non-judicial preventive mechanism alongside the existing reactive judicial mechanism of the ECtHR.

279. Of crucial significance is the fact that the Convention institutes a system of on-the-spot monitoring and encourages an ongoing dialogue between state officials of the country concerned and the CPT, with a view to improving the protection of human rights, notably the prevention of ill-treatment, in places of detention. In the twenty-five years since its establishment, the CPT has become an important safeguard for all persons deprived of their liberty throughout the European continent and an influential source for setting minimum standards in this field.

§2. Background

280. The inspiration for the CPT is drawn from the work of the International Committee of the Red Cross (ICRC), which pioneered the notion of protecting detained persons through a system of visits to places of detention by an expert and impartial body. The proposal for a European treaty was made by the Consultative Assembly of the CoE in September 1983,[305] based on a draft of a European Convention elaborated by the International Commission of Jurists and the Swiss Committee against Torture[306] (now renamed Association for the Prevention of Torture).

---

304. For the dates of the signatures and ratifications, please *see* the CoE Treaty Office website: CETS No. 126 on http://conventions.coe.int.
305. Recommendation 971(1983) on the protection of detainees from torture and from cruel, inhuman or degrading treatment or punishment, adopted on 28 Sep. 1983.
306. It was Jean-Jacques Gautier, a retired Swiss banker, who had the idea of a visit-based mechanism to assist States in preventing ill-treatment in places of detention. Through the Swiss Committee against Torture he campaigned tirelessly for such a mechanism to be established at the United Nations level, and when the process stalled, attention turned to the European level.

Member States were quick to ratify the Convention following its opening for signature in 1987, and it entered into force in 1989. The CPT first met in the same year, and carried out its initial visits to Austria, Denmark, Malta, Turkey and the UK in 1990. In the period up to June 2014 the CPT has carried out some 360 visits.

§3. How Does the CPT Function?

281. Article 1 of the Convention foresees the establishment of the Committee for the Prevention of Torture and states that 'the Committee shall, by means of visits, examine the treatment of persons deprived of their liberty with a view to strengthening, if necessary, the protection of such persons from torture and from inhuman or degrading treatment or punishment'.

282. As the Committee stated in its first General Report, its duty is broader than merely reporting on the allegations of torture or inhuman and degrading treatment; 'rather, it must look into the general conditions surrounding the alleged abuses and, if need be, suggest ways of both stopping the abuses in the immediate and of preventing their reoccurrence in the future'. It goes on to detail the four important consequences that 'follow from the fact that "prevention" constitutes the lynchpin of the whole monitoring system set up by the Convention':[307]

> First, the CPT must always look into the general conditions of detention existing in the countries visited. It must examine not only whether abuses are actually occurring but also be attentive to those 'indicators' or 'early signs' pointing to possible future abuses. For instance, it must – and indeed does – scrutinise the physical conditions of detention (the space available to detainees; lighting and ventilation; washing and toilet facilities; eating and sleeping arrangements; the medical care provided by the authorities, etc.) as well as the social conditions (e.g., relationships with other detainees and the law enforcement personnel; links with families, social workers, the outside world in general, etc.). The CPT also pays close attention to the extent to which certain basic safeguards against ill-treatment exist in the country visited e.g., notification of police custody; access to a lawyer; access to a medical doctor; the possibilities of lodging complaints about ill-treatment or conditions of detention.

Second, often one cannot understand and assess the conditions under which persons are deprived of their liberty in a given country without considering those conditions in their general (historical, social, economic) context. Although human dignity must be effectively respected in all Parties to the Convention, the background of each of these countries varies, and can account for differences in their response to human rights issues. It follows that, to fulfil its task of preventing abuses, the CPT must often look into the underlying causes of general or specific conditions conducive to mistreatment.

307. First General Report, CPT/Inf (1991) 3, paras 46–51.

The third consequence is closely associated with the two previous ones. In a number of instances the CPT – after investigating the conditions of detention in a particular country – may not find it appropriate to confine itself to merely suggesting immediate or short-term measures (such as, for example, administrative action) or even such measures as legislative improvements. It may find it necessary to recommend long-term measures, at least whenever it has become apparent that unacceptable conditions exist in a country as a result of deep-rooted factors that cannot be alleviated simply by judicial or legislative fiat or by resort to other legal techniques. In such cases, educational and similar long-term strategies may prove essential.

A fourth consequence flows from all the above remarks, namely that for the CPT to accomplish its preventive function effectively, it must aim at a degree of protection that is greater than that upheld by the European Commission and ECtHR when adjudging cases concerning the ill-treatment of persons deprived of their liberty and their conditions of detention.

283. The visits therefore represent the beginning of a process of ongoing dialogue with the States, and the CPT reports and state responses represent the formal means of communication between visits.

§4. Who Makes up the Committee?

284. The Convention provides that the Committee is to consist of persons of 'high moral character, known for their competence in the field of human rights or having professional experience' in the areas covered by the Convention.[308]

285. The CM of the CoE elects one member in respect of each country that has ratified the treaty (the lists of three candidates are drawn up by the national delegations to the Parliamentary Assembly, and submitted to the CM by the Assembly's Bureau). However, members serve in their individual capacities and not as State representatives. To further bolster their impartiality, 'national' members do not take part in visits to their own countries. Once elected, members serve for an initial term of four years, with the possibility of reappointment for two further terms.[309] While membership is currently a part-time responsibility, in practice many members spend considerable time on CPT business.[310]

286. A strength of the CPT lies with its composition, which brings together a wide range of knowledge and skills from among its members. In order to guarantee a genuinely multidisciplinary approach to its work, the Committee is concerned to

308. *See* Art. 4, para. 2, of the Convention.
309. Protocol No. 2 to the Convention increased the number of terms that a member could serve from two to three.
310. A busy member should count on approximately nine weeks away from home a year (three one-week plenary sessions, two two-week periodic visits, one one-week ad hoc visit and perhaps one week on country-specific delegation meetings). This does not include the time spent on writing up notes from visits, undertaking research on relevant issues or preparing for the three annual plenary sessions during which the visit reports are adopted.

ensure that its membership is balanced. While those with a legal background predominate, many members bring medical expertise to the work of the CPT. Others have served in their home countries as specialists in prison or police matters.[311] The Parliamentary Assembly also tries to ensure a gender balance on the lists and that neither men nor women fall below 40% of the membership.

287. The CPT's permanent Secretariat, composed of some twenty-four staff members, is based at the CoE's headquarters in Strasbourg.[312]

§5. The Mandate of the CPT

288. The CPT's mandate involves the *prevention* of torture and inhuman or degrading treatment or punishment, rather than formal condemnation of the treatment of any one detained person. It is interested in systems and processes that are practical and effective in preventing ill-treatment. Through visits to places of detention, the CPT assesses the treatment of persons deprived of their liberty and the conditions of detention, and obtains information on current legal and administrative procedures and operational practices. The information gathered forms the beginning of an ongoing dialogue with the State concerned.

289. The CPT implements its essentially preventive function through two kinds of visit – periodic and ad hoc. Periodic visits normally last two weeks, though they may be shorter or longer depending on the size of the country and the issues to be tackled, and allow the Committee to visit countries on a regular basis at roughly four-year intervals. Ad hoc visits are organized when they appear 'to be required in the circumstances' (*see* Article 7, paragraph 1, of the Convention). It is interesting to note that while the CPT is under an obligation to give notice of its intention to visit a particular country, the Convention does not lay down any minimum notice required.

290. Consequently, an ad hoc visit may be carried out immediately after notification has been made, thus permitting the CPT to respond rapidly when it receives information requiring a prompt investigation of a particular issue or of a place of detention. The Committee has resorted with increasing frequency to such visits and, as from 2018, it has reduced the number of periodic visits per year from ten to eight with the express purpose of increasing the number of ad hoc visits that may be carried out each year. For example, between January 2016 and December 2017 there

311. In the CPT General Reports, issued each spring, the Committee informs the State Parties of the types of expertise it believes would be beneficial. For example, in the twenty-sixth General Report of April 2017 it stated 'more members with first-hand knowledge of and experience in police matters (in particular investigation work) and/or prison matters (notably prison health care specialists), as well as prosecutors. Members with specific experience of working with vulnerbale groups in situation sof deprivation would also be an asset' (*see* CPT/Inf (2017) 5, para. 76).
312. Twenty-seventh General Report, CPT/Inf (2018) 4, para. 97 and Appendix 5.

were eighteen periodic visits (totalling 222 days) and seventeen ad hoc visits (totalling 110 days). The intention of the Committee is to have a programme of visits whereby each State Party receives at least a periodic visit every four years to five years.

291. The principles of *co-operation* and *confidentiality* lie at the heart of the system of visits by the CPT. The powers vested in the Committee to carry out its tasks are extensive. Article 2 of the Convention states that 'each party shall permit visits ... to any place within its jurisdiction where persons are deprived of their liberty by a public authority'. For the CPT, the notion of deprivation of liberty is understood within the meaning of Article 5 of the ECHR as elucidated by the case law of the ECtHR.[313] To date, these include places such as prisons and juvenile detention centres, police stations, immigration holding centres, psychiatric hospitals and homes for elderly or disabled persons.

292. As mentioned, the principle of *co-operation* is a core feature of the Convention mechanism (*see* Article 3). The substance of the co-operation is spelt out in Article 8, which makes clear that once the CPT has notified a State of a forthcoming visit it must be provided with:

(1) access to its territory and the right to travel without restriction;
(2) full information on the places where persons deprived of their liberty are being held;
(3) unlimited access to any place where persons are deprived of their liberty, including the right to move inside such places without restriction; and
(4) other information available to the Party which is necessary for the Committee to carry out its task.

293. Further, Article 8 states that the Committee 'may interview in private persons deprived of their liberty' and it 'may communicate freely with any person whom it believes can supply relevant information'.

294. These are exceptional powers, which the CPT has attempted to use judiciously. However, the ability of visiting delegations to be granted rapid access to places of detention they wish to visit, to the documentation it wants to consult and to individuals whom it wishes to interview represents a fundamental requirement for the Committee to function effectively. Consequently, the authorities in each State to

313. It is interesting to note that symbiosis between the CPT and the European Court of Human Rights may lead to the Committee taking a stance on an issue before the Court has had an opportunity to examine the matter. For example, the CPT's view that foreigners staying in a transit or international zone of an airport can, depending on the circumstances, amount to a deprivation of liberty within the meaning of Art. 5(1)(f) of the European Convention on Human Rights was vindicated by the judgment of 25 Jun. 1996 by the European Court of Human Rights in the case of Amuur against France. More recently, the CPT has stated that it cannot be ruled out that the cumulative effect of the obligations imposed by a control order on a given individual, under the Prevention of Terrorism Act 2005 in the UK, might in certain circumstances be considered as a deprivation of liberty (*see* CPT/Inf (2006) 28, para. 41).

be visited are encouraged to provide information about the *modus operandi* of the Committee and of its powers to all places where persons are deprived of their liberty. Further, visiting delegations are provided with credentials by the authorities explaining their mandate and granting them access to all such places. The result has been that the Committee now rarely encounters difficulties in obtaining access to a particular establishment. When problems in particular localities do occur, recourse can be had immediately by the CPT's delegation to a central government liaison officer who is empowered to resolve any difficulties relating to questions of access.[314]

295. Co-operation does not only relate to issues of access but also to the follow-up given by Governments to the recommendations made by the CPT in its visit reports. As a non-judicial mechanism focused on prevention, the Committee is interested in pursuing a meaningful dialogue with States on the issues it has found during a visit. Hence, the visits represent the starting point for any dialogue. However, it has become apparent that in a number of cases the recommendations made by the Committee are not being acted upon with due diligence or do not appear to be taken seriously by the respondent authorities. The Committee thus finds itself having to repeat its recommendations in consecutive visit reports. Where the State responses consistently ignore or do not address in an adequate manner the recommendations that have been made, the Committee may decide to initiate a procedure for issuing a public statement under Article 10, paragraph 2, of the Convention.[315]

296. The resort to a public statement is considered as a breakdown in the process of an ongoing dialogue and hence the Committee will strive to avoid such a scenario. To date, there have been only eight occasions on which the Committee has felt it necessary to issue a public statement, twice in relation to Turkey,[316] three times in relation to the Russian Federation,[317] one regarding Greece[318] and Bulgaria[319] and, most recently, one regarding Belgium.[320]

297. The corollary to co-operation is *confidentiality*, as laid down in Article 11 of the Convention. This means that the work of the Committee and its dialogue with

---

314. Issues of 'access' are always raised in the Section on Co-operation in all visit reports, and general aspects of concern or note may be raised in the general reports (*see* sixteenth General Report, para. 15).

315. 'If the Party fails to co-operate or refuses to improve the situation in the light of the Committee's recommendations, the Committee may decide, after the Party has had an opportunity to make known its views, by a majority of two-thirds of its members to make a public statement on the matter.'

316. On 15 Dec. 1992 (*see* CPT/Inf (93) 1) and 6 Dec. 1996 (*see* CPT/Inf (96) 34).

317. In relation to the Chechen Republic on all three occasions, 10 Jul. 2001 (*see* CPT/Inf (2001) 15); 10 Jul. 2003 (*see* CPT/Inf (2003) 33) and 13 Mar. 2007 (*see* CPT/Inf (2007) 17) respectively.

318. On 15 Mar. 2011 (*see* CPT/Inf (2011) 10) concerning the detention of irregular migrants and the state of the prison system.

319. On 26 Mar. 2015 (*see* CPT/Inf (2015) 17) concerning ill-treatment by the police and prison officials and the state of the prison system.

320. On 13 Jul. 2017 (*see* CPT/Inf (2017) 18) concerning the lack of a minimum service in prisons as a result of industrial action by prison staff.

the authorities of a country, including the visit reports, remain confidential and out of the public domain until such time as the State concerned authorizes the publication of a visit report and of its response(s) to such a report. Nevertheless, there has been a growing trend over recent years for States to authorize the publication of the visit reports along with their responses. In many instances such a publication is authorized immediately after reception of a State's response to the visit report. This means that roughly within a year of a visit taking place, both the visit report and the response will be in the public domain. As of July 2018, some 386 reports and responses have been published out of a total of 424 adopted visit reports.[321]

298. A further step in placing information on the findings of a CPT visit to a State in the public domain more rapidly was taken by Norway following the periodic visit of October 2005. The Committee has developed a practice of providing the authorities of a State with its preliminary observations at the end of a visit, which includes the main and most urgent findings of the visiting delegation. The Norwegian authorities are the first State to have published these preliminary findings, less than two months after the end of the visit.[322] Bosnia and Herzegovina, Denmark, Finland and Sweden have each published the preliminary observations made by the CPT following periodic visits to these countries. In 2012, Ukraine requested the publication of the preliminary observations after the 2011 ad hoc visit, and Greece did likewise following the April 2018 ad hoc visit. Moreover, a growing number of countries have decided to sign up to an 'automatic publication procedure' whereby the report of a visit to a country is placed in the public domain fifteen to thirty days following its transmission to the national authorities. As of July 2018, nine countries[323] have signed up the 'automatic publication procedure' with a number of other countries expecting to do so in the near future.

299. It should also be noted that the CPT may decide to place a visit report and the corresponding response in the public domain under certain circumstances; for example, if a part of the report is published by the authorities or the authorities provide an incomplete or misleading picture concerning the findings of the visit.

§6. The Chronology of a CPT Periodic Visit

300. For periodic visits, each December the CPT has so far published a list of countries that it intended to visit in the following twelve months. However, as from 2014 the Committee decided to publish the list of countries to be visited the following year already in March. The list is alphabetical and there is no indication as

321. It is notable that of the twenty-three visit reports submitted to the Russian Federation, it has, to date, only authorized the publication of three reports, namely the 2001 visit report, the 2011 visit report concerning the North Caucasus and the 2012 periodic visit report. It should also be noted that on 18 Jul. 2018, the six outstanding reports and responses concerning visits to Azerbaijan between 2004 and 2017 were published.

322. *See* CPT/Inf (2005) 20.

323. Austria, Bulgaria, Denmark, Finland, Luxembourg, the Republic of Moldova, Monaco, Sweden and Ukraine – *see also* twenty-seventh General Report, CPT/Inf (2018) 4, para. 28.

to the timing when the visit will take place. For the past few years the CPT has been announcing ten periodic visits per year, most of which are of some ten to twelve days duration. There is no further formal communication until two weeks before the visit is scheduled to start when a letter is sent to the authorities of the State concerned notifying them of the forthcoming visit and informing them of the names of the CPT's visiting delegation.

I. Composition of a Delegation

301. It has become usual practice that a visiting delegation will be composed on average of five members of the CPT, two members of the Secretariat and two experts. As the Committee's composition expanded in recent years, it is at times the case that visits contain more CPT members and fewer external experts. The important point is that the skills reflected by the delegation embrace the range of issues upon which it will focus during the visit. A typical periodic visit would be examining treatment of persons in establishments run by the law enforcement agencies (in some countries this may include a focus on places holding irregular migrants, or those held by specialized police units or intelligence services), several prisons and perhaps one or two psychiatric establishments. Thus the delegation must be able to competently cover the range of issues that such a visit engenders. For example, the 2013 visit to Turkey typifies the composition of such a delegation: two lawyers, a prosecutor, two forensic doctors, a psychiatrist, a prison expert and two Secretariat members.[324]

302. A CPT delegation is usually complemented by a number of interpreters (on average three to five, depending on the language skills of the group) for all non-English and non-French speaking countries. The interpreters represent an integral component of the delegation and the CPT has, in general, been able to count upon highly professional individuals to carry out this arduous task.

II. Information from a State to Be Visited

303. From the moment that it is announced that a periodic visit will occur to a State in the forthcoming year, there is usually some contact with the authorities. Important background information will be sought to ensure the Committee possesses the latest updates on all places where persons may be deprived of their liberty within the country, including the capacity of places of detention and the existing occupancy in each establishment. For example, the list of all police stations, the list of prisons and their categorization (pre-trial, sentenced, security status) as well as the number of men and women in such establishments, and the number of involuntary patients in each psychiatric institution will certainly be requested. Certain States might also furnish the CPT with extensive briefing papers on recent developments in their countries.

---

324. *See* News Flash of 26 Jun. 2013 http://www.cpt.coe.int/documents/tur/2013-06-26-eng.htm.

304. A few days prior to the start of a visit the CPT will notify the State concerned of some of the establishments it intends to visit – typically one or two prisons, a psychiatric institution and perhaps a general reference to police stations within a major urban area (often the capital city). The CPT will usually request more specific information concerning these notified establishments, such as a full breakdown of the inmate/patient population, the composition of the staff and the daily regime.

III. The Conduct of the Visit

305. At the outset of the visit the delegation will be provided with letters of accreditation by the authorities (in most States there will be one for each type of institution – Ministry of Defence for military detention facilities, Ministry of Interior for police stations and other law enforcement establishments, Ministry of Justice for Prisons and so forth). These letters of accreditation are essential as they ensure that the delegation can have swift and full access to those establishments it wishes to visit, regardless of whether they have been notified to the Government previously.

306. The first day-and-a-half of a visit is usually devoted to a series of discussions with relevant NGOs, government ministers and officials and other relevant interlocutors, such as the Ombudsman. In most cases, the delegation will divide into two sub-groups, one for example focusing on prison establishments and the other on psychiatric institutions and/or social care homes. Both sub-groups will probably examine issues relating to police custody. Throughout the course of the visit the sub-groups of the delegation will cross-reference information they are receiving and continue to assess whether additional places of deprivation of liberty need to be visited. The two sub-groups will invariable meet at least once, often on a Sunday, to debrief more fully on the progress of the visit. For each establishment visited there is a reference list of issues to be checked which include *inter alia* allegations of ill-treatment by staff, inter-prisoner/patient violence, material conditions, regime, healthcare provision, discipline, contact with the outside world, safeguards, and so on.

307. On the last day of the visit, the delegation will meet with ministers and officials to share its first impressions on the findings of the visit. This is also the occasion when the delegation will inform the authorities officially of any 'immediate observations'[325] it wishes to make concerning situations requiring urgent attention by the authorities. For example, it may concern a request to take out of commission certain cells or dormitories and transfer the persons concerned to more appropriate

325. Article 8, para. 5, of the Convention enables the Committee (via its delegation) to make certain observations during the visit itself which require immediate action.

accommodation;[326] or it may concern the treatment provided to a category of prisoners[327] as well as to individuals; or the necessity to improve the material conditions and/or regime in a particular establishment;[328] or to be informed of the outcome of an investigation into an incident.

308. In making an 'immediate observation', subsequently confirmed in writing by the CPT, the delegation is highlighting a matter of concern to the authorities which warrants urgent attention and cannot wait until the adoption of the visit report. States are usually requested to inform the Committee about the actions taken in respect of 'immediate observations' within one to three months, and the response provided is taken into account when drafting the visit report.

§7. CPT Reports

309. The drafting of CPT reports is an extensive collaboration effort, as the findings of all the members of the delegation are distilled and the essential elements of relevance for enhancing the prevention of ill-treatment are elaborated upon. The report sets down the precise findings by the delegation in the various establishments visited and includes recommendations for improvements, along with requests for information where the Committee either wants to have confirmation about a reform or a specific action. The Committee also makes comments on issues where it wants to engage the authorities in a discussion on how to tackle a particular matter. The recommendations, comments and requests for information contained in a report represent the basis for the ongoing dialogue with a State.

310. Following the adoption of a report, at one of the three plenary sessions of the CPT organized each year, the State concerned will be expected to make a full response within six months. Further correspondence may be entered into between the Committee and the State on specific issues requiring additional information or clarification.

311. The record of action taken in furthering dialogue is reviewed during the plenary sessions. Where appropriate, the Committee has initiated face-to-face discussions, known as high-level talks, to improve the quality of the dialogue and in recent years has placed more emphasis on such talks.[329] For example, in 2011/2012, it held

326. *See*, for example, Report on the visit to 'the Former Yugoslav Republic of Macedonia' of 21 Sep. 2010–1 Oct. 2010, CPT/Inf (2012) 4, para. 6.
327. *See*, for example, Report on the visit to the Czech Republic of 27 Mar.–7 Apr. 2006, CPT/Inf (2007) 32, para. 8.
328. *See*, for example, Report on the visit to Estonia of 30 May–6 Jun. 2012, CPT/Inf (2014) 1, para. 6.
329. Twenty-second General Report, paras 13–16:

high-level talks in Moscow and in Yessentuki (North Caucasus);[330] in 2016 in Brussels, Helsinki and Stockholm;[331] and in 2017 in Baku, Skopje, London, Tirana and Vilnius.[332]

§8. Ad Hoc Visits

312. As mentioned above, ad hoc visits relate to those visits that appear to be required in the circumstances and in recent years they amount to at least one-third of the visit days per year undertaken by the CPT, and this tendency is likely to rise further.[333] As compared to periodic visits, such visits tend to be shorter in duration (approximately one week) and carried out by smaller delegations composed of two or three members, a member of Secretariat and possibly an expert. The prior notification for ad hoc visits tends to be a week or less. The visits themselves follow the same scheme as for periodic visits, ending with a meeting to impart the first impressions of the delegation. The Committee will usually strive to adopt ad hoc visit reports within a three-month period and will usually request the authorities to respond within a similar timeframe.

§9. CPT Standards

313. Although the CPT is not a judicial body, it has developed a set of standards since its inception, which guide its work and inform governments as well as NGOs and other actors on what the Committee considers as good practice and minimum conditions. The standards are designed to assist in the prevention of ill-treatment and to build upon the formulations contained in existing European and international instruments. They are also dynamic rather than static statements evolving and developing over time, in the light of the reality on the ground as seen by the CPT's visiting delegations.

314. The CPT's standards are set out in its annual ('general') reports, published each spring (since 2015), and they reflect both the 'case law'-style accumulation of precedent found in the country visit reports and also highlight particular concerns to

---

> The discussions which CPT delegations hold with senior officials in the context of visits continue to be supplemented, in appropriate cases, by high-level talks between the national authorities and CPT representatives. Such direct contacts outside the context of a visit have frequently made it possible to clear up misunderstandings and enrich the ongoing dialogue with States.

330. Twenty-second General Report, para. 14.
331. *See* twenty-sixth General Report, CPT/Inf (2017) 5, paras 13–15.
332. *See* twenty-seventh General Report, CPT/Inf (2018) 4, paras 15–19.
333. Twenty-second General Report, para. 1; during the period 1 Aug. 2011 and 31 Jul. 2012, the CPT carried out ten periodic visits (totalling 102 days) and eight ad hoc visits (forty-four days). Twenty-seventh General Report, para. 1; during 2017, the CPT carried out ten periodic visits (totalling 105 days) and eight ad hoc visits (fifty seven days).

which the Committee wishes to draw attention. As the Committee has carried out more visits so have its standards become more elaborate and refined. Hence, it is not surprising that the initial thoughts on police custody[334] and imprisonment[335] outlined in the second General Report in 1992 were revisited in the eleventh and twelfth General Reports in 2001 and 2002 respectively.

315. As regards healthcare services in prisons,[336] the Committee has stated that:

> an inadequate level of health care can lead rapidly to situations falling within the scope of the term 'inhuman and degrading treatment'. Further, the health-care service in a given establishment can potentially play an important role in combating the infliction of ill-treatment, both in that establishment and elsewhere (in particular in police establishments).

Further, it is clear that a properly resourced and well-functioning healthcare service is well-placed to make a positive impact on the overall quality of life in the establishment within which it operates.

316. The CPT has consistently reiterated the importance it attaches to the general principle that prisoners are entitled to the same level of medical care as persons living in the community at large. Thus, it will always examine the state of health-care services in an establishment with regard to the 'equivalence of care' principle.

317. Other issues of concern that the Committee has come across, and continues to encounter, in the course of its visits have also been laid out in substantive sections in the general reports, such as:

– foreign nationals detained under aliens legislation;[337]
– involuntary placement in psychiatric establishments;[338]
– juveniles deprived of their liberty;[339]
– women deprived of their liberty; and[340]
– deportation of foreign nationals by air.[341]

318. In 2004, the CPT turned to a matter that it has referred to in many reports, notably the duty of the authorities in combating impunity.[342] Although the CPT is focused on prevention of ill-treatment, with eyes on the future rather than the past,

334. *See* second General Report, CPT/Inf (92) 3, updated description in twelfth General Report, CPT/Inf (2002) 15, paras 32–50.
335. *See* second General Report, updated description in eleventh General Report, CPT/Inf (2001) 16, paras 25–33.
336. *See* third General Report, CPT/Inf (93) 12, paras 30–77.
337. *See* seventh General Report, CPT/Inf (97) 10, paras 24–36.
338. *See* eighth General Report, CPT/Inf (98) 12, paras 25–55.
339. *See* ninth General Report, CPT/Inf (99) 12, paras 20–41.
340. *See* tenth General Report, CPT/Inf (2000) 13, paras 21–33.
341. *See* thirteenth General Report, CPT/Inf (2003) 35, paras 27–45.
342. *See* fourteenth General Report, CPT/Inf (2004) 28, paras 25–42.

assessing the effectiveness of action taken when ill-treatment has occurred constitutes an integral part of its mandate. In recent years, the CPT has had cause to reiterate its call for prompt, thorough and independent investigations into allegations of ill-treatment.[343]

319. More recently, the CPT has examined means of restraint in psychiatric establishments for adults,[344] elaborating upon the remarks it made in the eighth General Report when it addressed the issue of involuntary placement in psychiatric establishments for adults. In 2009, the CPT set out its views on the safeguards that should be afforded to detained irregular migrants, with an additional special emphasis on children.[345] In 2010, a special section on the use of electrical discharge weapons ('Tasers') by law enforcement officials was included in the General Report.[346] The standards on detained persons' access to a lawyer were updated in the light of the ECtHR's *Salduz v. Turkey* judgment.[347] Additionally, the 2011 General Report contained detailed guidelines on the use of solitary confinement of prisoners, highlighting the damaging effects of prolonged isolation.[348] Since the entry into force of the Optional Protocol to the UN Convention against Torture (OPCAT) in 2006, an increasing number of CoE Member States have established a so-called National Preventive Mechanism (NPM). In its twenty-second General Report the CPT supported the establishment of these monitoring bodies and set forth the principles of co-operation between the Committee and NPMs.[349] In 2013, the CPT laid out its standards on the documentation and reporting of medical evidence of ill-treatment.[350]

---

343. *Ibid.*, para. 25:

> The credibility of the prohibition of torture and other forms of ill-treatment is undermined each time officials responsible for such offences are not held to account for their actions. If the emergence of information indicative of ill-treatment is not followed by a prompt and effective response, those minded to ill-treat persons deprived of their liberty will quickly come to believe – and with very good reason – that they can do so with impunity. All efforts to promote human rights principles through strict recruitment policies and professional training will be sabotaged. In failing to take effective action, the persons concerned – colleagues, senior managers, investigating authorities – will ultimately contribute to the corrosion of the values which constitute the very foundations of a democratic society. Conversely, when officials who order, authorize, condone or perpetrate torture and ill-treatment are brought to justice for their acts or omissions, an unequivocal message is delivered that such conduct will not be tolerated. Apart from its considerable deterrent value, this message will reassure the general public that no one is above the law, not even those responsible for upholding it. The knowledge that those responsible for ill-treatment have been brought to justice will also have a beneficial effect for the victims.

344. *See* sixteenth General Report, paras 36–54.
345. *See* nineteenth General Report, paras 75–100.
346. *See* twentieth General Report, paras 65–84.
347. *See* twenty-first General Report, CPT/Inf (2011) 28, paras 18–23.
348. *Ibid.*, paras 53–64.
349. *See* twenty-second General Report, paras 27–52.
350. *See* twenty-third General Report, paras 71–84.

320. While the deprivation of liberty of children should always be a last resort, all European countries imprison young people and, in its 2014 General Report, the CPT lays out its thinking concerning juveniles deprived of their liberty under criminal legislation. It also addresses the very worrying phenomena of intimidation and reprisals against detainees following a CPT visit.[351] In the following General Report, the Committee looked at the situation of life-sentenced prisoners and called upon European countries to review their treatment of life-sentenced prisoners according to the individual risk they present, and to provide for their possible reintegration into society at some stage.[352] In the 2017 General Report, the CPT looked at remand detention and urged the forty-seven CoE Member States to use remand detention only as a measure of last resort and to provide remand prisoners with adequate detention conditions. During visits to prisons throughout Europe, the CPT has often found that remand prisoners are held under very poor conditions and an impoverished regime.[353] Most recently, in the twenty-seventh General Report, the Committee addressed the importance of complaint mechanisms and the onus on European states to ensure that persons deprived of their liberty have access to effective complaints mechanisms in prisons, police stations, immigration detention centres, psychiatric institutions and other places of detention.[354]

321. As a final remark on standards, it is worth noting that the CPT has not attempted to provide a definition for the terms 'torture' or 'inhuman and degrading treatment', leaving the interpretation of such legal terms to the UN Committee against Torture and the ECtHR.[355] Nevertheless, while being guided by the Court, the CPT is not confined to its definitions and given its preventative mandate has explored the environmental and cumulative conditions in which persons are deprived of their liberty. On occasion this has resulted in conditions in an institution being described as amounting to 'inhuman and degrading treatment'. For example, the CPT used such a designation in respect of the cumulative findings of overcrowding, poor sanitation, dilapidated and unhygienic cell conditions and the fact that inmates spent twenty-three hours per day locked in a cell in the case of certain prison establishments in Serbia, Ukraine, Georgia and Armenia;[356] but also with regard to the UK and Ireland.[357]

---

351. *See* twenty-fourth General Report, paras 96–132 and 41–46, respectively.
352. *See* twenty-fifth General Report, paras 67–82.
353. *See* twenty-sixth General Report, paras 52–73.
354. *See* twenty-seventh General Report, paras 68–91.
355. *See* Explanatory Report to the Convention, CPT/Inf (2002) 1, para. 25.
356. *See* Report to Serbia of 19–29 Nov. 2007, CPT/Inf (2009) 1, para. 48; Report to Ukraine of 9–21 Sep. 2009, CPT/Inf (2011) 29, para. 101; Report to Georgia of 5–15 Feb. 2010, CPT/Inf (2010) 27, paras 65–69; and Report to Armenia of 5–7 Dec. 2011, CPT/Inf (2012) 23, paras 14–15.
357. *See* Report to the United Kingdom of 29 Jul. 1990–10 Aug. 1990, CPT/Inf (1991)15, paras 36–57; and Report to Ireland on the visit of 26 Sep. 1993–5 Oct. 1993 CPT/Inf (95) 14, paras 77–104.

§10. Relationship with Other Bodies

322. The CPT has consistently advocated, as a fundamental safeguard against ill-treatment, the desirability for States to establish independent domestic monitoring bodies that would provide oversight in all places where persons are deprived of their liberty. A number of States have indeed established independent monitoring mechanisms and since the entry into force of OPCAT or Punishment on 22 June 2006, the number has risen. As of July 2018, thirty-eight CoE Member States have ratified OPCAT and thirty-seven have designated a NPM.[358] The OPCAT also establishes a Subcommittee with similar powers to the CPT. Moreover, it explicitly encourages co-operation between the Subcommittee and regional bodies like the CPT 'to consult and cooperate with a view to avoiding duplication'. To this end, the CPT has already proposed ideas for concrete co-operation with the Subcommittee and NPMs.[359]

323. On 6 November 2009, on the occasion of its twentieth anniversary, the CPT organized a meeting of the key and emerging actors in torture prevention in Europe, including representatives of the Subcommittee and the newly established NPMs, to discuss possible 'New Partnerships'. The matter was also addressed in the twenty-second General Report (*see* above) and, most recently, in July 2018 the SPT and CPT decided to reinforce complementarity and subsidiarity to reflect their respective strengths and added values.

324. The interaction between the ECtHR and the CPT is evolving and in recent years there has been an increased reference to CPT reports in Court proceedings and judgments.[360]

325. Within the CoE, the CPT is regularly consulted in the framework of the elaboration of new CoE standards by intergovernmental working groups. Examples include the Twenty Guidelines on forced return of foreign nationals[361] and the revised European Prison Rules[362] adopted by the CM on 4 May 2005 and 11 January 2006, respectively. There is also a close coordination with the CoE Commissioner of Human Rights and regular consultations with the PACE, as well as with the CM.

358. OPCAT foresees that every State Party should establish a national preventative mechanism possessing extensive monitoring powers in relation to places of detention.

359. *See* the Preface to the sixth General Report, CPT/Inf (2006) 35 and the twenty-second General Report, paras 27–52.

360. For example, the judgments of *Aerts v. Belgium* of 30 Jun. 1998; *Dougoz v. Greece* of 6 Mar. 2001; *Kalshnikov v. Russian Federation* ECHR 2002-VI; *Lorsé and Others v. The Netherlands* of 4 Feb. 2003; *Mouisel v. France* ECHR 2002-IX; *Poltoratskiy v. Ukraine* ECHR 2003-V; *Salduz v. Turkey* of 27 Nov. 2008; *M. v. Germany* of 17 Dec. 2009; *Vinter and others v. The United Kingdom* of 9 Jul. 2013; *Muršić v. Croatia* of 20 Oct. 2016; etc.

361. *See* Document CM (2005) 40; and for a comment on the Guidelines *see* fifteenth General Report, CPT/Inf (2005) 17, paras 43–48.

362. *See* Committee of Ministers Recommendation Rec (2006) 2; and for a comment on the Revised European Prison Rules *see* fifteenth General Report, CPT/Inf (2005) 17, paras 49–54.

326. More generally, the CPT is keen to maintain close links with NGOs and Ombudsman Offices on the ground, and with relevant international organizations such as the United Nations High Commission for Refugees (UNHCR) and, in a number of countries, the Organization for Security and Co-operation in Europe as well as the EU. It also maintains a constant link with the ICRC.[363]

§11. Conclusion

327. The CPT's unique visiting powers have enabled it to gain a rare insight into the operation and management of places of detention, which have in the past generally been outside the scope of public scrutiny and knowledge.[364] From this basis the CPT has engaged in a process of dialogue with States Parties to strengthen their procedures and mechanisms for preventing ill-treatment. Despite the progress made concerning the treatment of persons deprived of their liberty within Europe, there remain pressing challenges in all countries visited by the CPT. Ill-treatment, whether physical, psychological or environmental, requires constant vigilance and action if it is to be eradicated. The existence of independent monitoring mechanisms at the national level represents an important means of assisting governments in identifying where improvement are required and corrective action necessary. The CPT intends to support this process at the European level.

363. Article 17.3 of the Convention provides that the Committee shall not visit places which 'representatives or delegates of Protecting Powers or the International Committee of the Red Cross effectively visit on a regular basis by virtue of the Geneva Conventions of 12 Aug. 1949 and the Additional Protocols of 8 Jun. 1977 thereto'.

364. For a more extensive discussion of the CPT and its interaction with protection mechanisms, notably the European Court of Human Rights, *see* 'The treatment of prisoners: European standards' by Jim Murdoch (Council of Europe Publishing, May 2006) and 'Preventing Torture In Europe' by Christine Bicknell, Malcolm Evans and Rod Morgan (Council of Europe Publishing, 2018).

Part IV. Building a United Europe Without Dividing Lines

Chapter 1. Treaty-Making in the CoE

Christina Olsen, updated by Tanja E. J. Kleinsorge

§1. General Overview

328. Since the laying down of the Statute of the CoE in May 1949 and the opening for signature of the European Convention for the Protection of Human Rights in November 1950, the Council of Europe Treaty Series (CETS) has developed into an important body of common standards and rules of co-operation furthering the aim of creating a greater unity among the Member States of the CoE.

329. The legal foundation for the conclusion of treaties within the CoE is to be found in Article 15a of its Statute, which stipulates:

> On the recommendation of the Consultative Assembly [now the Parliamentary Assembly] or on its own initiative, the Committee of Ministers shall consider the action required to further the aims of the Council of Europe, including the conclusion of conventions or agreements and the adoption by governments of a common policy with regard to particular matters.

330. On 19 May 2006, with the opening for signature of the CoE Convention on the avoidance of statelessness in relation to State succession, the Series totalled 200 treaties.[365] These instruments deal with a wide and diverse array of subject matters, owing to the ample scope of action conferred upon the organization by its Statute, in particular Article 1b, under which terms:

> This aim [i.e., the aim of the organization] shall be pursued through the organs of the Council by discussion of questions of common concern and by agreements and common action in economic, social, cultural, scientific, legal and administrative matters and in the maintenance and further realisation of human rights and fundamental freedoms.

365. On 1 Jan. 2019, there were 223.

331. Although they have been prepared and negotiated within the institutional framework of the organization, CoE treaties are not instruments of the CoE as such. They are instruments whose content has been established and agreed upon by the CM of the CoE, but whose destiny ultimately lies in the hands of those states (and, in some cases, supranational institutions) entitled to sign and ratify them.

332. However, apart from constituting the international forum for the discussion and drafting of the treaty, the CoE may continue to play an important role in the life of the treaty after it is adopted, whenever the implementation thereof is followed or supervised by a monitoring mechanism set-up within the organization, such as the ECtHR or an expert committee.

333. CoE treaties are treaties according to the meaning given to the term by the Vienna Convention on the Law of Treaties. As such, they do not produce immediate legal effects upon states having concluded them, and require being signed and ratified before they can become legally binding upon states. Differences in the titles of the treaties, which may be referred to as 'conventions', 'agreements', 'codes' or 'protocols' are purely terminological, and do not reflect a difference in the legal nature and effects of the treaties.

334. Treaties listed in the CETS must be distinguished from partial agreements concluded within the organization (examples for such partial agreements would include the 'Venice Commission'[366] and the 'European Pharmacopoeia'). These agreements do not qualify as international treaties, but represent a particular form of intergovernmental activity, allowing those Member States who do not wish to participate to abstain from doing so.

§2. Subject Matters Covered by CoE Treaties

335. CoE treaties may deal with any of the areas of common concern in which the CoE is active. In pursuance of Article 1b of the Statute mentioned above, such areas include in particular human rights and fundamental freedoms, economic, social, cultural, scientific, legal and administrative matters.

336. The only explicit limit to the Organization's scope of action is that set by Article 1d of the Statute, which provides:

> Matters relating to national defence do not fall within the scope of the Council of Europe.

337. According to the classification used for searching purposes on the official website of the CoE Treaty Office (*see* http://conventions.coe.int), CoE treaties may be grouped according to the following fields of interest: arbitration, au pair work, audiovisual law, biomedicine, cinema, civil law, civil liability, commercial law, cor

366. In 2002, the 'Venice Commission' became an enlarged agreement.

ruption, court procedure, culture, cybercrime, data protection, enforcement of sanc tions, environment, European social charter, extradition, family law – rights of chi ldren, financial law, general international law, higher education, human rights, inte llectual property, legal co-operation in administrative, fiscal, civil and criminal mat ters, legal status of the CoE, local and regional authorities, migrant workers, mino rities, movement of persons, mutual assistance in criminal matters, nationality, pre vention of torture, protection of animals, protection of victims, public health, radio and television, refugees, social and medical assistance, social law, social protection of farmers, social security, sport, terrorism, testaments and transfer of proceedings.

338. During the third Summit of Heads of State and Government of the CoE (Warsaw, May 2005), three highly important instruments for the pursuit of the fight against terrorism and organized crime were opened for signature:

(1) The *CoE Convention on the Prevention of Terrorism* (CETS No. 196) was drafted with a view to increasing the effectiveness of existing international texts on the fight against terrorism. It aims to strengthen Member States' efforts to prevent terrorism and sets out two ways to achieve this objective: first, by establishing as criminal offences certain acts that may lead to the commission of terrorist offences, namely: public provocation, recruitment and training; second, by reinforcing co-operation on prevention both internally (national prevention policies), and internationally (modification of existing extradition and mutual assistance arrangements and additional means). It is grounded on the fundamental premise that it is possible and necessary to fight terrorism while respecting human rights, fundamental freedoms and the rule of law.
(2) The *CoE Convention on Action against trafficking in human beings* (CETS No. 197) is a comprehensive treaty mainly focused on the protection of victims of trafficking and the safeguard of their rights. It also aims at preventing trafficking as well as prosecuting traffickers. It applies to all forms of trafficking, whether national or transnational, whether or not related to organized crime.
(3) The *CoE Convention on laundering, search, seizure and confiscation of the proceeds from crime and on the financing of terrorism* (CETS No. 198) is the first international treaty covering both the prevention and the control of money laundering and financing of terrorism. The text addresses the fact that quick access to financial information or information on assets held by criminal organizations, including terrorist groups, is the key to successful preventive and repressive measures and, ultimately, is the best way to stop them.

339. Since then, several other important new treaties have been opened for signature:

(1) The *CoE Convention on the Protection of Children against Sexual Exploitation and Sexual Abuse* (CETS No. 201) is the first instrument to establish all the various forms of sexual abuse of children as criminal offences, including the solicitation of children for sexual purposes ('grooming') and 'sex tourism'. The Convention follows the comprehensive 'four P'-format, and thus

includes preventive measures, protection and support programmes for victims, measures related to prosecution (so that offenders can be prosecuted even when the act is committed abroad), and integrated policies – including child participation – to ensure meaningful implementation.

(2) The *CoE Convention on preventing and combating violence against women and domestic violence* (CETS No. 210) is a new landmark treaty which opens the path for creating a legal framework at pan-European level (and beyond) to protect women from all forms of violence, and prevent, prosecute and eliminate violence against women and domestic violence. It entered into force on 1 August 2014. The Convention, which has been accepted as the 'gold standard' in its field,[367] also establishes a specific monitoring mechanism ('GREVIO') in order to ensure effective implementation of its provisions by the Parties.

(3) The *CoE Convention on the counterfeiting of medical products and similar crimes involving threats to public health* – short: the MEDICRIME Convention (CETS No. 211) is the first international criminal law instrument to oblige States Parties to criminalize: the manufacturing of counterfeit medical products; supplying, offering to supply and trafficking in counterfeit medical products; the falsification of documents; the unauthorized manufacturing or supplying of medicinal products and the placing on the market of medical devices which do not comply with conformity requirements. The Convention provides a framework for national and international co-operation across the different sectors of public administration, measures for coordination at national level, preventive measures for use by public and private sectors and protection of victims and witnesses.

(4) The *CoE Council of Europe Convention against Trafficking in Human Organs* (CETS No. 216) calls on governments to establish as a criminal offence the illegal removal of human organs from living or deceased donors, where the removal is performed without the free, informed and specific consent of the living or deceased donor, or, in the case of the deceased donor, without the removal being authorized under its domestic law; where, in exchange for the removal of organs, the living donor, or a third party, receives a financial gain or comparable advantage; or where in exchange for the removal of organs from a deceased donor, a third party receives a financial gain or comparable advantage. The Convention also provides protection measures and compensation for victims as well as prevention measures to ensure transparency and equitable access to transplantation services.

Two Conventions in the realm of sports also deserve a mention here: the CoE Convention on the Manipulation of Sports Competitions (CETS No. 215) of 2014 and the CoE Convention on an Integrated Safety, Security and Service Approach at Football Matches and Other Sports Events (CETS No. 218) of 2016.

---

367. *See* press release 'Council of Europe 2013 Highlights – Gender Equality and Violence against Women Division', downloadable here: http://www.coe.int/t/dghl/standardsetting/convention-violence/Docs/Contribution_2013Highlights%20docxREV.pdf.

§3. Procedure for the Adoption of CoE Treaties

340. The adoption of a CoE treaty is a complex process involving the participation of several bodies of the organization. Central to this process is the role of the CM, the CoE's executive organ: any proposal to draft a new treaty must in fact receive the green light from the Committee before the drafting process can begin.

I. Initiative to Draw up a Treaty

341. An initiative to elaborate a new treaty may come from an individual Member State, the CM itself (or one of its subordinate committees), the Congress of Local and Regional Authorities of the CoE, a conference of specialized ministers, or – as has been the case for most CoE treaties – from the Parliamentary Assembly.

II. Drafting of the Treaty

342. The actual drafting of the text is normally carried out by a committee directly or indirectly answerable to the CM, and composed of governmental experts possessing the required expertise relative to the issues at stake, with the Parliamentary Assembly usually sending an observer. More and more often, participation in the work of any such committee is extended to non-Member States, intergovernmental or non-governmental and professional organizations, as well as the EU, which may be admitted as observers without the right to vote.

343. A drafting committee's activity is governed by Resolution Res (2005)47 on committees and subordinate bodies, their terms of reference and working methods, which was adopted by the CM on 14 December 2005, at the 951st meeting of the Ministers' Deputies. The relevant rules applying to the approval of a draft treaty by a committee are those laid down in Article 11, Appendix 1, of Resolution Res (2005)47: 'each member of the committee shall have one vote; however, where a government designates more than one member, only one of them is entitled to take part in the voting'; […] 'decisions of steering committees[368] are taken by a two-thirds majority of the votes cast' […] 'other committees shall not take decisions by voting but state their conclusions in the form of unanimous recommendations, or, if this proves impossible, they shall make a majority recommendation and indicate the dissenting opinions'. It should be emphasized, however, that recourse to voting is in principle left as a 'last resort' solution and that committees strive as much as possible to reach unanimity in endorsing a draft treaty. Unanimity enhances the chances of the treaty quickly entering into force and becoming operational among a wide circle of states.

368. Steering committees are committees which are answerable directly to the Committee of Ministers and responsible for a substantial portion of the Council of Europe's intergovernmental activity.

344. Once the drafting of the treaty is completed, the competent committee of experts and/or steering committee approves the text and submits it to the CM for final adoption.

III. Consultation of the Parliamentary Assembly

345. The adoption of the definitive text of a treaty by the CM will normally not occur before the CM has sought the opinion of the Parliamentary Assembly on it. Although such an opinion does not put the CM under any legal obligation to amend the draft treaty, it carries considerable political weight as it tests the future acceptability of the text at the level of national parliaments which will be called upon to ratify the treaty.

346. The legal framework governing the participation of the Parliamentary Assembly in the adoption of CoE treaties is set by the following rules:

(1) Article 23a of the Statute of the CoE, providing that 'the Consultative Assembly [now Parliamentary Assembly] [...] shall also discuss and may make recommendations upon any matter referred to it by the CM with a request for its opinion'.
(2) Paragraph 1 of Resolution (52)26 on Consultation of the Consultative Assembly, adopted by the Ministers' Deputies on 5 May 1952, under which terms:
   (a) The CM may, in appropriate cases, invite the Assembly to give its reasoned opinion, to be presented within a fixed time-limit, on draft Conventions drawn up by the CM.
   (b) Any draft Convention drawn up by the CM, and submitted by it to the Consultative Assembly for an Opinion, shall be accompanied by a detailed Explanatory Memorandum.
(3) The CM' reply to the Parliamentary Recommendation 1361(1998), adopted on 27 April 1999, in which the Committee undertook to 'consult the Parliamentary Assembly in the future on all draft treaties. However, in practice, a small number of treaties, of an exclusively technical nature, may not require such a consultation'.

347. It should be mentioned that a report by the Parliamentary Assembly's Committee on Rules of Procedures and Immunities (Doc. 11017 of 18 September 2006, *The institutional balance at the Council of Europe*) recalls the Assembly's dissatisfaction with the current system for involving it in the elaboration, adoption and implementation of CoE conventions. The report puts forward the proposal to conclude an agreement between the Assembly and the CM, which would enhance co-operation between the two organs at the various stages of the making of CoE treaties, by – *inter alia* – better associating the Assembly with the drafting work in intergovernmental expert committees and introducing a conciliation procedure in case of diverging opinions between the CM and the Assembly on the latter's proposals for amendments to a draft treaty. The report further suggests that the CM could, on an ad hoc basis, delegate to the Assembly the right to adopt conventions.

However, these proposals have not received any concrete follow-up recently, perhaps because the de facto situation at the level of the drafting committees has been improving of late when it comes to the committees taking the opinion of the Assembly (and its representative on the committee) into account.[369]

IV. Adoption and Opening for Signature by the CM

348. The adoption of a treaty text by the CM falls under the rule of Article 20d of the Statute of the CoE, which requires a two-thirds majority of the representatives casting a vote and a majority of the representatives entitled to sit on the Committee. In practice, however, there is a strong tendency towards ensuring that a draft treaty garners consensus or near consensus within the Committee. This practice reflects the realization that for a treaty to become truly effective, there should be a widespread agreement among negotiating states as to the substance of the treaty.

349. Discussions over a draft treaty within the CM are unlikely to fundamentally change the text of the draft. However, it may occur that the expert committee entrusted with the drafting of the treaty renounces, or fails to deal conclusively with an issue in view of its political rather than technical implications, in which case it will be up to the CM to take over the challenge of finding a solution to this issue.

350. For example, it was only at the level of the CM that an agreement was found around the formulation of the so-called disconnection clause[370] within the three treaties which were opened for signature during the third Summit of Heads of State and Government of the CoE, in Warsaw, in May 2005 (treaties CETS Nos 196, 197 and 198 mentioned above). Such a clause aims at regulating the relationship between treaty provisions and EC/EU law in the relations between parties to the treaty which are members of the EU. A similar clause has been included in the past in other CoE treaties dealing with matters for which Community law had been enacted. Upon the adoption of treaties CETS Nos 196, 197 and 198, the EC and the Member States of the EU made a declaration[371] clarifying the objective, the scope and the effects of the 'disconnection clause'. As an instrument made in connection with the conclusion of a treaty, within the meaning of Article 31, paragraph 2(b) of

369. With the notable exception of the draft Additional Protocol on the protection of human rights and dignity of persons with mental disorders with regard to involuntary placement and involuntary treatment, currently being finalised by the organization's Committee on Bioethics (DH-BIO) despite the Assembly's opposition.

370. The clause is worded as follows:

> Parties which are members of the European Union shall, in their mutual relations, apply Community and European Union rules in so far as there are Community or European Union rules governing the particular subject concerned and applicable to the specific case, without prejudice to the object and purpose of the present Convention and without prejudice to its full application with other Parties.

371. The text of this declaration has been published within the Explanatory Reports to all three conventions.

the Vienna Convention on the Law of Treaties, it was acknowledged that this declaration forms part of the 'context' of the conventions for the purpose of their interpretation.

351. According to the CM' Statutory Resolution (93)27 on Majorities required for Decisions of the CM, decisions on the opening for signature of conventions and agreements concluded within the CoE are taken by a two-thirds majority of the representatives casting a vote and a majority of the representatives entitled to sit on the Committee, as set out in Article 20d of the Statute. The date on which a CoE treaty is opened is the date by which it is known. CoE treaties remain open for signature indefinitely.

§4. Ways of Expressing Consent to Be Bound by a CoE Treaty

I. Member States of the CoE

352. In accordance with the Model Final Clauses for Conventions and Agreements concluded within the CoE,[372] Member States may usually express their consent to be bound by a treaty by signature followed by ratification, acceptance or approval. If the treaty provides for it, the signature alone can express the consent of a state to be bound by the convention.

II. Non-Member States of the CoE

353. Most CoE treaties foresee the possibility of non-Member States of the CoE taking part in them by way of accession, provided that they have been formally invited to accede by the CM. Generally, such an invitation can only be issued after the treaty has entered into force. The CoE convention for which the highest number of invitations to accede (nineteen) has been achieved is the Convention on the Transfer of Sentenced Persons (CETS No. 112).

354. Non-Member States which have taken part in the elaboration of the treaty will usually be entitled to directly sign and ratify it thereafter. This is the case, for example, of the Convention on Cybercrime (CETS No. 185), which has entered into force in six non-Member States: Australia, the Dominican Republic, Japan, Mauritius, Panama and the USA.

372. The Model Final Clauses were approved by the Committee of Ministers at the 315th meeting of the Ministers' Deputies in February 1980.

§5. Reservations

355. In accordance with the rules of international law, on acceding to an international convention states are entitled to make certain reservations.[373] To use the terms of Parliamentary Assembly Recommendation 1223(1993) on reservations made by Member States to CoE Conventions, 'the use of a reservation enables a state to circumvent the obstacle which it may encounter in a given convention provision. Thus the possibility of making reservations simplifies the accession of states to certain Council of Europe conventions'.

356. Nonetheless, the use of reservations carries the risk of impairing the unity and coherence of the convention. Furthermore, as reserving states are no longer bound by the same international undertakings, reservations interfere with the equality between parties and make it difficult to determine the obligations of each state.

357. Within the CoE, it could be said that there is a long-standing practice aimed at limiting the number and extent of reservations. This objective has been pursued in different ways. CoE treaties make extensive use of the so-called negotiated reservations. This means that many treaties will contain a reservation clause specifying which reservations are permitted.[374] Usually, this will be done by identifying those provisions which may be derogated from,[375] and sometimes by establishing the precise wording of any reservation.[376] Other treaties limit the validity of reservations for a certain period of time.[377] Finally, a CoE treaty may totally bar states from formulating reservations.[378]

358. In addition, a certain control over reservations entered into by states to CoE treaties is exercised by bodies entrusted – either directly, in pursuance of a conventional provision, or following a decision of the CM – with the task of ensuring the

---

373. Based on the definition established by the International Law Commission in 1998 (*see* Report of the International Law Commission on the work of its fiftieth session, UN Doc. A/53/10 (1998)), a reservation can be defined as 'a unilateral statement, however phrased or named, made by a state or an international organisation when signing, ratifying, formally confirming, accepting, approving or acceding to a treaty or by a state when making a notification of succession to a treaty, whereby the state or organisation purports to exclude or to modify the legal effect of certain provisions of the treaty in their application to that state or to that international organisation'.

374. An example of such a clause appears in the Model Final Clauses (Art. e).

375. For an example of such a reservation clause, refer to Art. 53 of the Council of Europe Convention on Laundering, Search, Seizure and Confiscation of the Proceeds from Crime and on the Financing of Terrorism (CETS No. 198).

376. Refer for instance to Appendix I to the European Convention on the Transfer of Proceedings in Criminal Matters (CETS No. 73) and to Appendix I to the European Convention on the International Validity of Criminal Judgments (CETS No. 70).

377. Refer to Art. 38 of the Criminal Law Convention on Corruption (CETS No. 173).

378. *See* for instance Art. 3 of Protocol No. 13 to the Convention for the Protection of Human Rights and Fundamental Freedoms, concerning the abolition of the death penalty in all circumstances (CETS No. 187).

follow-up to the convention. The ECtHR has notably asserted on a number of occasions its competence to examine and judge the validity of reservations made by parties to the Convention.[379]

359. Moreover, within the CoE, the Committee of Legal Advisers on Public International Law (CAHDI) operates as an observatory of reservations to multilateral international treaties.[380] The CAHDI is the only truly pan-European forum where legal advisors of the Ministers for Foreign Affairs of the Member States of the CoE and a significant number of observer States and Organizations can exchange and possibly coordinate their views regarding major issues of public international law.

360. Finally, in his role as depositary of CoE treaties, the Secretary General is responsible for ensuring the conformity of reservations with the treaty's rules on reservations and the general rules of international treaty law. Although the depositary is not in the position to decide on the admissibility or the legal effects of reservations, the Secretary General will refuse the deposit of an instrument of ratification if it contains reservations other than those expressly authorized or reservations which are expressly prohibited by the treaty. Where the envisaged reservation is found to be questionable in the light of the relevant rules, a process of informal consultation with the state concerned is engaged with a view to overcoming any difference of views between this state and the secretariat. If, however, the state maintains its reservation, the Secretary General proceeds to its registration and notification, leaving it to the other states party to determine whether they wish to object to the reservation.

§6. Succession of States: The Example of the Former State Union of Serbia and Montenegro

361. On 3 June 2006, following the Declaration of Independence adopted by the National Assembly of Montenegro, Montenegro separated from the State Union of Serbia and Montenegro. Pursuant to Article 60 of the Constitutional Charter of Serbia and Montenegro, activated by the Declaration of Independence, the membership of the State Union of Serbia and Montenegro in the CoE was continued by the Republic of Serbia.[381]

379. Refer to *Belilos v. Switzerland*, ECHR Ser. A, No. 132, 29 Apr. 1988.
380. The CAHDI has achieved an agreement between Member States on the question of inadmissible reservations and as a result, the Committee of Ministers adopted Recommendation No. R (99) 13 on responses to inadmissible reservations to international treaties.
381. Refer to the letters of 5 Jun. 2006 in which Mr Boris Tadic, President of the Republic of Serbia, informed respectively Mr Sergey Lavrov, Chairman-in-office of the Committee of Ministers, and Mr Terry Davis, Secretary General of the Council of Europe, of the continuation by the Republic of Serbia of membership of the Council of Europe previously exercised by the Union of States of Serbia and Montenegro, and to the decision of the Committee of Ministers taking note of such continuation (decision taken by the Deputies on 14 Jun. 2006 at their 967th meeting). It should be

362. Provided that none of the treaties concluded within the CoE contains any explicit provisions on state succession, the effects of the separation of Montenegro regarding CoE treaties which were binding upon Serbia and Montenegro, can be summarized as follows. Article 35 of the Vienna Convention on the Succession of States in respect of Treaties[382] provides that:

> When, after separation of any part of the territory of a State, the predecessor State continues to exist, any treaty which at the date of the succession of States was in force in respect of the predecessor State continues in force in respect of its remaining territory unless:
>
> (a) the States concerned otherwise agree;
> (b) it is established that the treaty related only to the territory which has separated from the predecessor State; or
> (c) it appears from the treaty or is otherwise established that the application of the treaty in respect of the predecessor State would be incompatible with the object and purpose of the treaty or would radically change the conditions for its operation.

363. As none of these exceptions applied, the Republic of Serbia remained a party to all the treaties ratified or acceded to by Serbia and Montenegro. As to treaties signed but not yet ratified by Serbia and Montenegro, the Republic of Serbia became entitled to ratify them at any time.[383]

364. As far as Montenegro is concerned, the newly independent State requested to become a member of the CoE by a letter of Mr Miodrag Vlahovic, Minister of Foreign Affairs of the Republic of Montenegro, dated 6 June 2006. The Vienna Convention on the Succession of States in respect of Treaties states in Article 16 that 'a newly independent State is not bound to maintain in force, or to become a party to, any treaty by reason only of the fact that at the date of the succession of States the treaty was in force in respect of the territory to which the succession of States relates'. However, in the aforementioned letter, Montenegro declared its determination to respect and implement all Conventions and Protocols of the CoE ratified by the State Union of Serbia and Montenegro.

365. With regard to the latter treaties, the same Convention specifies in Article 17 that subject to certain conditions, 'a newly independent State may, by a notification of succession, establish its status as a party to any multilateral treaty which at the date of the succession of States was in force in respect of the territory to which

---

noted here that according to Council of Europe practice, succession to membership of the Council of Europe, as well as to Council of Europe treaties, is not automatic and requires the agreement of the Committee of Ministers.

382. Serbia and Montenegro was a party to this treaty at the time of the separation of Montenegro.

383. The Committee of Ministers' decision of 14 Jun. 2006 mentioned above noted that the Republic of Serbia was either a signatory or a party to the Council of Europe conventions, to which Serbia and Montenegro had been a signatory or party.

the succession of States relates'. Pursuant to this provision and in line with its previous declaration, Montenegro notified its successor status to all CoE treaties by a letter from the Minister of Foreign Affairs of 12 June 2006.

366. In the case of those treaties which are open to the accession of States which are not members of the CoE, the CM agreed that the Republic of Montenegro was either a signatory or a party to such instruments, with effect from 6 June 2006, the date of the declaration of succession. Concerning those treaties to which only CoE Member States can become parties, when the CM decided, during its 994th *bis* meeting on 9 May 2007, to invite the Republic of Montenegro to accede to the CoE, it took the decision to consider Montenegro, with effect from 6 June 2006, as a party therefore. The treaties concerned are listed in the Note Verbale JJ6484C established by the CoE's Treaty Office which was notified to all Member States on 11 May 2007 (the Note Verbale is published on the Treaty Office's website, at: http://convention s.coe.int).

§7. Considerations on the Relations Between CoE Treaties and EU Legal Standards

367. Many treaties concluded within the CoE have contributed to the creation of an area of freedom, security and justice among its Member States. As this is a common goal of the CoE and the EU, they form part of the EU's *acquis* on the basis of which closer co-operation within the Union is being developed.

368. These include fundamental treaties relating to the fields of human rights, the prevention of torture, social rights, the rights of minorities and data protection. In the field of criminal law in particular, the EU *acquis* comprises a number of treaties vital to the fight against organized crime, such as:

- the European Convention on Extradition (CETS No. 54) and the European Convention on Mutual Assistance in Criminal Matters (CETS No. 30), each complemented by two protocols;
- the European Convention on the Suppression of Terrorism (CETS No. 90) and its amending protocol;
- the Convention on Laundering, Search, Seizure and Confiscation of the Proceeds from Crime (CETS No. 141) and the CoE Convention on Laundering, Search, Seizure and Confiscation of the Proceeds from Crime and on the Financing of Terrorism (CETS No. 198);
- the Criminal and Civil Law Conventions on Corruption (CETS Nos 173 and 174); and
- the Cybercrime Convention and its Additional Protocol concerning the criminalization of acts of a racist and xenophobic nature committed through computer systems (CETS Nos 185 and 189).

369. Other important conventions have been concluded in the field of judicial co-operation in civil matters, an area of Community competence, such as:

- the Convention on Recognition and Enforcement of Decisions concerning Custody of Children and on Restoration of Custody of Children (CETS No. 105), which ensures that children of divorced parents can be returned to their legal guardian quickly; and
- the Convention on Contact concerning Children (CETS No. 192), which complements the EU's work in the area of recognition and enforcement of judgments.

370. An increasing number of CoE conventions and agreements contain a clause allowing for the participation of the EC. The EC has already become a party to eleven CoE treaties.[384] Most of these treaties are 'mixed' agreements, covering certain subject matters for which the EC has competence and others for which its Member States have competence. The Convention on Information and Legal Co-operation concerning 'Information Society Services' (CETS No. 180), which the Community signed without reservation as to ratification on 22 March 2004, is a treaty for which the Community alone holds an exclusive competence.

371. The latter Convention offers an example of a CoE treaty which extends EU standards beyond the borders of the EU to all Member States of the CoE. The Convention, which aims at setting-up a legal information and co-operation system in the area of the new communication services, is widely based on the Directive 98/34/EC of the EP and of the Council of 22 June 1998 laying down a procedure for the provision of information in the field of technical standards and regulations (as modified by Directive 98/48/EC).

§8. Review of CoE Treaties

372. As part of the reform process of the CoE, the Secretary General launched the proposal of taking stock of the situation of CoE's conventions through a critical review of their relevance, with a view to providing the basis for decisions on follow-up, including measures to increase the visibility and the number of Parties to relevant conventions.

373. In February 2011, the CM took note of the general approach proposed by the Secretary General to the preparation of a full report on CoE conventions. This report was finalized in May 2012 and transmitted to the CM for examination.[385]

374. On 10 April 2013, the CM agreed on a series of measures relating to the promotion and management of conventions, the participation of non-Member States and reservations to conventions.[386]

384. The list of treaties to which the EC has become a party is available on the official website of the Council of Europe Treaty Office at: http://conventions.coe.int.
385. The report has been published on the Treaty Office's website, at: http://conventions.coe.int.
386. Refer to Res. CM/Res(2013)7 concerning financial arrangements for the participation of non-Member States in Council of Europe conventions.

Chapter 2. The Venice Commission

Schnutz Rudolf Dürr

§1. Introduction

375. The European Commission for Democracy through Law – widely known as the Venice Commission – is probably one of the CoE's most successful achievements. Created in 1990, it is an advisory body in the field of constitutional law providing opinions upon request by Member States and the organs of the CoE. Since then, it has become a reference in constitutional matters and is widely respected for its independent advice.

376. In several respects, the Venice Commission has specific features within the CoE. Composed of independent members rather than governmental experts[387] it is an enlarged agreement[388] of the Council and consequently has a geographical scope which largely exceeds that of Europe. The Commission thus reaches out to its full members and observers overseas.[389] Finally, it differs from other CoE bodies in its seat, which is in Venice, Italy, rather than in Strasbourg, France.

377. Nevertheless, the Venice Commission is fully part and parcel of the CoE as is witnessed by the high number of requests for opinions from the organs of the Council. As a legal expert body, the Commission is well embedded in the context of the political organs of the CoE, notably the Parliamentary Assembly, the CM and the Secretary General, which regularly use it as a tool to obtain a firm legal basis on which they can build their activity.

378. According to its Statute, the Member States and the organs of the CoE can ask the Venice Commission for opinions. As to states, usually parliaments, governments or individual government ministries request opinions but the Commission also accepts requests for opinion from constitutional courts. As regards the organs of the CoE, the Parliamentary Assembly and in particular its Monitoring and Legal Committees frequently ask for opinions.[390] The Secretary General requests opinions in particularly sensitive legal questions affecting the democracy or the rule of law in Member States. When requests for opinions come from the organs of the

387. There are, however, also other bodies within the Council of Europe with an independent membership, for example, the Committee for the Prevention of Torture, the Advisory Committee on the Framework Convention for the Protection of National Minorities or the Consultative Council on European Judges.
388. The Commission was created as a partial agreement. *See* https://www.coe.int/en/web/conventions/partial-agreements/-/conventions/ap/list.
389. Argentina, Canada, the Holy *See*, Japan and Uruguay. The European Union, the Palestinian National Authority and South Africa have a special co-operation status, which is similar to that of observers.
390. The Parliamentary Assembly and the Venice Commission have concluded a co-operation agreement to facilitate requests for opinions by the Assembly (CDL(2004)102).

CoE, the text examined often raises issues in respect of CoE standards. In such cases, the authorities of the state concerned are sometimes reluctant to work with the Venice Commission but the Commission takes special care to base its opinion purely on legal arguments, taking into account the views of all stakeholders in order to provide a balanced legal opinion. Following a period of rapid democratic development after the fall of the Berlin Wall, the Venice Commission is faced with an increase of such requests in recent years.[391]

379. We can distinguish two major forms of activity of the Commission:

(1) Constitutional co-operation with individual countries, that is giving advice to individual countries on draft constitutions, constitutional amendments as well as para-constitutional legislation, e.g., laws on the ombudsman, laws on the government, minority legislation, etc. (*see* paragraphs 400–404 below).
(2) Transnational opinions or studies, which often gave the Commission the opportunity to identify standards of the Common Constitutional Heritage (*see* paragraphs 405–407 below).

380. Two fields of the activity of the Commission stand out from the general constitutional co-operation, both because of the quantity of work done in these domains and because of the way in which the Commission co-operates with partner institutions:

(1) Constitutional justice, that is co-operation with constitutional courts and equivalent bodies in the framework of the Joint Council of Constitutional Justice (*see* paragraphs 408–410 below).
(2) Electoral law, including legislation on political parties, usually dealt with in the Council for Democratic Elections (*see* paragraph 413 below).

Over time, the Commission has consolidated its activity and has thus contributed to the Common Constitutional Heritage, which is based on the basic principles of the CoE: democracy, the protection of human rights and the rule of law.

---

391. For example, CDL-AD(2012)026, Opinion on the compatibility with Constitutional principles and the Rule of Law of actions taken by the Government and the Parliament of Romania in respect of other State institutions and on the Government emergency ordinance on amendment to the Law No. 47/1992 regarding the organization and functioning of the Constitutional Court and on the Government emergency ordinance on amending and completing the Law No. 3/2000 regarding the organization of a referendum in Romania; CDL-AD(2013)012, Opinion on the Fourth Amendment to the Fundamental Law of Hungary; CDL-AD(2016)026, Poland – Opinion on the Act on the Constitutional Tribunal; CDL-AD(2016)037, Turkey – Opinion on Emergency Decree Laws Nos 667–676 adopted following the failed coup of 15 Jul. 2016; CDL-AD(2017)004, Turkey – Opinion on the duties, competences and functioning of the criminal peace judgeships; CDL-AD(2017)031, Poland – Opinion on the Draft Act amending the Act on the National Council of the Judiciary; on the Draft Act amending the Act on the Supreme Court, proposed by the President of Poland, and on the Act on the Organisation of Ordinary Courts; CDL-PI(2018)007, Romania – Preliminary Opinion on draft amendments to Law No. 303/2004 on the statute of judges and prosecutors, Law No. 304/2004 on judicial organization, and Law No. 317/2004 on the Superior Council for Magistracy (J. Scholsem, H. Suchocka, K. Tuori, I. Cameron, C. Bazy-Malaurie).

§2. Founding and Statute

381. The idea to create a Commission for Democracy through Law in the form of a group of experts in the field of constitutional law was conceived by the then Minister of [European] Community Policy of Italy, Mr Antonio La Pergola, a professor of constitutional law of outstanding international renown who *inter alia* had been Judge and later President of the Constitutional Court of Italy.[392] His choice of the name for the Commission was to express his conviction that sustainable democracy can only be built in a sound constitutional framework based on the rule of law.

382. The establishment of co-operation in the field of constitutional law was however by no means obvious within the framework of an intergovernmental organization such as the CoE. Constitutional law is necessarily close to issues touching upon state sovereignty as it also deals with sensitive questions like the distribution of competencies between the executive and legislative branches of power.

383. Initially, not all Member States of the CoE were in favour of creating this body. Some may have feared that foreign governments might interfere in questions like the checks and balances between President and Parliament, which then were deemed to be internal affairs *par excellence.* Given Mr La Pergola's background as a constitutional court judge, others may have feared that the Commission would turn into a tool for the 'proliferation' of specialized constitutional courts (as opposed to Supreme Courts exercising constitutional review).[393] Out of the then twenty-three Member States of the CoE only eighteen were ready to participate in the Commission when it was established in 1990.[394]

---

392. The late Mr La Pergola was Member of the European Parliament from 1989 to 1994. Between 1994 and 2006 he was Advocate General and Judge at the Court of Justice of the European Communities.

393. Indeed all Central and Eastern European transition countries opted for various models of such a court (only Estonia established a Constitutional Review Chamber within its Supreme Court). While the Venice Commission certainly provided encouragement and advice to a number of states on how to set up a constitutional court, the decision to establish such a body was probably driven by the states' desire to move from their previous declaratory constitutions, which listed principles which were not observed in practice, to normative constitutions, which shape the functioning of society and are observed in real life. Constitutional courts are a key instrument in guaranteeing the implementation of a constitution in real life. For doctrinal reasons, however, some reject the idea of constitutional review by courts because this would contradict the sovereignty of parliament as the representative of the people (*see* for example, Art. 120 of the Dutch Constitution, which excludes constitutional review of laws adopted by Parliament). The reply to this argument is that the constituent power (parliament itself with a qualified majority or the people by way of referendum) enjoys an even higher legitimacy than the ordinary legislator and constitutional review – exercised by constitutional courts or Supreme Courts – is a mere tool to ensure that the ordinary legislator respects the limits established by the constituent power.

394. Austria, Belgium, Cyprus, Denmark, Finland, France, Greece, Ireland, Italy, Luxembourg, Malta, Norway, Portugal, San Marino, Spain, Sweden, Switzerland and Turkey.

384. Therefore, the Venice Commission was first created in the form of a partial agreement,[395] an instrument which allows for a 'variable geometry' within the CoE by permitting a group of Member States to pursue an activity only between them but nevertheless in the framework of the CoE thus benefiting from its institutional structure. In order to create such a partial agreement, these countries have to seek the agreement of the CM as a whole.

385. The formal proposal to create the Commission was made by Mr La Pergola's colleague, the Minister of Foreign Affairs of Italy, Mr Gianni de Michelis, who invited the Ministers of Foreign Affairs of the CoE's Member States to a Conference for the Constitution of the Commission for Democracy through Law, which was held in his hometown, Venice, on 31 March–1 April 1989.[396] In the light of the pressing need to assist Central and Eastern European countries in adopting new democratic constitutions after the fall of the Berlin Wall, the CM agreed to the creation of such a Commission in the form of a partial agreement at a further Conference in Venice on 19–20 January 1990. On 23 April 1990, the Ministers' Deputies unanimously authorized the establishment of a partial agreement for this purpose. Finally, on 10 May 1990, the CM adopted the Statute of the Commission.[397]

§3. Revision of the Statute: Geographical Scope

386. The Statute provided for its re-examination before 31 December 1992 with a view to an integration of the Commission into the intergovernmental programme of activities of the CoE. By then, all Member States had still not joined the Commission and a full integration of the Commission into the intergovernmental programme of the Council was thus excluded.[398]

387. Following the accession of the originally hesitating states and once the Russian Federation had joined the Commission on 1 January 2002, the membership of the Venice Commission and that of the CoE coincided. In the light of the strong interest expressed by non-Member States of the CoE in the work of the Venice Commission, the CM decided to convert the partial agreement into an enlarged agreement.[399] In its Resolution (2002)3 on the revised Statute of the Commission,[400] the CM wished 'to give to these states the possibility to take part in the work

395. For the legal basis for the creation of partial, enlarged partial and enlarged agreements *see* Statutory Res. (93)28 on Partial and Enlarged Agreements adopted by the Committee of Ministers on 14 May 1993 at its ninety-second Session.

396. *See* Document CM(89)82 on the Final Declaration of the Conference.

397. Resolution (90)6 on a Partial Agreement Establishing the European Commission for Democracy through Law, adopted by the Committee of Ministers on 10 May 1990 at its eighty-sixth Session.

398. By the end of 1992, Bulgaria, Germany, Hungary and Liechtenstein had joined the Commission and brought its membership to twenty-two states out of the then twenty-six Member States of the Council of Europe. Iceland, the Netherlands, Poland, which had become a member of the Council of Europe only shortly before, and the UK were not yet members of the Commission.

399. Full membership of a partial agreement is open only to Member States of the Council of Europe whereas an enlarged agreement necessarily comprises all Member States of the Council but allows for full membership of non-Member States of the Council (Art. I of Statutory Res. (93)28). New

of the Commission on an equal footing'. Indeed, by then the Commission had already a dozen non-European observers: Argentina, Canada, the Holy See, Israel, Japan, Kazakhstan, the Republic of Korea, Kyrgyzstan, Mexico, the US and Uruguay as well as South Africa with a similar co-operation status.[401] While observer status was abolished in the revised Statute, existing observers were allowed to retain this status.[402] However, in practice they are invited only to one of the four annual sessions in December.

388. The conversion of the partial agreement to an enlarged agreement allowed for the accession of non-European states as full members of the Commission. Therefore on 1 January 2004, Kyrgyzstan became the first non-European full Member State of the Venice Commission, followed by Chile in 2005, the Republic of Korea in 2006, Morocco and Algeria in 2007, Israel in 2008, Peru and Brazil in 2009, Mexico and Tunisia in 2010, Kazakhstan in 2012, the US in 2013, Kosovo[403] in 2014 and Costa Rica in 2016. This brings the current membership of the Venice Commission to sixty-one states.

389. In fact, the Venice Commission's activities go beyond non-European members and observer states. The interest of non-European constitutional courts and equivalent bodies was so strong that the Commission co-operates with bodies uniting such courts in Africa, Asia and the Americas,[404] and the Commission assisted in the establishment of the World Conference on Constitutional Justice for which it acts as the Secretariat. In the field of constitutional justice (*see* below), the activities of the Venice Commission are therefore of a global scope.

390. As concerns its opinions, the Commission remains most active in Central and Eastern Europe. This is understandable because after the fall of the Berlin Wall,

---

Member States of the Council of Europe become full members of an Enlarged Agreement by virtue of their accession to the Council itself (this implies also budgetary contributions). Montenegro as well as Monaco thus already automatically became full members of the enlarged agreement by virtue of their accession to the Council of Europe.

400. Adopted by the Committee of Ministers on 21 Feb. 2002 at the 784th meeting of the Ministers' Deputies.

401. The special co-operation status of South Africa stems from the time when the President of the Venice Commission, Mr La Pergola, was in the country together with Henry Kissinger and Lord Carrington to mediate between the ANC, Inkatha and the National Party. The Committee of Ministers then authorized the Commission to cooperate with South Africa. This mandate was the basis for a very intensive co-operation with that country, which eventually turned into co-operation with Constitutional and Supreme Courts of the Southern African region in general. Content with this state of affairs, South Africa never formally sought observer status; its special co-operation status is in fact equivalent to it.

402. Article 2.8 of the revised Statute.

403. The decision the Committee of Ministers on the accession of Kosovo to the European Commission for Democracy through Law (Venice Commission) stipulates that the Venice Commission should not refer to Security Council Res. 1244 in the name of the country, as this is the case in the rest of the Council of Europe (item 10.3, 1202nd meeting of the CM, 10–11 Jun. 2014).

404. *See* below in the Chapter Constitutional Justice, Regional Co-operation, paras 396–397.

former communist countries had an urgent need for the adoption of new, democratic constitutions and they often lacked the experience in drafting such texts. Following the first wave of new constitutions, the Commission is engaged in constitutional amendments, which adapt constitutions and implement legislation to the rapidly changing needs of society. The largest number of opinions relates to the Balkans, the Caucasus and Ukraine. Although the Commission's Statute does not restrict its activity to Central and Eastern Europe, in practice however, it has been active only in a few of the old Member States of the CoE. Opinions relating to Belgium,[405] France,[406] Monaco,[407] Liechtenstein,[408] Spain[409] were requested not by the countries concerned but by the Parliamentary Assembly. However, Finland,[410] Iceland,[411] Italy,[412] Malta,[413] Norway,[414] Luxembourg,[415] Switzerland[416] and the UK[417] themselves requested opinions. When the Government of Luxembourg requested three opinions in 2002,[418] they expressly pointed out that the Venice Commission is available for advice also to old Member States of the Council.

405. Opinion on Possible Groups of Persons to which the Framework Convention for the Protection of National Minorities could be applied in Belgium, adopted by the Venice Commission at its fiftieth Plenary Meeting, Venice, 8–9 Mar. 2002 (CDL-AD(2002)001). Note: All documents cited here are available on the public website of the Commission www.venice.coe.int. The Commission's docu ment codes always start with the abbreviation CDL (French acronym for *Commission européenne pour la Démocratie par la Loi*), which can be followed by a code designating the sub-commission to which the document was presented. Texts adopted by the Commission become public immedi ately after their adoption. Until 2002 they were published in the CDL-INF series, since then in the CDL-AD series.
406. CDL-AD(2016)006, Opinion on the Draft Constitutional Law on 'Protection of the Nation' of France.
407. CDL-AD(2013)018, Opinion on the balance of powers in the Constitution and the Legislation of the Principality of Monaco.
408. CDL-AD(2002)032, Opinion on the Amendments to the Constitution of Liechtenstein proposed by the Princely House of Liechtenstein.
409. CDL-AD(2017)003, Spain – Opinion on the law of 16 Oct. 2015 amending the Organic Law No. 2/1979 on the Constitutional Court.
410. Opinion on the Constitution of Finland adopted by the Venice Commission at its seventy-forth Plenary Session, Venice, 14–15 Mar. 2008 (CDL-AD(2008)010).
411. CDL-AD(2013)010, Opinion on the Draft New Constitution of Iceland.
412. CDL-AD(2015)009, Opinion on the Citizens' bill on the regulation of public participation, citizens' bills, referendums and popular initiatives and amendments to the Provincial Electoral Law of the Autonomous Province of Trento (Italy).
413. CDL-AD(2014)035, Joint Opinion on the Draft Act to regulate the formation, the inner structures, functioning and financing of political parties and their participation in elections of Malta; CDL-AD(2018)014, Malta – Opinion on the draft act amending the Constitution, on the draft act on the human rights and equality commission, and on the draft act on equality.
414. CDL-AD(2010)046, Joint opinion on the electoral legislation of Norway.
415. CDL-AD(2009)057, Interim Opinion on the Draft Constitutional Amendments of Luxembourg.
416. CDL-INF(2001)016, Opinion on the Electoral Law of the Canton of Ticino.
417. CDL-AD(2010)045, Opinion on the Code of Practice on observing elections of the United Kingdom; CDL-AD(2007)046, Opinion on the Electoral Law of the United Kingdom.
418. CDL-AD(2002)019, Opinion on the Draft Law of Luxembourg on the Protection of Persons in Respect of the Processing of Personal Data; CDL-AD(2002)018, Opinion on the Draft Law of Luxembourg on Freedom of Expression in the Media and CD-LAD(2002)022, *Avis sur le projet de la Loi no. 4832 relative à la mise en place d'un médiateur au Luxembourg*.

§4. Venice as the Seat of the Commission

391. According to Article 8.3 of the revised Statute, the seat of the European Commission for Democracy through Law is Venice and Article 6.3 provides that:

> the Regione Veneto shall put a seat at the disposal of the Commission free of charge. Expenditure relating to the local secretariat and the operation of the seat of the Commission shall be borne by the Regione Veneto and the Italian Government, under terms to be agreed between these authorities.

Since its creation, with two exceptions,[419] the Venice Commission has held all its meetings in Venice. The seat of the Commission is the *Scuola Grande San Giovanni Evangelista* in Venice,[420] which the Regione Veneto puts at the disposal of the Commission for its four annual sessions, usually in March, June, October and December.

392. Article 8.1 of the revised Statute provides that '[t]he Commission shall be assisted by the Secretariat General of the Council of Europe … '. Given that the CoE has its seat in Strasbourg the offices of the Secretariat of the Commission are located there as well. The Commission has no offices in Venice.[421]

§5. Independent Membership

393. Article 2 of the revised Statute provides that:

> [t]he Commission shall be composed of independent experts who have achieved eminence through their experience in democratic institutions or by their contribution to the enhancement of law and political science. The members of the Commission shall serve in their individual capacity and shall not receive or accept any instructions.

Indeed, the list of members of the Venice Commission reads like an excerpt from the 'who's who' in constitutional law. It seems that governments pride themselves on appointing high-level experts of great renown. A large majority of the members are either judge at a Constitutional or Supreme Court or eminent professor of law. While the statute mentions law and political science on an equal footing, the Commission has a clear majority of lawyers. Political scientists as members are rather the exception. This fact has certainly contributed to shaping the working methods of the Commission, which coherently uses a legal methodology. The organs of the

419. Thirteenth Meeting, held in Warsaw on 21–22 May 2003. The 100th session took place in Rome upon invitation by the Italian Government in October 2014.

420. The Scuola Grande di San Giovanni Evangelista was the seat of an important law guild founded in 1261. The magnificent interior includes the grand staircase by Codussi (around 1498), which leads to the hall, restyled around 1787 by Massari.

421. And not even a postal address, which is sometimes difficult to understand for interlocutors who would like to contact the Commission at its seat.

CoE, especially the Parliamentary Assembly, which is at the origin of the highest number of requests, welcome this approach, insisting that from the Venice Commission they expect a sound legal basis for their own political assessment.

394. A few countries have chosen to appoint high-level civil servants or even active Ministers. While such appointments could cast doubt on the independence of these persons, in practice the Commission experienced only few problems as to their independence, probably due to the high-level of professionalism in the Commission and a feeling of collegiality between the members. A member who would blindly defend the interests of the government that appointed him or her would quickly lose all credibility within the Commission.[422]

395. The members are appointed by the governments for a period of four years. They can be reappointed. The Member States shall also appoint a substitute member. On two occasions, governments did try to replace their member who had fallen into 'disgrace' at home. The Commission vigorously rejected these attempts. After the expiry of the term of office, the Member State is however free to appoint a different person.[423]

§6. STANDARDS

396. The standards which the Venice Commission applies are first and foremost those of the CoE: democracy, the protection of human rights and the rule of law.[424] In the field of human rights, the ECHR and the case law of the Strasbourg Court of course provide guidance. In other fields, the Commission has had to identify elements of the Common Constitutional Heritage.

397. The Commission has learned to live with the diversity of constitutional systems in Europe, which it does not see as a problem but as a rich asset. The Commission never provides a model solution but will only comment on basic choices made within the country concerned. Therefore, the Venice Commission fully accepts for instance various systems of governance, be they presidential, semi-presidential or parliamentarian. What it will however insist on, is that the concrete implementation of such a system within a country remains coherent and allows for sufficient checks and balances between the state powers. When the Commission criticizes texts, which give important powers to the executive, without adequate control mechanisms, the drafters of these texts sometimes refer to another European

422. Nevertheless, during the preparation of the revised statute, Mr Jurgens, then representative of the Parliamentary Assembly at the Plenary Sessions of the Venice Commission, suggested that the members of the Commission be elected by the Assembly in order to enhance their status and their independence. However, the Committee of Ministers did not follow this useful suggestion.

423. It is to be regretted that out of the sixty-one members (not counting substitute members) only thirteen are women.

424. CDL-AD(2016)007, Rule of Law Checklist; *see also* CDL-JU(2017)011, Measuring the immeasurable: the Venice Commission's Rule of Law Checklist, Report, Ms Simona Granata-Menghini, Minsk, Belarus, 27–28 Apr. 2017.

country with a semi-presidential system as a model. The Commission will then typically reply that that country has the benefit of settled legal traditions, which will restrain the political forces from abusing the possibilities the Constitution might offer. A country without a developed constitutional culture, however, typically still lacks such legal traditions. Often, it will therefore be necessary to provide for more explicit rights of mutual control. The Venice Commission is thus open to various solutions but will insist on 'minimum standards' of the Common Constitutional Heritage.[425]

398. In addition to recommendations based on these standards, the Commission will also provide practical advice. The common knowledge of its members enables it to point out any elements in a draft constitutional setup which might prevent it from functioning efficiently without being contrary to any standard. This comparative method enables the Commission to point out that certain solutions have worked more or less smoothly in other states.

399. Usually, the Commission adopts its opinions by consensus. Voting on opinions is rather rare within the Commission. Objections to specific parts of an opinion are often taken into account in the final version of the adopted text.

§7. Constitutional Co-operation with Individual Countries

400. The Venice Commission assists and advises its Member States in constitutional and para-constitutional matters. The Commission endeavours to assist these countries in bringing their constitution and legislation as close as possible to the principles of the CoE and the Common Constitutional Heritage. The Commission never imposes a solution on a country, but adopts a non-directive approach based on dialogue. Its rapporteurs typically visit the country concerned, where they meet not only with the authorities but also with the opposition and civil society. These visits allow the rapporteurs to adapt their comments to the specific situation and needs in each country.

401. Upon receipt of a request for an opinion, the Commission will first establish a small group of rapporteurs – usually between two and four of its members – and sometimes also outside experts.[426] These rapporteurs first draft their individual comments.[427] On the basis of the members' comments and the results of the rapporteurs' visit to the country concerned, the Secretariat in Strasbourg will draw up a single, consolidated draft opinion.

425. *See* CDL-AD(2004)015, Opinion on the possible follow-up to Parliamentary Assembly Recommendation 1629(2003) on 'Future of Democracy: Strengthening Democratic Institutions', paras 9–11; CDL-AD(2005)038, Opinion on Draft Constitutional Amendments concerning the Reform of the Judicial System in 'the Former Yugoslav Republic of Macedonia', para. 47.

426. Outside experts intervene in joint opinions when they are appointed by the partner organization (e.g., OSCE-ODIHR) or when the Commission needs specific expertise that is not available among its members.

427. Members' individual comments are not available to the general public.

402. Following its approval by the rapporteurs, this draft opinion is forwarded to all members and the Member States' Permanent Representations with the CoE, including the authorities of the country concerned who may make any remarks. Depending on the complexity of the issue, the draft opinion is then either referred to a sub-commission[428] or directly presented to the Plenary Session, which will discuss and adopt the opinion, often with the participation of representatives of the country concerned. Whenever there are new developments concerning an adopted opinion (e.g., adoption or final rejection of the text examined), the Secretariat will report to the Plenary Session under the agenda item 'Follow-up to previous opinions'.

403. Occasionally, the Venice Commission also acted as a legal advisor to the EU in its mediation efforts for the settlement of ethno-political conflicts. In such cases, the advice of the Commission is sought to mould possible political compromise between the parties of the conflict into constitutional shape.[429] Standard models like autonomy or federalism are often rejected from the outset by one of the parties. Tailor-made agreements have therefore to be offered in order to convince both sides. This advice often does not result in the formal adoption of an opinion but is directly reflected in the results of the negotiations. However, the Venice Commission also adopted a large number of formally adopted opinions in the field of the protection of minorities.[430] More and more often the European Commission seeks assistance from the Venice Commission on the constitutional and legal set-up of candidate countries or countries negotiating association agreements. Usually the European Commission invites the country concerned to work with the Venice Commission[431] but the European Commission itself has also requested opinions from the Venice Commission.[432]

---

428. In addition to the two joint organs (Joint Council on Constitutional Justice and Council for Democratic Elections) the following sub-commissions have been established: Democratic Institutions, Fundamental Rights, Gender Equality, Judiciary, Federal and Regional State, Protection of Minorities, International Law, Rule of Law, Working methods, Latin America, Mediterranean Basin.

429. For example, Bosnia and Herzegovina, Kosovo, 'the Former Yugoslav Republic of Macedonia', State Union of Serbia and Montenegro.

430. For an overview *see* CDL-PI(2018)002, Compilation of Venice Commission opinions and reports on national minorities. Recent examples are CDL-AD(2015)033, Opinion on the Draft Law Amendments to the Law on Minority Rights and Freedoms of Montenegro; CDL-AD(2016)035, Republic of Moldova – Opinion on the Draft Law on the Ethno-Cultural Status of the District of Taraclia; CDL-AD(2017)030, Ukraine – Opinion on the provisions of the Law on Education of 5 Sep. 2017, which concern the use of the State Language and Minority and other Languages in Education.

431. For example, One of the conditions for the signature of an association agreement between Ukraine and the European Union was the implementation of recommendations of the Venice Commission on the reform of the prosecution system in Ukraine: CDL-AD(2013)025, Joint Opinion on the Draft Law on the Public Prosecutor's Office of Ukraine adopted by the Venice Commission at its ninety-sixth Plenary Session (Venice, 11–12 Oct. 2013).

432. CDL-AD(2011)038, Opinion on the draft code of constitutional procedure of Bolivia; CDL-AD(2011)007, Opinion on the Draft Organic Law of the Public Prosecutor's Office of Bolivia; CDL-AD(2012)014, Opinion on Legal Certainty and the Independence of the Judiciary in Bosnia and Herzegovina.

404. Sometimes the Commission's assistance is needed within very short deadlines.[433] This is why the Venice Commission is also referred to as a 'constitutional fire brigade' or as a provider of 'constitutional first-aid'. As such, the opinions of the Venice Commission are non-binding but sometimes the political organs of the CoE, the EU, other international organizations or individual Member States will refer to them and press for the implementation of the recommendations made by the Venice Commission.[434]

§8. Transnational Studies and Opinions: Defining the Common Constitutional Heritage

405. While the majority of requests for opinions[435] relate to individual states, over time, requests for general opinions or studies have given the Commission the opportunity to identify – if not to define – standards in the field of constitutional law, which constitute the Common Constitutional Heritage.

406. Important examples of such studies are the Report and Checklist on the Rule of Law,[436] which provides a list of concrete questions in order to evaluate the development of the rule of law in a given country. The Report on the Preferential Treatment of National minorities by their kin-State, which for the first time comprehensively dealt with the issue of kin-minorities.[437] Moreover, in its Opinion on PACE Recommendation 1713(2005) on the Democratic Oversight of the Security Sector in Member States,[438] the Commission has undertaken a study on internal

433. For instance, within a week when the President of Georgia requested an opinion to be available within the ten day deadline which he had for the veto of a draft law: CDL-PI(2016)005, Georgia – Preliminary Opinion on the Amendments to the organic Law on the Constitutional Court and to the Law on Constitutional Legal Proceedings (Ch. Grabenwarter, E. Tanchev, H. Gstöhl).

434. For example, the International Monetary Fund made a credit line totalling four billion US Dollars (together with other creditors) dependant on the implementation of the Venice Commission's recommendations in its opinion on anti-corruption courts in Ukraine, CDL-AD(2017)020, Ukraine – Opinion on the Draft Law on Anticorruption Courts and on the Draft Law on Amendments to the Law on the Judicial System and the Status of Judges (concerning the introduction of mandatory specialization of judges on the consideration of corruption and corruption-related offences); for other references to international organizations or individual States supporting the work of the Commission, *see* https://www.venice.coe.int/WebForms/pages/?p=02_references&lang=EN.

435. Article 3.1 of the revised Statute allows the Commission to undertake studies at its own initiative as was the case, for example, with its Study on the Composition on Constitutional Courts, *Science and Technique of Democracy*, No. 20.

436. CDL-AD(2011)003rev, Report on the Rule of Law; CDL-AD(2016)007, Rule of Law Checklist.

437. CDL-INF(2001)019.

438. CDL-AD(2005)033.

security services, which complements its study of 1997 on Internal Security Services in Europe[439] in the light of new challenges since 9/11. In the field of the judiciary, the Commission prepares general reports on judicial independence[440] and reports on specific issues, such as the freedom of expression of judges.[441] As concerns constitutional justice, the Commission adopted a report on the composition of constitutional courts[442] and a study on individual access to them,[443] which deals *inter alia* with the issue of how individual complaints at the national level can be a relief for the overburdened European Court of European Rights.

407. Sometimes, such studies were presented and discussed during Universities for Democracy (UniDem) seminars and later published in the Commission's *Science and Technique of Democracy* series.[444] Following the footsteps of its UniDem Campus held in Trieste, where the Venice Commission trained civil servants from the Balkans on issues of constitutional law and on other topics related to the activities of the CoE,[445] the Commission organizes a series of conferences called UniDem Med Campus for senior civil servants of seven partners in the MENA region (Algeria, Jordan, Lebanon, Mauritania, Morocco, Palestinian National Authority and Tunisia). The purpose of UniDem Med programme is to contribute to an efficient administration and good governance while respecting human rights.[446]

§9. Constitutional Justice

408. An important branch of the Commission's activities includes co-operation with constitutional courts and equivalent bodies. Since its creation, the Venice Commission has been aware that it is not sufficient to assist states in the adoption of democratic constitutions but that these texts have to be implemented in society. While the implementation of a constitution is incumbent on all state agencies, constitutional courts and equivalent bodies are key players for the control of this implementation.

---

439. CDL-INF(1998)006.
440. CDL-AD(2007)028, Report on Judicial Appointments; CDL-AD(2010)040, Report on European Standards as regards the Independence of the Judicial System: Part II – the Prosecution Service; CDL-AD(2010)004, Report on the Independence of the Judicial System Part I: The Independence of Judges.
441. CDL-AD(2015)018, Report on the Freedom of expression of Judges.
442. CDL-STD(1997)020, The Composition of Constitutional Courts – Science and Technique of Democracy, No. 20 (1997).
443. CDL-AD(2010)039rev, adopted by the Venice Commission at its eighty-fifth Plenary Session (Venice, 17–18 Dec. 2010).
444. https://www.venice.coe.int/webforms/documents/?series=23&year=all.
445. Seminars were held on: Interregional and Transfrontier Co-operation: Promoting Democratic Stability and Development (February 2010); The Protection of the Fundamental Rights of Irregular Migrants (November 2009); The Independence of the Judicial System from the Executive and Legislative Power (September, 2009).
446. https://www.venice.coe.int/WebForms/pages/?p=03_CampusUniDem&lang=EN.

409. As early as 1991, the Commission started to collect and disseminate constitutional case law and to organize seminars with constitutional courts.[447] The Commission fosters mutual exchanges between the constitutional courts and – when necessary – supports courts under undue pressure by other state powers.[448] Three times a year, it publishes the now electronic *Bulletin on Constitutional Case-Law* and the database CODICES, which report on important constitutional decisions. The fully searchable database CODICES www.CODICES.CoE.int already contains about 10,000 judgments, court descriptions, constitutions and the laws on the courts searchable via the Systematic Thesaurus of the Commission and in full text.

410. The Commission's activities in the field of constitutional justice are directed by the Joint Council on Constitutional Justice, which is a mixed body, composed of members of the Venice Commission and liaison officers appointed by courts from more than seventy countries,[449] as well as the ECtHR, the Court of Justice of the European Communities and the Inter-American Court of Human Rights.

411. Due to the strong interest from non-European constitutional courts in its activities, the Venice Commission has established, in addition to co-operation with the Conference of European Constitutional Courts, the Association of Constitutional Courts using the French language (ACCPUF), the Southern African Chief Justices Forum, the Conference of Constitutional Control Organs of Countries of New Democracy (Commonwealth of Independent States (CIS) countries), the Association of Asian Constitutional Courts and Equivalent Institutions, the Union of Arab Constitutional Courts and Councils, the Ibero-American Conference of Constitutional Justice, the Conference of Constitutional Jurisdictions of Portuguese-Speaking Countries and the Conference of Constitutional Jurisdictions of Africa. The partner courts are usually invited to contribute to the CODICES database. In January 2009, the Venice Commission invited all its partner courts as well as Commonwealth courts to the first World Conference on Constitutional Justice in Cape Town, hosted by the Constitutional Court of South Africa. On the basis of a declaration adopted there, a Bureau uniting these groups was mandated to prepare a Statute for the World Conference as a permanent body.

447. CDL-STD(1990)001, Meeting with the Presidents of Constitutional Courts and other Equivalent Bodies (Piazzola sul Brenta, 8 Oct. 1990) – Science and technique of democracy No. 1.

448. For example, Declaration on behalf of the Constitutional Court of Ukraine: www.venice.coe.int/files/2005_12_17_ukr_declaration_appointment_cc_judges_E.htm; President's Statement on behalf of the Constitutional Court of Romania 2012: https://www.venice.coe.int/webforms/events/default.aspx?id=1557; President's Statement on behalf of the Constitutional Court Moldova 2013: https://www.venice.coe.int/webforms/events/default.aspx?id=1703 and 2017; https://www.venice.coe.int/webforms/events/?id=2466.

449. Participation in the Joint Council is open to constitutional courts and equivalent bodies in the Venice Commission sixty-one Member States, the associated Member State (Belarus), observer states and states/entities with a special co-operation status (South Africa and the Palestinian National Authority) as well as the European Court of Human Rights, the Court of Justice of the European Union and the Inter-American Court of Human Rights.

412. The Statute[450] of the World Conference was discussed at the second Congress in January 2011 in Rio de Janeiro, Brazil, adopted by the Bureau at its meeting in Bucharest on 23 May 2011 and entered into force on 24 September 2011. The Statute establishes a General Assembly, a Bureau and provides that the Venice Commission acts as the Secretariat for the World Conference. Membership is open to the members of ten regional and linguistic groups as well as the courts participating in the Joint Council on Constitutional Justice. The World Conference has already more than 110 constitutional courts, constitutional councils and Supreme Courts as members on all continents.[451] When they need assistance, the member courts can call for good offices from the World Conference. They contribute an annual membership fee between EUR 200 and 2,000 to the budget of the Conference. The World Conference promotes constitutional justice as a key element for democracy, the protection of human rights and the rule of law. Member courts which violate these principles in a flagrant way can be suspended. The third Congress on the topic 'Constitutional Justice and Social Integration' was held on 28 September–1 October 2014 in Seoul, Republic of Korea, the 4th Congress dealt with 'the Rule of Law and Constitutional Justice in the Modern World' (Vilnius, Lithuania, 11–14 September 2017). The 5th Congress will deal with 'Constitutional Justice and Peace' in Algiers, Algeria, in 2020.

§10. Electoral Matters

413. For any democratic society, free and fair elections are of paramount importance. Therefore, the Commission made electoral legislation an important field of its activity and promotes European electoral standards within its Member States. The Commission defined the principles applicable to democratic elections in its Code of Good Practice in Electoral Matters[452] and a number of other electoral

450. CDL-WCCJ-GA(2017)010, Revised statute of the World Conference on Constitutional Justice, as amended by the 2nd General Assembly, Vilnius, 12 Sep. 2017.
451. https://www.venice.coe.int/WebForms/pages/?p=02_WCCJ.
452. CDL-AD(2002)023rev2, Code of good practice in Electoral Matters: Guidelines and Explanatory Report.

standard-setting texts[453] as well as a Code of Good Practice and guidelines on political parties.[454] It also drafts Opinions and Recommendations on the electoral legislation of member countries and organizes training seminars targeting all the actors involved in the electoral process. To a large extent these activities are carried out through the Council for Democratic Elections, a joint body set-up in co-operation with the Parliamentary Assembly and the Congress of Local and Regional Authorities of the CoE. The Commission assists PACE with legal advice during electoral observation mission in countries where the Commission provided opinions on the electoral legislation. Since 2002, the Venice Commission also organizes the annual European Conferences of Electoral Management Bodies in order to share knowledge and expertise on international standards, domestic legislation and good practice in the electoral field. Each Conference gathers together electoral administrators and experts from the Venice Commission Member States and beyond.

§11. Conclusion

414. Several factors have contributed to the Venice Commission's success: its independent membership, its integration into the structures of the CoE, its flexibility and capacity to react rapidly, its open approach based on dialogue and the acceptance of constitutional diversity. Over the years, the experience gained in co-operating with the new CoE Member States has allowed the Commission to identify common standards, which are applicable and needed all over Europe. This consolidation of the Common Constitutional Heritage is far from completed and will probably remain a major lasting achievement of the Venice Commission.

415. Following a period of rapid democratic progress during the first twenty years of the work of the Venice Commission, the so-called democratic backlash resulted in an increase of requests for opinions from the organs of the CoE. In such

453. CDL-AD(2006)018, Report on Electoral Law and Electoral Administration in Europe – Synthesis study on recurrent challenges and problematic issues; CDL-AD(2005)028, Opinion on Parliamentary Assembly Recommendation 1704(2005) on Referendums: towards good practices in Europe; CDL-AD(2005)034, Report on Referendums in Europe – An analysis of the legal rules in European States; CDL-AD(2008)037, CDL-AD(2010)007, Report on Thresholds and other features of electoral systems which bar parties from access to Parliament; CDL-AD(2011)022, Report on out-of-country voting; CDL-AD(2012)005, Report on measures to improve the democratic nature of elections in Council of Europe Member States; CDL-AD(2015)001, Report on Proportional Electoral Systems: the Allocation of Seats inside the Lists (open/closed lists); CDL-AD(2016)004, Joint Guidelines for preventing and responding to the misuse of administrative resources during electoral processes.

454. CDL-AD(2009)021, Code of Good Practice in the field of Political Parties; CDL-AD(2010)024, Guidelines on political party regulation, by OSCE-ODIHR and Venice Commission; CDL-INF(2000)001, Guidelines on prohibition and dissolution of political parties and analogous measures; CDL-INF(2001)008, Guidelines and Report on the Financing of Political Parties; CDL-AD(2004)007rev, Guidelines and Explanatory Report on Legislation on Political Parties: some specific issues; CDL-AD(2006)025, Report on the Participation of Political Parties in Elections.

opinions, the Venice Commission sometimes came to the conclusion that the applicable standards had not been followed.[455] As the opinions of the Venice Commission are based on thorough legal arguments, they provide a sound basis for the work of the organs of the CoE and other international bodies in their political dialogue with the country concerned. The work of the Venice Commission thus becomes even more relevant for maintaining and defending democracy, the protection of human rights and the rule of law in Europe.

455. CDL-AD(2016)001, Opinion on amendments to the Act of 25 Jun. 2015 on the Constitutional Tribunal of Poland; CDL-AD(2017)031, Poland – Opinion on the Draft Act amending the Act on the National Council of the Judiciary; on the Draft Act amending the Act on the Supreme Court, proposed by the President of Poland, and on the Act on the Organisation of Ordinary Courts; CDL-AD(2016)037, Turkey – Opinion on Emergency Decree Laws Nos 667–676 adopted following the failed coup of 15 Jul. 2016; CDL-AD(2017)004, Turkey – Opinion on the duties, competences and functioning of the criminal peace judgeships; recently CDL-PI(2018)007, Romania – Preliminary Opinion on draft amendments to Law No. 303/2004 on the statute of judges and prosecutors, Law No. 304/2004 on judicial organization, and Law No. 317/2004 on the Superior Council for Magistracy (J. Scholsem, H. Suchocka, K. Tuori, I. Cameron, C. Bazy-Malaurie).

Chapter 3. The Congress of Local and Regional Authorities: European Co-operation Close to the Citizen

Sylvie Affholder, updated by Maren Lambrecht-Feigl and Tim Lisney

§1. Introduction

I. Historical Background

416. Promoting democracy at the local and regional levels, which are close to the citizen, contributes to the political stability in Europe and is one of the CoE objectives. As early as 1957, the 'Conference of Local and Regional Authorities of Europe' was created by the CoE, bringing together the elected representatives of the local and regional communities of CoE Member States. Following the fall of the Berlin Wall in 1989, the revival and consolidation of subnational levels of democracy, according to the principle of subsidiarity, became one of the prerequisites for the integration of the new democracies of Central and Eastern Europe in the CoE. In 1994, the Congress of Local and Regional Authorities ('the Congress') succeeded the Conference as a CoE consultative body. In their final Declaration, the Heads of State and Government gathering in Strasbourg in 1997 acknowledged 'the fundamental role of the institutions of local democracy in the preservation of stability in Europe'.[456]

417. This contribution will explain the structure and functioning of the Congress and highlight some of the core areas of action where the Congress is promoting CoE values at local and regional level.

II. Structure and Functioning

418. The Congress is a political assembly composed of representatives holding an elected mandate as members of a local or regional authority (which may vary greatly in size, denomination and responsibilities) each appointed by a specific national procedure, determined by each Member State, which has to respect the criteria of geographical and gender balance and reflect the results of the most recent local and regional elections, as stipulated in Article 2 of the Congress Charter.[457] Its 324 full members and 324 substitute members, representing over 200,000 European municipalities and regions, are grouped by national delegation and by political

456. Final Declaration of the Second Summit of Heads of States and Government, Strasbourg, 10–11 Oct. 1997.
457. https://rm.coe.int/16807b308d.

groups. A Statutory Resolution[458] adopted by the CM in 2000 brought greater clarity to the functioning of the Congress. It reinforced regional participation in the Congress, as well as the stipulated electoral character of the mandate held by the Congress members.

419. The Congress appoints its President from the members of one of its two Chambers (of Local Authorities and of Regions respectively) on an alternating basis and remains in office for two ordinary sessions (i.e., for a period of two years). Since 2009, it holds two sessions per year, normally in March and October. The Secretariat is headed by a Secretary General (elected for a five-year mandate). The Congress provides a forum for dialogue where representatives of local and regional authorities discuss common problems, compare experiences and then put their points of view to the national governments.

420. The Congress performs several functions within the CoE:

- It helps the Organization's new Member States in tangibly introducing and reinforcing local and regional self-government according to European democratic standards. It delivers its support in founding the actual units of local and regional self-government or accompanying ongoing reforms while encouraging consultation and political dialogue between the national governments and the territorial entities.
- The Congress performs a function of keeping watch on local democracy in Europe, by producing 'monitoring reports' on the situation in the Member States. In this way, it verifies the effective application of the principles set forth in the main legal instrument of the Congress – the European Charter of Local Self-Government [the Charter hereafter], containing major principles of local democracy.
- It is also in charge of local and regional election monitoring and of setting the standards for Europe in electoral matters.
- The Congress organizes hearings and conferences at the local and regional levels to reach the general public whose participation remains essential if true democracy is to be established, and acts in close co-operation with the national and international organizations representing local and regional authorities.
- The Congress regularly undertakes fact-finding missions to explore concerns related to the Charter, promotes concrete action at local level and provides assistance to new democracies.
- Finally, it advises the CM on all aspects of local and regional policy.

421. Being intended to represent both local and regional authorities, it comprises two chambers: the Chamber of Local Authorities and the Chamber of Regions. Since 2010, the Congress has three statutory committees, which carry out the substantial work of the Congress http://www.coe.int/t/congress:

458. Statutory Res. (2000)1 and Charter of the Congress of Local and Regional Authorities of Europe, Strasbourg, 2002, Council of Europe.

- The Committee on the Honouring of Obligations and Commitments by Member States of the European Charter of Local Self-Government, known as the 'Monitoring Committee', responsible, in particular, for monitoring the application of the Charter as well as institutional developments in Europe's regions, for preparing reports on the situation of local and regional democracy in Europe, and following missions to observe local and regional elections, and monitoring specific questions related to local and regional democracy in the Member States.
- The Governance Committee is responsible for affairs falling within the scope of the Congress' statutory mandate, such as governance, public finance, cross-border and interregional co-operation, citizen participation and e-democracy as well as co-operation with intergovernmental bodies.
- The Current Affairs Committee is responsible for studying the role of local and regional authorities with regard to the major challenges of our society and preparing work on thematic issues such as social cohesion, education, culture and sustainable development from the point of view of the CoE's core values.

§2. Enforcing the CoE Legal Instruments to Promote Local and Regional Democracy Throughout Europe

I. The European Charter of Local Self-Government, a Milestone in Promoting Local Democracy in Europe

422. CoE Member States are organized in different ways throughout Europe. The principles of local self-government contained in the *European Charter of Local Self-Government*[459] [hereafter 'the Charter'] apply to all categories of local authorities, whether they belong to unitary, centralized or federal States.

423. The Charter sets out the principle that effective local self-government is essential to democracy. Local authorities are to be elected by universal suffrage. Local authorities, acting within the limits of the law, should be able to regulate and manage public affairs under their own responsibility in the interests of the local population. Consequently, the Charter considers that public responsibilities should be exercised by the authorities closest to the citizens, the higher level being considered only when the coordination or discharge of duties is impossible or less efficient at the level immediately below (subsidiarity principle). To this end, it sets out the principles concerning the protection of local authority boundaries, the existence of adequate administrative structures and resources for the tasks of local authorities, the conditions under which responsibilities at local level are exercised, administrative supervision of local authorities' activities, financial resources of local authorities and legal protection of local self-government.

424. Opened for signature by CoE Member States on 15 October 1985, the Charter came into force on 9 September 1988. This is the instrument in which the signatory States undertake to recognize the principle of local self-government in

459. *See* 'European Charter of Local Self-Government', CETS No. 122, http://conventions.coe.int.

domestic legislation. The Charter has also served as a model for legislative reform in the new democracies, with some states even incorporating its principles into their constitutions. The Charter is the reference instrument that the CoE uses as its basis in this field. By the end of 2013, all forty-seven Member States had ratified the Charter, thus creating a single legal space for local democracy in Europe.[460]

425. The Congress began monitoring the implementation of the Charter in 1995.[461] This task has been formalized in the Statutory Resolution governing the Congress, which specifies, in its Article 2, paragraph 3, that:

> the Congress shall prepare on a regular basis country-by-country reports on the situation of local and regional democracy in all member States and in States which have applied to join the Council of Europe, and shall ensure, in particular, that the principles of the European Charter of Local Self-Government are implemented.[462]

Monitoring reports on local democracy are regularly drawn up country-by-country (around 120 reports since 1995). In 2010, the Congress began to systematically monitor the application of the European Charter in every Member State on a regular basis.

426. The monitoring exercise, involving up to a dozen country visits in a year, provides an important basis on which to enter into a constructive political dialogue with the authorities of Member States in connection with local and regional democracy issues. This enables the Congress to familiarize governments, parliaments, associations, elected representatives and the media with its main conventions and legal instruments concerning local and regional institutional issues. Numerous legislative reforms have been set in motion by Member States in the light of the conclusions in these reports.

427. General reports providing an across-the-board analysis of the application of the European Charter of Local Self-Government in Member States and countries applying to join the CoE are also prepared. Some of the recent issues tackled include the monitoring of the principle of 'consultation of local authorities'[463] or the institutional framework of local democracy.[464] The Group of Independent Experts of the Charter, bringing together experts on local democracy, assists the Monitoring and Governance Committees with their statutory tasks, gathering information on local and regional self-government, providing elected representatives with technical

460. An updated chart of signatures and ratifications can be consulted on the website of the Treaty Office: http://conventions.coe.int.

461. *See* Res. 18 and Recommendation 12(1995) on local democracy in Romania.

462. Statutory Resolution CM/Res(2015)9 relating to the Congress of Local Authorities of the Council of Europe: https://rm.coe.int/16807b308f.

463. Sixth General Report on implementation of the European Charter of Local Self-Government (Arts 4.6, 5, 9.6 and 10) 'Consultation of Local Authorities' – CPL (12) 5 Part II.

464. Report on relations between the public, the local assembly and the executive in local democracy (the institutional framework of local democracy) – CPL (9) 2 Part II.

assistance, and helping to interpret and exploit the potential of the provisions of the European Charter of Local Self-Government.

428. The Congress has recently supplemented its monitoring activities with a process that it refers to as 'post-monitoring dialogue', in which it develops targeted assistance programmes on issues of common interest identified during the monitoring visits, in order to provide concrete assistance to local and regional authorities and to ensure the effective follow-up of its recommendations. As Resolution 353 (2013) on the 'Congress post-monitoring and post-observation of elections: developing political dialogue' states, post-monitoring seeks to ensure more impact and effectiveness towards the pursuit of political dialogue with national authorities and other relevant national stakeholders involved in monitoring and election observation activities, in order to improve the implementation of recommendations and resolutions.

II. Promoting Regionalization

429. The Congress has also promoted regional democracy and the regionalization process, in accordance with the principle of subsidiarity. In 1996, the Congress initiated the drafting of a 'European Charter of Regional Self-Government,' whereby regional self-government should 'denote[s] the right and actual ability of the largest territorial authorities within each State, having elected bodies, administratively placed between central government and local authorities, and enjoying prerogatives either of self-organization or of a type normally associated with the central authority, to manage, under their own responsibility and for the benefit of their populations, a substantial share of the matters of general interest, in particular in view of favouring the regional sustainable development'.[465] Both the Parliamentary Assembly (in its Recommendation 1349(1997) and Resolution 146(2002)) and the Committee of the Regions of the EU (in its opinion of 13 December 2000) supported the adoption of this new Charter in the form of a convention. This Charter was supposed to supplement the machinery set in place with the European Charter of Local Self-Government in order to establish the fundamental principles of regional democracy more firmly, while taking account of the specific circumstances of the Member States.[466] In 2008, the Congress adopted a Draft European Charter of Regional Democracy. However, this new instrument did not find the support of all delegations in the intergovernmental sector of the CoE, including the competent Steering Committee and the CM. However, in November 2009 in Utrecht (Netherlands), the Ministers responsible for Local and Regional Government were ready to adopt a Reference Framework on Regional Democracy which had been elaborated in close consultation with the Congress.

465. Article 3.1 of the Appendix of Res. 37(1996)[1] on the European Charter of Regional Self-Government.

466. *See* Recommendation 156(2004) on the Council of Europe convention on regional self-government.

III. Fostering Cross-Border and Interregional Co-operation

430. The Congress works to promote a Europe without dividing lines. Enabling co-operation between neighbouring countries separated by a border is at the centre of its work. *The European Outline Convention on Transfrontier Co-operation between Territorial Communities or Authorities* (1980) and its three Additional Protocols recognize the right of local and regional authorities to co-operate across frontiers in providing public services and environmental protection. The Congress promotes the ratification and implementation of these legal instruments. In addition to having organized a series of conferences in this field, the Congress has also encouraged the creation of Associations of Local and Regional Authorities such as the Local Democracy Agencies (LDA), the Network of Associations of Local Authorities of South-East Europe, the European Network of Local and Regional Authority Training Organisations (ENTO), and the National Association of Local Authorities of Georgia (NALAG), but also the establishment of Euroregions around seas such as, the Adriatic Euroregion and the Black Sea Euroregion project. These initiatives continue to be supported by the Congress, notably with a view to providing specific training to national stakeholders.

IV. Observing Local and/or Regional Elections

431. The Congress regularly observes local and/or regional elections in member and applicant countries, a key factor in its objective of monitoring progress towards, and the state of, local and regional democracy in the countries concerned.

432. Such observation always includes an analysis of the election campaign and involves discussion at the highest level with representatives of parties and groups contesting the elections, election commissions, media and civil rights groups. Reports and proposals are subsequently adopted by the Congress Bureau and made known to the relevant authorities in the countries concerned. On average, the Congress conducts five or six such observations per year and has concluded around 150 such missions to date.

§3. Fostering Co-operation among Local and Regional Authorities in Europe

I. Voicing the Interests of Local and Regional Authorities in Europe

433. The Congress has the mandate to represent the interests of the local and regional authorities in the CoE. It promotes their interests in the policy-making of the organization. Voicing the interests of European local and regional authorities in Europe relies on an active co-operation with European associations of local and regional authorities. International associations of local and regional authorities, which have consultative status with the CoE, also have observer status with the Congress. Observer status may also be granted to other associations on application to the Congress Bureau. This status gives them the right to take part in the work of the Congress, submit memoranda and comment on issues discussed at plenary sessions, without voting rights. The Congress has, for example, developed co-operation with various international associations, including Eurocities, the Union of capitals of the EU, the Alps-Adriatic Working Community, the Twin cities international association or the International Association of French-speaking mayors.

434. The Congress is closely following the developments related to local and regional democracy in the EU and promoting the principles in the Charter in its Member States. A contact group has been mandated to improve high-level contacts between the members of the Congress and the Committee of the Regions in order to develop co-operation between the two institutions. Based on a co-operation agreement between the Congress and the EU Committee of the Regions aimed at mutual support between the two institutions, these have, in recent years, prepared joint election observation missions and co-operated on interregional co-operation in the Black Sea area, multilevel governance and local and regional democracy in 'Eastern Partnership' countries, as well as on countering corruption at the local and regional levels.[467]

435. In his report of 2006,[468] then Prime Minister of Luxembourg Jean-Claude Juncker had identified several potential areas of co-operation between the Congress and the EU Committee of the Regions, among which the development of new-style 'Euroregions,' covering regions in both EU and non-EU countries, the establishment of the Centre for Interregional and Cross-Border Co-operation in Saint Petersburg, the promotion of new networks of local authority associations, especially in the South Caucasus and the Western Balkans and had called for further support of the EU to the Association of Local Democracy Agencies (ALDA) operating in South-Eastern European countries – 'since they may eventually join it'.

II. Preserving Europe's Diversity at Local Level

436. Local and regional authorities have a key role to play to promote social cohesion and cultural diversity at local level. In this context, the Congress has promoted instruments strengthening social cohesion. These instruments include:

- *The European Charter for Regional or Minority Languages* (1992) aims to preserve regional and minority languages as a unique component of Europe's cultural heritage, extending their use in law, in schools, in public, cultural, economic and social life, and in the media.

467. Agreement on the co-operation between the Committee of Regions and the Congress of Local and Regional Authorities of the Council of Europe, signed on 13 Apr. 2005.

468. Jean-Claude Juncker, *Council of Europe – European Union: A Sole Ambition for the European Continent*, Report by the Prime Minister of the Grand Duchy of Luxembourg to the attention of the Heads of State or Government of the Member States of the Council of Europe, Doc. 10897 of the Parliamentary Assembly, 11 Apr. 2006.

- *The European Landscape Convention* (2000) sets forth an obligation for public authorities to adopt policies and measures at local, regional, national and international level for protecting, managing and planning landscapes throughout Europe.
- *The European Urban Charter II – Manifesto for a new urbanity* (2008) defines citizens' rights in European towns and cities. It provides a practical guide to good urban management, covering housing, urban architecture, transport, energy, sport and leisure, pollution and street security.

Among its more recent, non-binding texts in this field, the Congress has, for example, adopted Resolution 280(2009) on Intercultural cities or Recommendation 365(2014) – Promoting diversity through intercultural education and communication strategies.

III. Promoting Citizen's Participation at Grass-Roots Level

437. As pointed out in the Juncker Report:

> the Congress might serve as one platform to promote the intercultural and interreligious dialogue which is vitally needed at local level. It might, for example, draw up codes of conduct for managing intercultural conflicts, and also take action to promote integration and participation of immigrants and foreign residents.[469]

The Congress is emphasizing the active participation of citizens, holding a voting right or not. Therefore special attention has been paid to groups which need to be included in the decision-making process, like young people, migrants and Roma. Two instruments illustrate the CoE commitment to pursue this goal:

(1) *The Charter on the Participation of Young People in Municipal and Regional Life* (1992), revised in 2003, sets out guidelines to encourage young people to play their part in decisions affecting them and to be actively involved in social changes in their neighbourhood, municipality or region.

(2) *The European Convention on the Participation of Foreigners in Public Life at Local Level* (1992) puts forward the principle of progressively granting civil and political rights to foreign residents, including the right to vote. An important part of the work of the Congress is devoted to the issue of the integration of migrants. The Congress also continues to follow these issues on a regular basis and has adopted a number of resolutions relating to citizen participation in recent years, including on youth participation and the empowerment of young Roma (Resolutions 346(2012) on Youth and democracy (17 October 2012) and Resolution 366(2014) on Empowering Roma youth through participation (26 March 2014)).

469. *Ibid.*

§4. Selected Highlights of Congress Action

438. In addition to the institutional work carried out by the Congress and its statutory committees, in recent years the Congress has developed a series of projects aiming at providing assistance and support programmes, often with the support of voluntary contributions granted by CoE Member States, and has addressed topical issues, such as the financial and economic crisis and its impact on local and regional democracy, human rights at the local level and local democracy in the 'digital age'.

I. Creation of Cross-Border Regions

439. The Congress is committed to promoting cross-border co-operation. Euroregions provide opportunities to elected representatives but also socio-economic actors, public institutions and NGOs to set up a working community across borders. The Congress contributed to the setting-up of the Black Sea Euroregion, on 3 November 2006 in Samsun (Turkey), and the Adriatic Euroregion on 30 June 2006,[470] bringing together local and regional authorities from Albania, Croatia, Italy, Montenegro and Slovenia, aiming to reinforce stability in the Adriatic and Balkan regions, promoting sustainable development and ensuring social and economic cohesion in the region. The growing role of interregional co-operation for developing territorial cohesion in Europe was underlined in the 2014 Congress 'Dickson' report on this subject.[471]

II. Local Democracy Agencies

440. During the Yugoslavian conflict, the Congress developed a comprehensive range of actions to support the municipalities and regions in the transition, post-conflict period. In southeast Europe, a series of projects was developed to contribute to restoring dialogue and co-operation at local level post-conflict. Local Democracy Embassies (which later became LDAs) were set up with support of the Congress. Local authorities throughout Europe were invited to establish twinning programmes to provide assistance for municipalities stricken by the war and promote democracy at local level. The LDA programme still aims at promoting intercultural dialogue and democratic practices at local level, in the spirit of the values defended by the CoE. As of 2018, there are fourteen LDAs operating in southeast Europe and the Caucasus, developing a wide range of activities involving local elected representatives and NGOs. They are supported by the European ALDA,[472] created in 1999, which gathers more than a hundred local and regional authorities and NGOs and has received wide support from the CoE and the EU. From its beginnings in southeast Europe, the programme expanded to the South Caucasian countries, starting with the Kutaisi LDA in Georgia. The LDA Association has been

470. *See* www.adriaticeuroregion.org.
471. https://rm.coe.int/1680718921.
472. *See* www.alda-europe.eu.

granted observer status with the Bureau of the Congress and promotes European integration in a wider sense. Further to supporting these organizational projects, the Congress entered into dialogue with local and regional elected representatives of southeast Europe, as well as the South Caucasus, and organized several Forums of Cities and Regions of southeast Europe, providing valuable fora for international exchanges.

III. Supporting National Associations of Local Authorities

441. Local authorities' right to associate is provided in Article 10 of the European Charter of Local Self-Government, which stipulates that they are entitled, 'in exercising their powers, to co-operate and, within the framework of the law, to form consortia with other local authorities in order to carry out tasks of common interest'. National associations of local authorities are regarded as key players for developing local and regional democracy and partners for monitoring the situation in their respective countries.[473]

442. These associations should play an active part in legislative processes relating to local self-government. They would thus ensure that their members' needs and aspirations are taken into account in their dealings with central government, *inter alia* producing comments on draft legislation and providing expert advice expressing their needs and requests. They can help foster a culture of partnership between local and central government and build on best practice in terms of local democracy. In particular, they should be a key partner for central government in the discussion and implementation of decentralization reforms.

443. These associations should enable a better representation of local authorities at national level and promote, at international level, dialogue and better co-operation among the various organizations with an interest in local self-government issues, but also with citizens, so as to spread good practice and to compare successful local democracy experiments. Therefore the Congress has promoted the setting-up of national associations in countries such as Georgia and Azerbaijan, with the support of many international organizations and donor countries.

A. *Georgia*

444. In 2003, the Congress was instructed by the CoE and the European Commission to assist the setting-up of the NALAG. To this end, a steering group of some twenty Georgian local and regional representatives was set up. Institutions invited to take part in the steering group as observers, included the State Chancellery of Georgia, the parliamentary committee on local self-government and regional policy, Georgian associations of local and regional authorities, local and international

473. Opening speech of Congress President Giovanni Di Stasi, at the Conference of National Associations of Local and Regional Authorities (Strasbourg, 23 Feb. 2006).

NGOs (Urban Institute, National Democratic Institute, GTZ, the national association of local and regional authorities of Norway) and some international organizations (EU, OSCE). NALAG came into being in 2004.

B. Azerbaijan

445. The National Association of Norwegian Local and Regional Authorities and the Congress launched a joint activity in Azerbaijan with the support of the Norwegian government to establish a national association of local authorities, to ensure compliance with the principles of the European Charter of Local Self-Government and raise the profile of local authorities at national level. A steering group comprising representatives of local authorities and observers, international organizations and NGOs, was entrusted with the preparations for the establishment of the association. However, the negotiations took an unexpected turn, with the result that, in 2006, not one but three associations were set up, namely the National Associations of City, Settlement and Village Municipalities.

446. Further programmes fostering constructive co-operation between municipalities have been launched in Albania, Armenia, Georgia, Republic of Moldova and Ukraine, in the framework of national action plans adopted by the CoE in general to which the Congress makes substantial contributions at the local and regional levels. A recent initiative in this field was the launch of the European Alliance of Cities and Regions for Roma Inclusion in March 2013.

IV. Neighbourhood Policy

447. In the wake of the historic events in the southern Mediterranean in 2011, and in the framework of the resulting new CoE policy towards its immediate neighbourhood of North Africa, the Congress began to intensify its co-operation with Morocco and Tunisia, with a view to assisting the development of territorial democracy in these countries. In October 2014, a 'Partner for Local Democracy' status was adopted, with a view to enabling elected representatives of local authorities to participate in Congress activities. The Congress Bureau subsequently appointed a thematic spokesperson on the South-Mediterranean Partnership and, in February 2017, adopted a co-operation programme for southern Mediterranean countries to meet the objectives of the neighbourhood policy. This co-operation led to the Congress approving, in June 2018, a request for granting of Partner for local democracy status to the Kingdom of Morocco. The Moroccan delegation will accordingly be attributed six seats for its representatives, and six seats for substitutes.

448. The co-operation programme with Morocco, launched by the Congress, includes providing assistance with its decentralization reforms, in the form of the sharing of expertise and good practice examples. Similarly for Tunisia, the Congress has been helping to reinforce local governance in the country, namely in the fields of legislative assistance, the training of political agents, and the undertaking of awareness-raising activities.

V. Developing Policy Replies to Current Challenges of Society at the Local Level

449. With social changes occurring at an increasing pace, stakeholders at all levels need to be more and more reactive in developing public policy responses. Through its activities in recent years, the Congress has shown that it is able to listen to the concerns of citizens and decision-makers at the local and regional levels and reply to their needs:

- In 2007, the Congress launched the European Local Democracy Week, an initiative promoting proactive local policies to foster citizen participation across Europe. Around 110 European towns and cities participated in its 2018 edition on ‘Citizen participation, consultation and commitment for a thriving democracy’, which shows the continuous success of this Congress project (www.coe.int/demoweek).
- In 2012, the Congress launched its ‘Pact of towns and regions to stop sexual violence against children’, thus joining the transversal CoE ONE in FIVE campaign to stop sexual violence against children (www.coe.int/oneinfive). Since 2012, several towns and regions have signed up to the Pact and made active use of the online platform developed to facilitate the European exchange on good local and regional practice in this field. The activity is part of the efforts aimed at raising awareness of human rights at the local level, one of the current political priorities of the Congress.
- The Congress has organized debates and made substantial contributions to different fora on issues related to territorial democracy, including the World Forum for Democracy, for example at the November 2018 Forum on gender equality.

450. The Congress recently published ‘Handbook on Human rights’, focusing on the right to non-discrimination for refugees, asylum seekers and migrants; Roma and travellers; and LGBTI people.[474] It has also turned its attention to developing local responses to Europe’s migration crisis, responding to the upsurge in movements of migrants and refugees and examining and proposing different integration strategies. The Congress plenary sessions in 2018 debated and adopted reports on ‘Border regions facing the migration phenomenon’, promoting an ‘integrated approach,’ involving cross-border co-operation and collaboration between local stakeholders, NGOs and civil society; on ‘Voting rights at local level as an element of successful long-term integration of migrants and IDPs in Europe’s municipalities and regions’, inviting associations to engage in promoting political participation and

474. https://rm.coe.int/promoting-human-rights-at-local-and-regional-level-monitoring-committe/168079416a.

voting rights of migrants and IDPs; and on 'Unaccompanied Refugee Children, the role and responsibilities of local and regional authorities'.

451. Transparency and open government is one of the priority areas that the Congress identified in its roadmap of activities on the 'prevention of corruption and the promotion of public ethics at local and regional levels,' adopted in October 2016. In the context of this roadmap, the Congress has also prepared reports, recommendations and resolutions on various aspects of the fight against corruption, including use of administrative resources in election campaigns, transparency in procurement, conflicts of interest, transparency and open government, whistleblower protection and preventing nepotism.

452. In 2018 it launched the 'European Code of Conduct for all Persons Involved in Local and Regional Governance', an extension and thorough revision of its 1999 'Code of Conduct for the political integrity of local and regional elected representatives', which had served as a reference text for many of its operational and training activities.

§5. Conclusion

453. The Congress has come to be regarded as the 'third pillar' of the CoE, having evolved from a consultative body to a well-recognized institution within the Organization. Local and regional authorities are becoming increasingly important stakeholders in Europe, responsible for implementing numerous social, cultural and economic policies at local and regional level. The implication of the Congress in CoE Campaigns, such as those against trafficking of human beings and domestic violence against women, illustrates a growing recognition of the role of local authorities in many of the policy areas covered by the CoE. Human rights, social cohesion, intercultural and interreligious dialogue are other subjects that require the proactive action of local authorities. Whether unitary or federal, the CoE Member States have to work with cities and regions. In this context, the Congress will continue to play a key role in the CoE to take up challenges that Europe will face in the coming years. As a body of international co-operation it has also shown that it has been able to flexibly adapt to evolutions and challenges by significantly changing its work structure and adapting its agenda over recent years.

454. In recent years the Congress has proven that it can contribute to the process of European integration through its networks of its elected members and experts. It continues to seek to ensure that local and regional democracy develops in a Europe without dividing lines, in compliance with the principles and goals of the CoE. Democracy has to start at the local level and encompass all citizens. This is the challenge that faces all democracies in Europe – and the goal that all local and regional authorities have to aim for.

Part V. Bringing Europe Closer Together

Chapter 1. The CoE and the Protection of National Minorities

Antti Korkeakivi, updated by Charlotte Altenhöner-Dion and Agnes von Maravić

§1. Introduction

455. The protection of national minorities is a key issue in today's Europe, and this is also reflected in the programme of activities of the CoE. The CoE has designed a variety of tools to address minority questions, ranging from treaty-based monitoring to assistance activities and intergovernmental co-operation, all reflecting the idea that the protection of national minorities is an integral part of the international protection of human rights.

456. Although the CoE has been engaged in minority issues from the outset of its activities, its most concrete achievements in this domain are relatively young. The CoE's action on minority questions was markedly stepped up in the early 1990s, prompted by appalling manifestations of extreme nationalism in certain parts of Europe. Inter-ethnic violence and hostility in parts of former Yugoslavia and of the former Soviet Union strengthened the conviction that the protection of national minorities was not only a crucial element of human rights protection but also essential for stability, security and peace in Europe.

457. The Heads of State and Government of the CoE responded to these developments at their first Summit Meeting, held in Vienna in October 1993, by launching both standard-setting and co-operation activities aimed at protecting national minorities. The increased attention given to minority issues within the CoE resulted in a number of accomplishments, including the adoption of the Framework Convention for the Protection of National Minorities and the European Charter for Regional or Minority Languages. With the entry into force of these two conventions in 1998, the respective treaty-monitoring bodies started their country-specific work, contributing substantially to advancing legislative and administrative frameworks for the protection of national minorities in Europe. Since the above-mentioned developments, the protection of national minorities has consolidated its place among the CoE's key areas of action.

458. In addition to its specific minority instruments and the ECtHR, discussed below, the CoE's other human rights instruments and mechanisms more and more often take up issues related to national minorities. The Human Rights Commissioner of the CoE, for instance, has tackled a number of minority issues in his thematic and country-specific reports, and the collective complaint mechanism under the European Social Charter, introduced through a Protocol that came into force in 1998, has been invoked, *inter alia*, in relation to the housing situation of Roma.

§2. The European Convention on Human Rights

459. The bedrock of the CoE's human rights system, for majorities and minorities alike, is the ECHR. Although the Convention does not include any specific articles devoted to the protection of national minorities, its standards and the jurisprudence of the ECtHR have benefited national minorities in such key fields as freedom of expression and freedom of association. Furthermore, the Court's case law regarding non-discrimination under Article 14 of the Convention, which prohibits discrimination also on the ground of association with a national minority, is developing. The Court's recent jurisprudence includes, *inter alia*, significant cases regarding persons belonging to the Roma minority.[475]

460. The Convention's importance for persons belonging to national minorities has increased further as a result of the entry into force of Protocol No. 12 to the Convention on 1 April 2005. Whereas the non-discrimination guarantees of Article 14 are limited to the enjoyment of the rights guaranteed by the Convention, Protocol No. 12 widened the scope of such guarantees by introducing a general prohibition against discrimination. It is to be noted, however, that only twenty State Parties to the Convention have ratified the said Protocol, while a further eighteen have signed it.[476]

§3. The Framework Convention for the Protection of National Minorities

461. While the ECHR provides the general human rights guarantees (also) for persons belonging to national minorities, significantly more specific human rights provisions pertaining to national minorities can be found in the Framework Convention for the Protection of National Minorities, opened for signature in 1995.

475. *See*, for example, *Nachova and Others v. Bulgaria*, Application No. 43577/98, Grand Chamber Judgment, 6 Jul. 2005. *See also* the regularly updated factsheet on ECHR case law regarding Roma at: www.echr.coe.int/Documents/FS_Roma_ENG.pdf.

476. As of 1 Jan. 2018.

I. Content of the Framework Convention

462. The Framework Convention for the Protection of National Minorities entered into force on 1 February 1998, after twelve ratifications. Since then, the number of ratifications has grown steadily, and, on 1 May 2015, there were thirty-nine parties to the Convention,[477] and only four Member States of the CoE (Andorra, France, Monaco and Turkey) had not signed it, while four Member States had signed but not ratified. The Framework Convention remains unique within the ranks of human rights instruments, being the only multilateral treaty that is devoted to national minorities coupled with an operational monitoring mechanism.

463. The Framework Convention sets out principles to be respected as well as goals to be achieved by the Contracting Parties, in order to ensure the protection of persons belonging to national minorities, while fully respecting the principles of territorial integrity and political independence of States. It is important to stress that the Framework Convention's provisions on the protection of national minorities are to be implemented in a manner that encourages the spirit of intercultural dialogue, emphasized in Article 6 of the Framework Convention rather than supporting isolationist tendencies.

464. The main operative part of the Framework Convention is section II, containing specific principles on a wide range of issues. It includes provisions devoted to general human rights that are of particular relevance for persons belonging to national minorities, such as the freedoms of assembly, association, expression, thought, conscience and religion, which are to be interpreted in accordance with the corresponding articles of the ECHR. At the same time, the Framework Convention stipulates additional guarantees that reflect the specific situation and concerns of persons belonging to national minorities.

465. Articles 4, 5 and 6 are often regarded as cornerstones of minority protection: while Article 4 explicitly envisages positive measures to promote the full and effective equality of persons belonging to national minorities, Article 5, containing a prohibition of forced assimilation, requires Member States to promote the necessary conditions for the preservation and development of minority cultures, as well as religions, languages and traditions. Article 6 calls for efforts to promote tolerance and intercultural respect in society and guarantees protection from discrimination and ethnically based hostilities to all persons (i.e., not only persons belonging to national minorities).

466. The Framework Convention's provisions on the access to, representation in, and use of media have particular significance when it comes to the promotion of

477. Parties to the Framework Convention: Albania, Armenia, Austria, Azerbaijan, Bosnia and Herzegovina, Bulgaria, Croatia, Cyprus, Czech Republic, Denmark, Estonia, Finland, Georgia, Germany, Hungary, Ireland, Italy, Latvia, Liechtenstein, Lithuania, Malta, Moldova, Montenegro, the Netherlands, Norway, Poland, Portugal, Romania, Russian Federation, San Marino, Serbia, Slovakia, Slovenia, Spain, Sweden, Switzerland, 'the former Yugoslav Republic of Macedonia', Ukraine and the UK. Belgium, Greece, Iceland, and Luxembourg are signatories to the Framework Convention.

tolerance and intercultural understanding and respect between majority and minority populations. Article 9 contains undertakings in respect of broadcast, print and electronic media which have also been invoked in relation to 'new media', including the Internet. A number of the Framework Convention's following provisions relate to the use of the languages of national minorities. Article 10 of the Convention guarantees the right to use minority languages in private and in public and, in certain circumstances, the right to use minority languages in contacts with administrative authorities. The right to use personal names and to display information of a private nature in minority languages is stipulated in Article 11, which, furthermore, envisages minority language street names and other topographical indications in areas inhabited by a substantial number of persons belonging to a national minority.

467. The Framework Convention further devotes particular attention to equal access to education and to minority language education. These issues are addressed in Articles 12–14, which contain principles on both public and private education. Another key principle is the effective participation of persons belonging to national minorities, guaranteed in Article 15 of the Framework Convention, which covers participation not only in public life but also in economic, cultural and social life.

468. In addition, the Framework Convention protects national minorities against any changes in the proportion of population that are aimed at restricting the rights of persons belonging to national minorities. Finally, Articles 17 and 18 guarantee the right to pursue transfrontier contacts and encourage bilateral and other co-operation in fields pertaining to national minority protection such as education.

II. The Framework Convention's Monitoring Mechanism: The Advisory Committee

469. Most of the provisions of the Framework Convention are formulated in a flexible manner, and there are certain questions that are left open in the Convention. For example, the Convention does not provide a definition of the term national minorities. However, the results of the monitoring mechanism of the Convention are a source of authoritative interpretation of the Convention's provisions in various contexts and they provide specific guidance on the optimum implementation of the Framework Convention.

470. The monitoring mechanism of the Framework Convention is based on Articles 24–26 of the Framework Convention and on the CM Resolution (97)10. The evaluation of the adequacy of the implementation of the Framework Convention by the State Parties is the responsibility of the CM, which is assisted by the Advisory Committee. The Advisory Committee is composed of eighteen independent and impartial experts, elected by the CM, and in practice it is the Advisory Committee that carries out the most detailed monitoring work under the Convention.

471. Each State Party is required to submit, every five years, a report on legislative and other measures taken to give effect to the principles of the Framework Convention. These state reports are made public and examined by the Advisory Committee, which prepares an Opinion on the measures taken by each reporting State. Having received the Opinion of the Advisory Committee and the comments from the respective State, the CM adopts conclusions and recommendations in respect of the State Party concerned.

472. The first cycle of monitoring started in 1999 and, in respect of most States, the fourth cycle of monitoring has now been completed while for some, the fifth has already begun. Over the last twenty years, the Advisory Committee has adopted almost 150 detailed Opinions on the evolving level of implementation of the Framework Convention in the Member States. The Advisory Committee's Opinions contain specific recommendations, designed for each particular situation and following a logical progression: an invitation to take certain steps in the first cycle may turn into a recommendation to do so in the second cycle, which then evolves into an urgent recommendation in the third. In its work, the Committee follows the same procedure in respect of all States Parties. Its work covers not only numerically larger minorities, such as Roma or sizeable Hungarian and Russian minorities in certain States, but also numerically smaller minorities, some of which consist of only a few hundred persons. Overall, the Advisory Committee has argued that the implementation of the Framework Convention requires a nuanced, article-by-article approach. In this context, the Committee has repeatedly highlighted principles contained in Article 3 of the Framework Convention, including the right of every person belonging to a national minority freely to choose to be treated or not to be treated as such.

473. An important step in creating an effective monitoring mechanism under the Framework Convention was the introduction of country visits by working groups of the Advisory Committee. The Advisory Committee has visited almost all the countries under review during the first cycle of monitoring, and this practice has since continued, with systematic visits not only to capitals but also to those regions of State Parties where minorities reside compactly. During these visits, the Advisory Committee has extensive contacts with both governmental and non-governmental interlocutors, which enables the Committee to collect comprehensive information, with a view to preparing a quality Opinion on the State in question. Once the Opinion has been adopted in a plenary meeting of the Advisory Committee, it is submitted to the CM, which uses the Opinion as a basis for its conclusions and recommendations.

474. Aside from its standard-monitoring activities, the Advisory Committee has developed monitoring practices for specific situations falling outside the scope of its regular monitoring work. Following an agreement reached in 2005 between the United Nations Interim Administration Mission in Kosovo (UNMIK) and the CoE, the Advisory Committee has adopted three specific Opinions on the implementation of the Framework Convention in UNMIK-governed Kosovo,[478] after which the CM issued its corresponding Resolutions. In March 2014, at the request of the Ukrainian authorities, the CM instructed the Advisory Committee to review the situation of national minorities in Ukraine in an ad hoc monitoring procedure.

475. The Opinions of the Advisory Committee used to be made public at the same time as the conclusions and recommendations of the CM, together with any comments the Contracting Party may have submitted in respect of the opinion delivered by the Advisory Committee. However, the CM amended the procedure in 2009, when it adopted Resolution (2009)3, according to which the Advisory Committee's Opinion is published as a rule four months after having been submitted to the concerned State, jointly with the Government's comments but irrespective of whether the CM has adopted the respective Resolution or not. In addition, States may agree to make the Opinions of the Advisory Committee public at an even earlier date. In fact, such early publication has become increasingly common, and in 2006 certain Governments started the practice of publishing the Opinion immediately upon its receipt. These steps have helped to improve the transparency of the monitoring process, which is a principle emphasized also in the Explanatory Report of the Framework Convention.

476. The Advisory Committee has observed that most of the countries concerned welcomed the Opinions of the Advisory Committee and provided constructive comments on them, in many cases indicating that the Opinion has already prompted increased action to address specific shortcomings in the implementation of the Framework Convention. The Opinions appear to have stimulated fresh rounds of interdepartmental discussions within governments and in some cases they have prompted an immediate dialogue with national minorities on the issues raised. This is often facilitated by the fact that the Opinions, together with the Resolutions of the CM, are translated into the language(s) of the countries concerned.

477. In its resolutions on the implementation of the Framework Convention, the CM regularly echoes the more detailed findings of the Advisory Committee and urges the country concerned to 'continue the dialogue in progress' with the Advisory Committee and to keep the Advisory Committee informed of the measures taken in response to the conclusions and recommendations of the CM. A majority of States have continued this dialogue by organizing, in co-operation with the CoE, so-called follow-up seminars, bringing together governmental representatives, representatives from civil society, members of the Advisory Committee and other key actors, to discuss how to advance the implementation of the results of the monitoring of the Framework Convention.

478. The Advisory Committee's country-specific activities are complemented by its thematic work. The Committee's first thematic commentary, issued in March

---

478. Throughout this text, all reference to Kosovo, whether to the territory, institutions or population shall be understood in full compliance with United Nations Security Council Res. 1244 and without prejudice to the status of Kosovo.

2006, is devoted to education, focusing on such questions as how to find the right balance between the need to guarantee minority language education and the need to ensure that there is no unnecessary separation along ethnic lines within the educational system.[479] A second thematic commentary on the effective participation of persons belonging to national minorities in economic, social and cultural life and in public affairs[480] (Article 15 of the Framework Convention) was adopted in February 2008, followed by the third thematic commentary on the language rights of persons belonging to national minorities under the Framework Convention in May 2012.[481] The fourth thematic commentary, adopted in May 2016, is entitled 'The Framework Convention: A Key to Managing Diversity Through Minority Rights' and deals with the scope of application of the Framework Convention.[482] All commentaries are the result of extensive consultations, including with experts working in other related bodies as well as minority representatives and civil society, and a number of follow-up measures have been taken to engage governmental and other interlocutors in further dialogue on these issues.

III. The Effect of the Framework Convention

479. There are a number of practical examples showing that the Framework Convention's monitoring mechanism is having a concrete impact on Europe's minority protection. The mechanism has, in many cases, improved dialogue between governmental agencies and national minorities and stimulated new good practices. It has also prompted the adoption of new laws devoted to the protection of national minorities and encouraged States to improve their legislation and policies in such fields as language and non-discrimination. It is also noteworthy that the Framework Convention and the Opinions of the Advisory Committee, as well as its thematic commentaries, are today a central reference in the work of other international bodies, including the OSCE-HCNM (High Commissioner on National Minorities) and the European Commission, which often relies on the Framework Convention, notably when it examines the implementation of the Copenhagen criteria related to the protection of national minorities in candidate countries.

480. The work of the monitoring bodies under the Framework Convention is completed by a range of CoE co-operation and assistance activities, aimed at facilitating the ratification and/or implementation of the Framework Convention. For

479. Commentary No. 1 on Education under the Framework Convention for the Protection of National Minorities, 2 Mar. 2006, ACFC/25DOC(2006)002.
480. Commentary No. 2 on the Effective Participation of Persons belonging to National Minorities in Cultural, Social and Economic Life and in Public Affairs, 27 Feb. 2008, ACFC/31DOC(2008)001.
481. Commentary No. 3 on the language rights of persons belonging to national minorities under the Framework Convention, 24 May 2012, ACFC/44DOC(2012)001.
482. Commentary No. 4 on the scope of application of the Framework Convention for the Protection of National Minorities, 27 May 2016, ACFC/56DOC(2016)001.

example, the Secretariat of the Framework Convention provides legislative assistance to authorities, including detailed expertise on draft laws pertaining to national minorities and it has assisted bilateral commissions with the examination of minority's situation in the respective States.

§4. The European Charter for Regional or Minority Languages

481. The European Charter for Regional or Minority Languages was opened for signature in November 1992 and it entered into force in March 1998. It has been ratified so far by Armenia, Austria, Bosnia and Herzegovina, Croatia, Czech Republic, Cyprus, Denmark, Finland, Germany, Hungary, Liechtenstein, Luxembourg, Montenegro, the Netherlands, Norway, Poland, Romania, Serbia, Slovakia, Slovenia, Spain, Sweden, Switzerland, Ukraine and the UK. It has also been signed by eight other States.[483]

I. Content of the Charter

482. The purpose of the Charter is to protect and promote the various regional and minority languages spoken in the different countries of Europe. The Charter provides for a definition of the languages covered by this treaty (Article 1): these are the languages which have been traditionally used within a given territory of a State by nationals of that State who form a group numerically smaller than the rest of the State's population and which are different from the official language(s) of that State. The definition explicitly excludes the languages of migrants and the dialects of the official language(s) of the State. The protection of regional and minority languages must respect the territorial integrity and traditions of each State without interfering with the development of the official language(s) of that State.

483. Part II of the Charter lays down the main principles and objectives upon which States must base their policies, legislation and practice. These principles and objectives are regarded as providing the necessary framework for the preservation of the languages concerned, and they include, *inter alia*, the recognition of the regional and minority language as an expression of cultural wealth, the respect for the geographical area in which each language is spoken, the facilitation and/or encouragement of the use of regional or minority languages, in speech and writing, in public and private life, and the teaching and study of these languages at all the appropriate stages. In addition, States are required to eliminate discrimination in respect of the use of regional or minority languages. Although the Charter is principally concerned with languages which are historically identified with a particular territory of the State, it was considered necessary to grant 'non-territorial languages' protection as far as possible, and they are therefore subject to the protection under Part II of the Charter.

483. Azerbaijan, France, Iceland, Italy, Malta, Moldova, Russian Federation and 'the former Yugoslav Republic of Macedonia'.

484. Part III contains more specific provisions for the languages identified by the States at the time of ratification. The undertakings entered into by the States under Part III require concrete positive measures for the protection and promotion of regional and minority languages, including in the following fields: education, justice, dealings with the administrative authorities and public services, media, cultural activities and facilities, economic and social life and transfrontier co-operation.

II. The Charter's Monitoring System: The Committee of Experts

485. According to the Charter's system of monitoring, each Party is required to present, every five years,[484] a report on the measures taken in order to fulfil obligations. After a first examination of the State report, the Committee of Experts, established under the Charter, may decide to visit the relevant State in order to meet with representatives of the users of the various regional or minority languages and to consult with the authorities on the contents of the information that the Committee has received. In the context of the fact-finding process, the Committee can be approached by bodies or associations legally established in the respective State Party wishing to supply additional information or to give their views on specific situations relating to the implementation of the Charter.

486. After this process of information gathering, the Committee adopts a report which is then sent to the CM of the CoE together with proposals for the recommendations to be addressed by the CM to the State concerned. Additionally, the Secretary General of the CoE is required to report every two years to the Parliamentary Assembly on the implementation of the Charter.

487. The Charter being a rather complex instrument for States to ratify, information seminars are regularly organized by the Secretariat in those States which are approaching ratification.

§5. European Commission Against Racism and Intolerance

488. The ECRI is the CoE's independent monitoring body devoted to combating racism, xenophobia, anti-Semitism and intolerance. ECRI develops standards in the fight against racism and racial discrimination, notably in the framework of its country monitoring reports and of its General Policy Recommendations. Although its mandate extends beyond national minorities, ECRI deals frequently with racism and intolerance affecting persons belonging to national minorities and makes recommendations to address shortcomings this area.

---

484. On 28 Nov. 2018, the CM decided to extend the reporting period from three to five years with effect from 1 Jul. 2019 and to align the due dates for state reports with those for the Framework Convention. *See* CM/Del/Dec(2018)1330/10.4e.

§6. Work Related to Roma and Travellers

489. The CoE has created certain structures to work on particularly important minority questions. For example, as regards Roma questions, the monitoring work of the Advisory Committee, ECRI and others is complemented by the activities of the Committee of Experts on Roma and Travellers, composed of representatives of some forty Member States. It has the mandate to study, analyse and evaluate the implementation of governmental policies and practices on Roma and Travellers. One of the priorities of the Committee is the monitoring and evaluation of national strategies on Roma, many of which were instigated by the CoE. The Committee has also initiated a number of CM recommendations on Roma issues. Its work is supplemented by various specific projects, such as 'JUSTROM – Access to Justice of Roma and Traveller Women', 'ROMACT – Strengthening the Capacity of Local and Regional Authorities', and 'INSCHOOL – Inclusive Schools: Making a Difference for Roma Children'.

490. The CoE has also promoted the European Roma and Travellers Forum, set up in 2004 at the initiative of the President of Finland. It is an independent international association, which works in partnership with the CoE. In April 2018, the European Roma Institute for Arts and Culture, a joint initiative of the CoE and the Open Society Foundation, was inaugurated in Berlin, Germany.

§7. The Venice Commission

491. The European Commission for Democracy through Law (the Venice Commission) provides Member States of the CoE with assistance in the adoption of constitutions and related legislation. It has, on a number of occasions, carried out activities in the field of minority protection. Prior to the adoption of the Framework Convention, the Commission made proposals for new European legal standards in this area, and, since then, it has adopted opinions on the conformity with European standards of several draft pieces of legislation relating to the rights of persons belonging to national minorities. Several important reports and studies have been prepared, such as the report on the 'Preferential treatment of national minorities by their kin-State' (2001), the study on the topic 'non-citizens and minority rights' (2004), and the Report on Dual Voting for Persons belonging to National Minorities (2008).

§8. The Parliamentary Assembly

492. The Parliamentary Assembly has repeatedly promoted additional standard-setting and improved monitoring to strengthen minority rights in Europe. The Parliamentary Assembly's Recommendation 1201(1993) on an additional protocol on the rights of national minorities to the ECHR is probably its most well-known text concerning minorities, but there are also a number of more recent Assembly recommendations in this domain, including Recommendation 2040 (2014) on the situation and rights of national minorities in Europe and Recommendation 2118 (2018) on the protection and promotion of regional or minority languages in Europe. The Assembly frequently promotes the ratification and implementation of the Framework Convention for the Protection of National Minorities and of the European Charter on Regional or Minority Languages, and questions of national minorities are also addressed in the Assembly's own monitoring work.

§9. The Congress of Local and Regional Authorities of Europe

493. The Congress deals frequently with issues pertaining to minority protection It has, for example, adopted Recommendation 410 (2017) on regional and minority languages in Europe today and taken a number of other initiatives, often stressing that the principle of subsidiarity can contribute to the protection of national minorities and highlighting the role of local and regional authorities in advancing minority rights.

494. For a more extensive bibliography than the selected bibliography, please visit the web site of the Secretariat of the Framework Convention at: www.coe.int/minorities.

Chapter 2. Cultural Co-operation

Rüdiger Dossow

§1. Introduction

495. Reaffirming their devotion to the spiritual and moral values which are the common heritage of their people and the true source of individual freedom, political liberty and the rule of law, principles which form the basis of all genuine democracy:[485] when the founders of the CoE formulated this principle as one of the fundamental reasons for the creation of the CoE in 1949, Europe was still far from recognizing and living common spiritual and moral values or, in the language of today, a shared European culture. Europe had just been liberated from the culture of Nazism in Germany and occupied and collaborating countries – a culture which included the burning of books, the removal of 'degenerated' art from museums and the persecution of artists and indeed many others on racist and political grounds, as well as from fascist culture in Italy which ranged from Mussolini's personality cult to architecture. At the same time, Stalinist culture was able to spread to new countries that became part of the so-called East Block, as symbolized for example by the gigantism of buildings, squares, streets and monuments dedicated to Stalin in Warsaw, Berlin, Prague, Bucharest and Sofia. Official propaganda culture existed besides exiled and underground culture, hence making culture a reflection of the political system.[486]

496. Some forty years after the start of European integration through the CoE, the Berlin Wall had come down and all formerly communist countries, with the exception of Belarus, were able to join the CoE. A vast transition towards genuine democracy in Europe was assisted by the CoE since the early 1990s. However, Europe also witnessed warfare, including ethnic and thus cultural warfare, in former Yugoslavia and the Caucasus, hence showing that the same spiritual and moral values were not yet shared all over Europe, whereas such terrible concepts as 'ethnic cleansing' were still pursued by a few regional leaders. Today, European society often struggles with its greater cultural diversity caused by globalization, migration and media. Several hundred young Europeans decided to become jihadist mercenaries in a religiously framed and horrendously brutal war in Syria and neighbouring countries, thus increasing also the number of terrorist attacks in Europe. Therefore, culture and education have been and are a major backbone of CoE action 'to achieve a greater unity between its members for the purpose of safeguarding and realizing the ideals and principles which are their common heritage'.[487] This role is stipulated, for instance, in the Treaty on the Functioning of the EU, which provides

485. Statute of the Council of Europe.
486. *See* for instance the twenty-third Council of Europe Art Exhibition 'Art and Power, Europe under the Dictators 1930–45' (London, Berlin, Barcelona, 1996).
487. Citation from the definition of the aim of the Council of Europe under Art. 1 of its Statute.

that the EU and its Member States shall foster co-operation with the CoE in the sphere of culture (Article 167(3)) as well as in the field of education and sport (Article 165(3)).

§2. Historic Achievements in the Field of Culture

497. The ECHR is not only the most important CoE achievement, but also the first legal treaty dealing with fundamental cultural rights. Article 9 of the Convention guarantees the right of everyone to freedom of thought, conscience and religion.[488] Under Article 2 of its Protocol of 1952,[489] Member States committed themselves to guarantee the right of everyone to education. At UN level, such a right was only later included in Article 13 of the International Covenant on Economic, Social and Cultural Rights of 1976.

498. Two years after the right to education had been recognized by the ECHR, the European Cultural Convention[490] was opened for signature by the CM, enabling signatory states 'to pursue a policy of common action designed to safeguard and encourage the development of European culture'. For this purpose, also non-Member States in Europe were invited to accede to this Convention.[491]

499. Following from the right to education, the European Convention on the Equivalence of Diplomas Leading to Admission to Universities[492] was opened for signature in 1953. In 1956, the European Convention on the Equivalence of Periods of University Study[493] was opened for signature, thus completing the European recognition of secondary and higher education together with the European Convention on the Academic Recognition of University Qualifications[494] of 1959, the European Convention on the General Equivalence of Periods of University Study[495] of 1990 and the Convention on the Recognition of Qualifications concerning Higher Education in the European Region[496] of 1997. The latter 1997 Convention provides the current legal foundation for student exchange programmes, such as those funded by the EU under the Erasmus Programme. The European Agreement on Continued Payment of Scholarships to Students Studying Abroad[497] of 1969 enabled many students to benefit from the mutual recognition of university studies abroad achieved by the other conventions.

488. European Treaty Series No. 5, 4 Nov. 1950.
489. European Treaty Series No. 9, 20 Mar. 1952.
490. European Treaty Series No. 18, 19 Dec. 1954.
491. The former Socialist Federal Republic of Yugoslavia became party to the Cultural Convention in 1987. Belarus is party since 1993 and Kazakhstan since 2010.
492. European Treaty Series No. 15, 11 Dec. 1953.
493. European Treaty Series No. 21, 15 Dec. 1956.
494. European Treaty Series No. 32, 14 Dec. 1959.
495. European Treaty Series No. 138, 6 Nov. 1990.
496. European Treaty Series No. 165, 11 Apr. 1997.
497. European Treaty Series No. 69, 12 Dec. 1969.

500. Cultural policies put special emphasis on young people both in formal education at school and institutions of higher education as well as in informal education, for instance by facilitating international contacts. The CoE responded to this challenge through the European Agreement on Travel by Young Persons on Collective Passports[498] of 1961 and the creation of the European Youth Foundation and Centre in 1972. More than 300,000 young people, aged between fifteen and thirty years and mostly from Member States, have benefited directly from activities supported by the European Youth Foundation since its creation.

501. The CoE specifically protects the cultural rights of language minorities through the European Charter for Regional or Minority Languages[499] of 1992 and the Framework Convention for the Protection of National Minorities[500] of 1995.

502. Media, which are an essential part of culture, developed rapidly in the second half of the twentieth century. The CoE Member States recognized this importance not only under Article 10 of the ECHR, but drafted the European Agreement concerning Programme Exchanges by means of Television Films[501] of 1958, the European Agreement on the Protection of Television Broadcasts[502] of 1960 and the European Agreement for the Prevention of Broadcasts Transmitted from Stations outside National Territories[503] of 1964. In 1989, the European Convention on Transfrontier Television[504] was opened for signature to Member States as the first European legal framework for the transmission and retransmission of television programme services.

503. One year earlier, the CoE Fund for the Co-production, Distribution and Exhibition of European Cinematographic Works (Eurimages) was set up in order to provide financial support for the European film industry. Co-productions were also supported through the European Convention on Cinematographic Co-Production[505] of 1992. In the same year, the European Audiovisual Observatory was created, which provides information about film and broadcasting to European policy-makers and the media.

504. Early achievements of the CoE also concern cultural heritage. In 1969, the CM opened for signature the European Convention on the Protection of the Archaeological Heritage and, in 1985, the Convention for the Protection of the

498. European Treaty Series No. 37, 16 Dec. 1961.
499. European Treaty Series No. 148, 5 Nov. 1992.
500. European Treaty Series No. 157, 1 Feb. 1995.
501. European Treaty Series No. 27, 15 Dec. 1958.
502. European Treaty Series No. 34, 22 Jun. 1960.
503. European Treaty Series No. 53, 22 Jan. 1967.
504. European Treaty Series No. 132, 5 May 1989.
505. European Treaty Series No. 147, 2 Oct. 1992.

Architectural Heritage of Europe.[506] The European audiovisual heritage was protected through the European Convention for the Protection of the Audiovisual Heritage [507] of 2001. On the occasion of the meeting of the European Ministers for Culture in Faro, Portugal, in 2005, the CoE Framework Convention on the Value of Cultural Heritage for Society [508] was opened for signature. In Nicosia, Cyprus on 19 May 2017, the CoE Convention on Offences Relating to Cultural Property[509] was opened for signature, which criminalizes the illicit trafficking and destruction of cultural property. It had been initiated because of terrorist attacks on cultural monuments in northern Africa and related plundering and trafficking of cultural objects.

505. Through internal restructuring of the CoE secretariat, environment protection has become part of the protection of the natural heritage and thus part of the Directorate General of Democracy which is dealing with culture in the broad sense. The milestone set by the CoE in this field is the Bern Convention on the Conservation of European Wildlife and Natural Habitats[510] of 1979, which brings together not only Member States, but was signed by the EU and the non-European states Burkina Faso, Morocco, Senegal and Tunisia.

506. Finally, the CoE was the first to develop legal standards concerning sport through its European Convention on Spectator Violence and Misbehaviour at Sports Events and in particular at Football Matches of 1985, which was updated in 2016 through the CoE Convention on an Integrated Safety, Security and Service Approach at Football Matches and Other Sports Events.[511] The CoE Anti-Doping Convention[512] of 1989 is the only standard in public international law and hence goes beyond the non-governmental World Anti-doping Code of the World Anti-doping Agency (WADA). Under Resolution 2011/C 372/02 by the Council of the EU and the Representatives of the Governments of the EU Member States of 20 December 2011, therefore, the 'coordination of European continent positions prior to WADA meetings takes place within the Council of Europe with due regard for any applicable EU legislation'. In 2007, the CoE established the Enlarged Partial Agreement on Sport (EPAS), which serves as a platform for intergovernmental sports co-operation and dialogue with sports federations and NGOs. Reacting to a growing threat by organized crime in sports, the Convention on the Manipulation of Sports Competitions (CETS No. 215) was opened for signature in 2014.

§3. CoE Bodies Dealing with Culture

507. Similar to the working structure of the CoE in other areas, cultural co-operation in a wide sense is mainly dealt with by the CM and its subordinate

506. European Treaty Series No. 66, 6 May 1969; European Treaty Series No. 121, 3 Oct. 1985.
507. European Treaty Series No. 183, 11 Aug. 2001.
508. European Treaty Series No. 199, 27 Oct. 2005.
509. Council of Europe Treaty Series No. 221, 19 May 2017.
510. European Treaty Series No. 104, 19 Sep. 1979.
511. European Treaty Series No. 120, 19 Aug. 1985.
512. European Treaty Series No. 135, 16 Nov. 1989.

Steering Committees as well as the Parliamentary Assembly and its Committee on Culture, Science Education and Media. The latter committee awards annually since 1977 the CoE Museum Prize, rewarding museums which have made a significant contribution to the understanding of European cultural heritage. In addition, the CoE serves meetings of specialized ministers, such as the Standing Conference of European Ministers of Education, the European ministers of culture, the European ministers responsible for sport, the European ministers responsible for media and the European ministers responsible for regional planning. Finally, specific partial agreements dealing with culture in a wide sense were set up for North-South co-operation (European Centre for Global Interdependence and Solidarity, Lisbon) in 1989, for the promotion of modern languages (ECML, Graz) in 1994, for the support of the co-production, distribution and exhibition of European cinematographic works (Eurimages, Strasbourg) in 1989, for gathering and distributing information about the audiovisual industry in Europe (European Audiovisual Observatory, Strasbourg) in 1992, for promoting youth mobility (Partial Agreement on the Youth Card for the Purpose of Promoting and Facilitating Youth Mobility in Europe, Strasbourg) in 1991, for mutual assistance concerning natural and technological disasters (European and Mediterranean Major Hazards Agreement, Strasbourg) in 1987 as well as the EPAS in 2007.

508. Each of these bodies adopts decisions, policy recommendations and action plans that have an impact on national or regional cultural, educational, sports and media policies in Europe. European co-operation in the field of 'culture' under the umbrella of the CoE, therefore, means a multilateral discussion and coordination of common policies on the basis of common European values. National ministries, national parliaments and local or regional authorities maintain their competencies and powers while co-operating with each other across national borders in Europe or even beyond. This approach has not been replaced by the geographical enlargement and further legal integration of the EU, because Member States of the EU have not and will probably not transfer their legislative powers to the EU in the field of culture.[513] Cultural diversity in Europe, although based on common values, lends itself to co-operation and subsidiarity rather than centralized decision-making.

§4. Major Legal Standards in the Cultural Field

509. Through its specific conventions and recommendations, the CoE developed common standards in several sectors which determine the practice in Member States. In particular, this applies to the international recognition of studies and degrees, minority languages, the protection of cultural heritage, fair play in sport and broadcasting.

510. As mentioned before, the mutual recognition of school and university diplomas has been a field of excellence of the CoE for some sixty years. Today, the Convention on the Recognition of Qualifications concerning Higher Education in

513. *See* Arts 165 and 167 of the Treaty on the Functioning of the European Union.

the European Region[514] of 1997 serves as the leading legal instrument for Europe since its entry into force on 1 February 1999. It was drawn up by the CoE together with United Nations Educational, Scientific and Cultural Organization (UNESCO) in order to streamline the legal framework at European level and to replace the earlier six conventions adopted in this field by the CoE and UNESCO. The Convention is open for signature by the Member States of the CoE, the Member States of the UNESCO Europe Region, and any other contracting state or party to the European Cultural Convention of the CoE or to the UNESCO Convention on the Recognition of Studies, Diplomas and Degrees concerning Higher Education in the States belonging to the Europe Region, which were invited to the Diplomatic Conference entrusted with the adoption of this Convention, in Lisbon, on 11 April 1997.

511. Two bodies oversee, promote and facilitate the implementation of the Convention: the Committee of the Convention and the European Network of National Information Centres on Academic Mobility and Recognition. The Convention defines the common standards for the recognition of qualifications giving access to higher education, the recognition of periods of study, the recognition of higher education qualifications as well as the recognition of qualifications held by refugees, displaced persons and persons in a refugee-like situation. It also addresses the assessment of higher education institutions and programmes.

512. Besides the Framework Convention for the Protection of National Minorities[515] of 1995, which is dealt with in detail in Part V, Chapter 1 above, minority languages are protected through the European Charter for Regional or Minority Languages[516] of 1992. This Convention aims to protect and promote the historical regional or minority languages of Europe. It was adopted in order to maintain and develop Europe's cultural traditions and heritage as well as to respect an inalienable and commonly recognized right to use a regional or minority language in private and public life. For this purpose, it enunciates objectives and principles which all signatory parties must apply to the regional or minority languages spoken within their territory, in particular the respect for the geographical area of each language and the facilitation and encouragement of the use of such languages in public and private life, for instance through teaching and transnational exchanges with other states where such languages are used in identical or similar form. Furthermore, the Charter sets out a number of specific measures to promote the use of regional or minority languages in public life in education, justice, administration and public services, media, cultural activities and facilities, and economic and social activities – also across national borders. Enforcement of the Charter is under the control of a committee of experts which periodically examines reports presented by the signatory parties.

---

514. European Treaty Series No. 165, 11 Apr. 1997. This convention has also been signed by the non-Member States Australia, Belarus, Canada, Holy *See*, Israel, Kazakhstan, Kyrghyz Republic, New Zealand, Tajikistan and United States of America.
515. European Treaty Series No. 157, 1 Feb. 1995.
516. European Treaty Series No. 148, 5 Nov. 1992.

513. In the area of cultural heritage, the CoE Framework Convention on the Value of Cultural Heritage for Society[517] of 2005 is the latest of a series of legal treaties opened for signature by the CoE. This Framework Convention reflects a shift from the question 'How and by what procedure can we preserve the heritage?' to the question 'Why should we enhance its value, and for whom?' It is based on the idea that knowledge and the use of heritage form part of everybody's human right to participate in cultural life. It presents heritage as a resource for human development, the enhancement of cultural diversity and the promotion of intercultural dialogue. Cultural heritage is seen as part of an economic development model based on the principle of sustainability. In this sense, the Convention stipulates policy recommendations in a legal treaty, thus giving these recommendations a secure framework. The CM, pursuant to Article 17 of the Statute of the CoE, shall nominate an appropriate committee or specify an existing committee to monitor the application of the Convention, which will be authorized to make rules for the conduct of its business. It will enter into force once ten parties have acceded to the Convention.

514. Since its entry into force on 1 May 1993, the European Convention on Transfrontier Television[518] creates a legal framework for the free circulation of transfrontier television programmes in Europe through minimum common rules in fields such as programming, advertising, sponsorship and the protection of certain individual rights. It entrusts the contracting states with the task of ensuring that television programme services transmitted comply with its provisions. In return, freedom of reception of programme services is guaranteed as well as the retransmission of the programme services which comply with the minimum rules of the Convention. The Convention applies to all transfrontier programmes regardless of the technical means of transmission used including satellite, cable, terrestrial transmitters, et al. All signatory states recognize under this Convention freedom of expression, reception, and retransmission, the right of reply, the prohibition of pornography, violence and incitement to racial hatred, youth protection and the screening of European works and cinema films.

515. The Convention also sets common advertising standards, in particular the prohibition of advertising for tobacco, medicines and medical treatments available only on prescription as well as restrictions on the advertising of alcoholic beverages. It stipulates the permissible advertising time, which is normally not more than 15% of the daily transmission time and not more than 20% of any one-hour period, and advertising breaks, for example twice during a ninety-minute feature film, none during a news or current affairs programme lasting less than thirty minutes. Finally, it regulates programme sponsorship. This normative framework has been aligned with the EU Directive on Television without Frontiers and needs further revision in accordance with the EU Directive on Audiovisual Media Services.

517. European Treaty Series No. 199, 27 Oct. 2005.
518. European Treaty Series No. 132, 5 May 1989.

516. On 9 July 2014, the CoE adopted its Convention on the Manipulation of Sports Competitions, which has the objective to prevent, detect, punish and discipline the manipulation of sports competitions. It also strives to enhance the exchange of information between public authorities and to provide a normative framework for co-operation with sports organizations and sports betting operators.

§5. Conclusion

517. Cultural standards in a wide sense can be put into legal norms, although their enforcement will always require a margin of appreciation by the contracting states. This is, however, not a weakness of international treaties dealing with cultural matters, but rather their strength. This factor will allow contracting states to take account of their historic situation and other circumstances and respond to national or regional requirements. Therefore, the CoE provides added value in serving as a platform for European states, often including neighbouring states, interested in co-operating on the basis of common shared values.

518. This wider dimension in multilateral co-operation will become more and more relevant for Europe through globalization, migration and mobility of persons. Intercultural dialogue, cultural responses to overcoming conflicts and the impact of cultural values on state legislation are just a few examples of the current priority areas of activity of the CoE. In essence, human rights and democracy are concepts which can only be acquired through education and culture. Most of the CoE's work dwells on multilateral exchanges and concrete action programmes, thus leading to recommendations and other policy guidelines by the appropriate bodies under the umbrella of the CoE referred to above. Several legal standards have been set for Europe and beyond, and this standard-setting is an ever ongoing process which reflects the cultural progress and challenges European societies are facing.

Chapter 3. Achieving Social Cohesion Through the Protection of Vulnerable Groups: The Example of Children

Elda Moreno, updated by Maren Lambrecht-Feigl

519. 'When we speak of social cohesion, we are not just speaking about the technicalities of social security systems, of social policy or employment programmes. […] Social cohesion is also built on equal rights and equal opportunities; on a life without discrimination; on shared social responsibilities; on social dialogue, democratic decision-making and full participation for all: the weak and the strong, young and old, rich and poor. Promoting social cohesion in this wide sense is the approach to which the CoE and its Member States have committed themselves in the "New Strategy for Social Cohesion" adopted in 2010. This approach is the leitmotif of all our activities and instruments within the Council of Europe.' Gabriella Battaini-Dragoni, Deputy Secretary General of the CoE in her address to the second CoE Conference of Ministers responsible for Social Cohesion in Istanbul on 12 September 2012.

520. The importance of social cohesion is explained by the term itself. It describes a society which is pulling together, not falling apart. Social cohesion in Europe is based on the European social model, which balances economic growth and social justice. The CoE defines social cohesion as the capacity of a society to ensure the well-being for all its members, minimizing disparities. It also accentuates the importance of 'social actors' joint responsibility for its attainment. Our primary task is thus improving the quality of life in Europe through the genuine enjoyment of fundamental human rights and the respect of human dignity. This is fulfilled in particular through the promotion of European standards in the social and health fields, the support of ethnic and cultural diversity, and the exchange of good practice in the area of social policies. Most recently, national action contributing to more social cohesion has been overseen by the European Social Cohesion Platform, which promotes the European Social Charter.

521. Through its action, the CoE also seeks to develop multidisciplinary and innovative policies and to give practical support to policy-makers, professionals and field workers across Europe. The combination of all CoE tools (standard-setting, monitoring, policy development, awareness-raising and technical assistance to individual countries) is a must when it comes to addressing issues related to specific vulnerable groups such as children, people with disabilities, national minorities, migrants or people living in extreme poverty. The transversal Programme 'Building a Europe for and with children' is a perfect illustration of how human rights, education, youth, culture and social policies can combine in a transversal manner to effectively protect a vulnerable group. It also illustrates the joint responsibility and the importance of the combined effort of all stakeholders.

§1. 'Building a Europe for and with Children'

I. The Mission and the Vision

522. Since January 2006, the programme 'Building a Europe for and with children' is being implemented further to the Third Summit of Heads of State and Government of the CoE (Warsaw, May 2005). It is a response to both the mandate assigned to the organization to guarantee an integrated approach to promoting children's rights and the decision to launch an action programme covering the social, legal, and educational as well as the health dimensions of the various forms of violence against children. After the initial Strategy (2006–2009), the programme has subsequently been following the Stockholm Strategy (2009–2011), the Monaco Strategy (2011–2015) and, most lately, the current Sofia Strategy (2016–2021). It is being followed up by the Ad hoc Committee for the Rights of the Child (CAHENF) which focuses, in its work programme, on topical child-related issues: children in vulnerable situations (such as migration), responses to violence against children, child participation, equal opportunities for all children and children's rights in the digital environment.

523. The objective of the programme 'Building a Europe for and with children' has always been to help decision-makers and other parties concerned to design and implement national strategies for the protection of children's rights and the prevention of violence against children. Most of the activities within the programme concern all Member States. Country-specific projects are developed to analyse and assess practices, to launch pilot projects, to provide technical assistance and to evaluate the impact of the programme in a specific country.

II. Promoting Children's Rights

524. The Member States of the CoE have entered into numerous commitments to children's rights under universal and regional legal instruments. The CoE has an exceptionally broad base of *standard-setting texts* whose purpose is to promote and protect children's rights, including protection from all forms of violence. The most important of these are *conventions*, some of which establish monitoring mechanisms which strongly influence the development of standards.

525. Conventions that allow individuals and/or legal entities to lodge complaints are of particular interest. The *ECHR* has established the ECtHR. Individuals (including children) or legal entities which are victims of a violation of the rights and guarantees set out in the Convention may lodge applications with the Court. The violation must have been committed by one of the forty-seven states bound by the Convention. The case law of the ECtHR relates to individual cases, but gives an indication of the interpretation of standards set by the Convention and the remedies needed to avoid future violations.

526. The *European Social Charter* guarantees social and economic human rights. The ECSR is the body responsible for monitoring compliance of states parties to the European Social Charter. Under a protocol, which came into force in 1998, 'collective complaints' of violations of the Charter may be lodged with the ECSR. Certain organizations are entitled to lodge complaints with the committee, such as NGOs enjoying participatory status with the CoE.

527. The CoE conventions of particular relevance for children's rights are: the Convention on the protection of children against sexual exploitation and sexual abuse of 2007, the so-called Lanzarote Convention (2007), the Convention on Action against trafficking in human beings (2005), the Convention on contact concerning children (2003), the Convention on Cybercrime (2001), the Convention on the exercise of children's rights (1996), the Convention on the adoption of children (revised) as well as, more lately, the Convention on preventing and combating violence against women and domestic violence (2011).

528. The Organization's two statutory bodies, the CM and the Parliamentary Assembly, have also adopted an impressive list of *recommendations* and *resolutions* on children's rights. Over recent years, the Congress of Local and Regional Authorities has continued to focus on topical issues of relevance for children at the local level, including child sexual abuse, violence in the urban environment, children in migration and, as a continuous issue, young people's participation. Although resolutions and recommendations are non-binding legal texts, they serve as significant guidelines for policy development in the Member States.

529. The impressive amount of standards is certainly the result of the importance attached to the subject. It is, however, clear that each new legal instrument represents a considerable burden for States who have to adapt their legislative, institutional and policy frameworks. For instance, to comply with the child-related provisions in the Convention on action against trafficking in human beings, countries may have to introduce changes not only in their criminal, civil and administrative codes but also in their training, education, health and social assistance and immigration policies. The setting-up of an integrated national strategy for the protection of children's rights would very much facilitate this constant 'upgrading process'. Like the UN Committee on the Rights of the Child, the CoE promotes the setting-up of such strategies at national level and wishes to help countries to define their own strategies, based upon three pillars: (1) a coherent and comprehensive legal framework; (2) an effective institutional framework; and (3) an operational policy negotiation and implementation framework involving all stakeholders.

530. The programme 'Building a Europe for and with children' endeavours to help states to honour their commitments by assisting them in devising integrated children's policies and legal frameworks, establishing the requisite institutions and structures, developing networks and producing tools and working methods, as well as resources for informing, training and raising the awareness of the general public and the players directly concerned. Special attention is paid to the consultation and participation of children and their access to information.

III. Protecting Children Against All Forms of Violence – A Long-Standing Priority

531. Violence against children takes many forms. Some of these, such as trafficking or organized sexual exploitation and abuse receive extensive media coverage. Others are more insidious and less easily identifiable. Up to 80% of such crimes takes place under cover of places that should be havens for children, such as the school, the family or residential institutions, the so-called 'circle of trust', where they are all too often shrouded in secrecy. In many European countries, society tolerates and even silently approves of some recurrent forms of violence against children, in particular those inflicted in the family setting, sometimes called 'ordinary educational violence' (such as slapping children). Violence against children remains a human rights violation. Albeit to different degrees, violence can deprive children of their well-being and the ability to learn and socialize normally, and it can leave an indelible imprint on the way their adult lives are lived.

532. In spite of the many international and regional treaties that protect children's rights, violence against children remains widespread. It occurs in every country in Europe, irrespective of people's geographical origin or social stratum. For the CoE, no tradition, religion, belief, economic situation or 'educational' method can ever justify hitting, smacking, spanking, mutilating, abusing, humiliating, or any other practice that violates children's dignity. Europe must become a continent where practices such as corporal punishment (whether at home, at school or in institutions) no longer exist.

533. Through its standard-setting, promotion and co-operation activities, the CoE intends to assist states in implementing their obligations under the above-mentioned treaties in particular by developing integrated prevention policies, alerting professional circles and the general public to topical issues and providing them with the appropriate tools, by regularly referring to four well-known basic principles (the 'four Ps'): protection of children, prevention of violence, prosecution of criminals and participation by children. Follow-up has always been ensured at Pan-European level to the recommendations included in the UN Secretary General's study on violence against children. As a response to one of the Study's recommendations, the CoE adopted in 2009 the European Policy Guidelines for integrated national strategies on the protection of children from violence, a text which continues to inspire governments in Europe and beyond. In the framework of the upcoming mid-term evaluation of the Sofia Strategy (2016–2021), the CoE also evaluates the progress made by Member States in the area of responses to violence against children.

534. To reinforce the effectiveness of national strategies, the CoE has always campaigned against different forms of violence against children, with a particular focus on awareness-raising, education, training and capacity-building to promote a culture of non-violence and reach a zero level of tolerance. In pursuing these objectives, the CoE formulates instruments and methodologies suited to the different places where violence takes place (family, school, residential institutions, the community, media and cyberspace), paying attention to vulnerable children (such as children with disabilities, or migrant and Roma children).

535. Among recent CoE campaigns, the ONE in FIVE Campaign to stop sexual violence against children (2010–2015) deserves special attention. Aimed at raising general awareness of the fact that one child in five experiences sexual violence of some degree throughout her or his lifetime and at promoting the Convention on the protection of children against sexual exploitation and sexual abuse (Lanzarote Convention), the initiative had considerable success in changing legislation and policies. By 2018, all Member States had signed the Convention and forty-four had ratified, among others thanks to the strong messages sent out by the Campaign at European and national level and to the most useful tools it put at the disposal of national stakeholders (State and local authorities, NGOs, etc.). The Campaign also is an excellent example of a transversal initiative: next to intergovernmental bodies, both the Parliamentary Assembly and the Congress of Local and Regional Authorities took full ownership of the project and developed a broad range of activities addressed to their members and partners (www.coe.int/oneinfive).

536. A similar partnership approach is being followed in the current Parliamentary Campaign to End Immigration Detention of Children (since 2015). The campaign, which is part of the Global Campaign to End Immigration Detention of Children (launched during the 19th Session of the UN Human Rights Council in 2012), seeks to raise awareness of this issue in Europe and to encourage States to adopt alternatives to detention that fulfil the best interests of the child and allow children to remain with their family members and/or guardians in non-custodial, community-based contexts while their immigration status is being resolved.

§2. The Methodology

537. Transversal work, coordination, integrated approaches, co-operation and communication are the key words of the CoE's working methods in the area of children's rights. The programme 'Building a Europe for and with Children' has been designed to use the existing resources in the most efficient manner, establishing the necessary links between activities, using all available tools to address specific issues and establishing strategic partnerships with external actors.

I. Internal Co-operation

538. All CoE bodies, institutions and major administrative entities share the programme vision and are contributing to meet its objectives. This 'team work' at the organization level is inspired by a Task Force (in which all relevant secretariat services are represented) and a coordination unit for the Programme (within the Directorate General of Democracy and its Directorate of Anti-discrimination).

539. The CoE is the best-placed organization in Europe to properly address the issue of children's rights, as it can:

- Combine very relevant tools: Standards setting – Monitoring – Policy development – Co-operation and assistance programmes – Outreach (Education, training and communication).
- Easily mobilize four main actors (the four pillars): Governments, Parliamentarians, Local Authorities and Civil Society (NGOs, the business community and professional networks).

II. External Co-operation

540. At present there is an interesting momentum in the international arena generated by the strong commitment of governments and intergovernmental organizations to children's rights. The EU and other Organizations (such as the United Nations International Children's Emergency Fund (UNICEF), the United Nations Office of the High Commissioner for Human Rights (OHCHR) and the World Health Organization (WHO)) have set their agenda in this respect and there is an enormous potential for fruitful co-operation with these other players.

541. Over the past years, co-operation has been stepped up and consolidated in particular with the European Commission, the OCHCR (assisting the UN Committee on the Rights of the Child), UNICEF (which is working on child protection relating to many urgent and long-term issues), the European Network of Ombudsmen for Children, and major NGOs such as Save the Children or Eurochild.

542. Of special interest is the role that the CoE is playing in support of the UN Secretary General Special Representative on Violence against Children. The CoE played a leading role in the preparatory process for the UN Study on Violence against Children published in 2006, based on which the CoE later prepared its Policy guidelines on integrated national strategies for the protection of children from violence to support the implementation of the UN study's recommendations as far as the European region is concerned.

543. The programme 'Building a Europe for and with Children' also regularly calls for the development of partnerships with other stakeholders: children, parents, private companies, professional networks and the media.

§3. The Action

I. Standard-Setting

544. The most important asset of the CoE is probably its capacity to set widely accepted standards. Among the various legal texts concerning children prepared over recent years, we could notably highlight:

– a convention on the protection of children against sexual exploitation and abuse;
– a recommendation to respect, protect and fulfil the rights of the child in the digital environment;
– a recommendation on the participation of children and young people under the age of 18;
– a recommendation on children's rights and social services friendly to children and families;
– further standards, in the format of policy guidelines, on child-friendly justice and child-friendly health care;
– a recommendation on positive and non-violent parenting;
– a recommendation on empowering children in the new media environment and other standards for the protection of children in this context;
– a CoE Charter on Citizenship and Human Rights Education.

545. The Parliamentary Assembly also regularly adopts recommendations (to the CM), resolutions (to national governments) or opinions concerning children's rights. The following texts by the Assembly may be highlighted (non-exhaustive list):

– a resolution on the best interest of the child and the need to keep families together;
– a resolution on protecting children affected by armed conflicts;
– a recommendation on protecting children against over-sexualization;
– a resolution on protecting children against forced marriage;
– a recommendation on including children's rights into national constitutions;
– a resolution on ending child poverty;
– a recommendation on children's rights to physical integrity;
– a recommendation on combating 'child abuse images' through committed, transversal and internationally coordinated action;
– a recommendation on child abuse in institutions: ensuring full protection of the victims;
– a recommendation on children who witness domestic violence;
– a recommendation on the promotion of Internet and online media services appropriate for minors;
– a recommendation on the participation by children in decisions affecting them;
– a recommendation on child victims: stamping out all forms of violence, exploitation and abuse.

II. Monitoring

546. Monitoring compliance by Member States with human rights standards is of outmost importance. The CoE's statutory bodies (the CM and the Parliamentary Assembly) have established various monitoring systems (country-based, thematic or treaty-based). Of particular importance are the case law of the ECtHR and the decisions and conclusions adopted by the ECSR.

547. An independent institution, the CoE Commissioner for Human Rights greatly contributes to assessing the situation in the countries he visits. In his reports and activities, the Commissioner regularly highlights children's rights issues. Since 2018, this function is held by Ms Dunja Mijatović who has put issues related to children's rights very high up on her work agenda, in particular with regard to stateless children, the placement of some groups of children, including Roma and children with disabilities, in segregated educational settings and the human rights situation of migrant children, especially unaccompanied minor migrants.

548. Monitoring bodies are being encouraged to pay a particular attention to violence against children. The programme objective is to conduct a systematic review of decisions, reports and recommendations concerning children's rights. The online database 'Theseus' was precisely created to give further visibility to the Court case law concerning children.

III. Policy Development

549. The CoE has cumulated impressive expertise in the field of policy development. The bulk of the work is undertaken by Steering Committees which are composed of representatives of governments and observers from NGOs and other intergovernmental organizations. The Steering Committees are the architects of the CoE's sectoral policies. The Steering Committees in the fields of legal co-operation, human rights, culture, education and youth, as well as their subordinate committees and expert groups, address within their respective agenda many of the various topical children's rights issues, including access to education by Roma children, education for democratic citizenship, rights of children with disabilities, rights of children in institutions, integration of migrant children, participation of children (methodology, networks and tools), international reviews of national youth policies, analysis of legal and institutional frameworks at national and local levels, identification of best practices and elaboration of models of national strategies for the protection of children's rights, including for the prevention of violence, elaboration of a set of tools for decision-makers on citizenship and human rights education, and development of family policies in the best interest of the child. Since many years, the CoE regularly has set up specific bodies dedicated to children's rights; most recently, since 2016, the CAHENF, in charge of the implementation and follow-up of the current Strategy for the Rights of the Child (2016–2021).

IV. Technical Assistance and Targeted Co-operation

550. Upon request, the CoE co-operates with individual countries to support the review of their legislation, the design of policies and institutional frameworks or the training of professionals. Several co-operation projects are currently running, notably in countries of Eastern Europe.

V. Outreach (Communication, Education and Training)

551. Standards and policies need to be accompanied by communication, education and training strategies. Activities include:

- Continuous development of a website devoted to children's rights: www.coe.int /children.
- Development of a child-friendly website and online tools, such as the game 'Through the Wild Web Woods' now available in twenty-four languages, or a new tool coming up in 2019, called 'Online with the Websters', intended to increase children's awareness of Internet safety.
- Publication of handbooks: Internet literacy, violence in schools, democratic governance at school, and soon a handbook for the rights of the child in the digital environment (to be published in 2019).
- Production of manuals for trainers: on human rights education for and with children (Compasito), on gender-based violence, on violence in schools, etc.
- Publication of a children/youth-friendly version of legal instruments, including the UN Convention on the Right of the Child standards on the rights of children in institutions, the Charter on the participation of young people in local and regional life, etc.
- Communication campaigns on specific issues, such as sexual abuse, corporal punishment, violence in schools, violence in the media or children in the context of migration.
- Organization of events at national level, such as a high-level event for the mid-term evaluation of the current strategy in November 2019 (in Paris, France).

§4. The Impact

552. One of the CoE's weakest points is certainly the lack of resources to disseminate the results of its work and the absence of tools to assess the real impact of legal texts, monitoring reports, policies and campaigns. Implementation of standards still depends very much on individual governments' commitment and the role played by NGOs and the business sector. To foster social cohesion effectively, the real challenge remains to mobilize all actors, to pull all resources together and make them work in the interest of society as a whole.

553. The CoE has a vision of Europe based on freedom, social justice and respect for human dignity and human rights; its ambition is to help Member States translate this vision into reality. Building and consolidating social cohesion is neither simple, nor easy and it does not come for free. The stakes are huge and we are working under pressure – but after all – social cohesion, built on truly equal rights, equal opportunities and responsibilities and full participation in society, is a complex challenge and a long-term vision for our societies. It must start with our children to anchor fundamental values in them and help and allow them to shape peaceful societies in the future.

Appendix: Illustrating transversality
Objective: Eradication of corporal punishment of children in Council of Europe Member States (launched in 2008)

Stakeholders involved:

(1) *Internal*: Committee of Ministers, Parliamentary Assembly, Congress of local and regional authorities, INGOs Conference, Court of Human Rights, Commissioner for Human Rights, different Directorates General.
(2) *External*: UN Study against violence, UNICEF, OHCHR, WHO, NGOs, children, private companies, media, parents, professional networks.

Tools used:

(1) UN and Council of Europe *standards* condemn corporal punishment.
(2) *Monitoring* bodies confirm that corporal punishment should be banned.
(3) *Policies* are developed to eradicate and prevent corporal punishment, for instance through the drafting of guidelines on positive parenting and on education in the best interest of the child, education for and on children's rights.
(4) *Technical assistance* is offered to countries facing specific difficulties (to review legislation, build institutions, design policies, train professionals, etc.).
(5) *Education and training* programmes, pedagogical material and *targeted communication* are developed to accompany policy objectives and support implementation of standards.

Action:

(1) all Council of Europe actors were encouraged to produce results in their respective areas of expertise
(2) once the results were available, a thematic campaign against corporal punishment was launched. It not only reminded countries of their legal obligation to ban corporal punishment and protect children but also provided them with a package of measures helping them to address all dimensions of the problem.

Results:

In 2018, thirty-two Member States had fully prohibited corporal punishment of children through legislation, Supreme Court Ruling or public commitment, which left only fifteen countries that are not yet fully committed and need to step up action and awareness in this field. National authorities are pursuing their promotional activities in this field and regularly referring back to UN and Council of Europe standards (https://www.coe.int/en/web/children/corporal-punishment).

Conclusions

Chapter 1. The CoE's Place in Europe and the World

Jack Hanning, updated by Tanja E.J. Kleinsorge and serving staff in the External Relations Department

§1. An Overview of the External Relations of the CoE

554. When CoE Heads of State and Government met in Warsaw in May 2005 for the last CoE summit, they pledged both to continue building a united Europe based on common values and to ensure complementarity between the CoE and the other organizations involved in this process. They also said they were open to co-operation with Europe's neighbouring regions (i.e., the Southern Mediterranean, the Middle East and Central Asia) and the rest of the world.

555. This commitment to 'close co-operation and coordination in international action' is in marked contrast to the CoE's 1949 Statute which to all intents and purposes is silent on the Organization's external or international relations. The only reference to other international organizations is to be found in Article I(c) which stipulates that 'participation in the CoE shall not affect the collaboration of its Members in the work of the UN and of other international organizations to which they are parties'.

556. Article I(d) which states that 'matters relating to National Defence do not fall within the scope of the CoE' may be construed as an indirect reference to NATO which was set up one month before the CoE. Finally, Article 23 provides that the Assembly, in drawing up its agenda, 'shall have regard to the work of other European intergovernmental organizations to which some or all the Members of the Council are parties'.

557. However, with the rapid proliferation of international and European intergovernmental and NGOs, it soon became apparent that some form of coordination and rationalization was needed. This led to the adoption by the CM, at its eighth Session in May 1951, of a Statutory Resolution authorizing the CM, on behalf of the CoE, to conclude with any intergovernmental organization agreements on matters which are within the competence of the Council.

558. The Resolution also states that the CoE, or any of its organs, shall be authorized to exercise any functions coming within the scope of the CoE which may be entrusted to it by other European intergovernmental organizations. Furthermore, the CM was also authorized to make suitable arrangements for consultation with INGOs.

559. Following these decisions, an Agreement between the CoE and the International Labour Organization (ILO) was concluded in November 1951 and the following month there was an agreement between the UN per se and the Council through an exchange of letters. This provided for exchange of information, mutual consultation, exchange of observers and technical co-operation.

560. In parallel with these arrangements with the UN family, the Council also developed relations with the ECSC which would subsequently become the EU as well as with a whole host of other intergovernmental organizations.

561. As regards NGOs, the arrangements introduced in the CoE, initially on a consultative basis, were inspired in part by the system then prevailing in the UN where such organizations were granted consultative status with the Economic and Social Council. However, strictly speaking, the CoE's external relations only cover relations with other international intergovernmental organizations or public international institutions, as well as with non-Member States.[519]

562. The May 1951 Statutory Resolution was further refined in a Statement of Policy on Relations with Other International Organizations adopted by the CM in May 1954. The underlying philosophy aimed to 'make of the CoE a framework for the elaboration of common solutions of European problems, to be sought and put into effect by the international organization most appropriate in each case'.

563. As regards non-Member States of the CoE, in the early years a major cause for concern was the fate of the countries of central and Eastern Europe which were de facto barred from joining because of the nature of their political regimes. This resulted in the Assembly establishing a Special Committee in 1950 to watch over the interests of these countries. Its room for manoeuvre was necessarily limited but by following political developments and reporting on them it ensured that human rights abuses by the so-called democratic republics were denounced and made known in the West.

564. During those years a number of west European countries, including Austria, Switzerland, Spain and Portugal, remained outside the CoE either because they

519. The definition of 'non-Member State' has also changed over the years. After 1989, and in particular after the Parliamentary Assembly Recommendation 1247(1994) on the Council of Europe's enlargement, the notion of 'non-Member State' has been reserved for States having no possibility of applying for membership because of their geographical position outside Europe. Belarus is currently not a Member State, but could one day become one, and is thus not usually referred to as a 'non-Member State' in the classical sense.

would not or could not join for differing reasons. However, with time intergovernmental and/or parliamentary relations developed with the authorities or with opposition leaders of those countries thus facilitating their later accession to the Council when the political conditions were right.

565. Beyond Europe, the CoE began by attempting to build bridges in what was a very different world from today's. In 1950 the Assembly proclaimed the need for close liaison between the democratic nations of Europe and the countries of North America and this policy was endorsed by the CM. This led to the November 1951 Strasbourg Conference on 'The Union of Europe: its progress, problems, and place in the Western World' which brought together more than a dozen US Senators and Congressmen and a similar number of senior European politicians. Meanwhile, the CoE was also making overtures to the rest of the world, particularly through the Commonwealth. The Assembly for its part urged that 'the governments concerned should consult the Governments of the overseas countries with which they have links of a constitutional character, in order to study ways and means of ensuring that their interests are adequately represented in the CoE.'

566. It was in this context of a divided continent rebuilding itself after the moral and physical devastation of World War II and against the background of a world freeing itself from the chains of colonialism that the CoE gradually expanded and established its reputation as the standard bearer of Human Rights.

567. However, with the fall of communism in 1989, Europe's institutional landscape changed dramatically. The CoE, NATO and the EU enlarged. The all-embracing Conference on Security and Co-operation in Europe (CSCE) born of the Cold War was 're-founded' under the Charter of Paris in 1990, becoming the OSCE in 1994 and growing in membership with the collapse of the Soviet Union.

568. In 1989, the original founding principles and values of the European project which had been enshrined in the Statute of the CoE forty years earlier could finally be shared by all. Since then the quest for a 'Europe without dividing lines' uniting more than 800 million people which was proclaimed in Budapest in 1999 when the CoE turned fifty has also become EU policy for its neighbourhood relations since 2003.

569. East-West divisions had to a large extent shaped the history and culture of Europe's various organizations and institutions. Needless to say they had to adapt to the new realities and the needs of the new Europe. As from 1990 there were regular calls for the OSCE, NATO, the CoE and the EU to act as 'interlocking institutions', that is complementary and mutually supporting structures of the new pan-European co-operation.

§2. RELATIONS WITH THE EU

570. As already mentioned, the establishment of the ECSC marked the beginning of relations between the CoE and what is today the EU. Initially such relations focused on issues not specifically dealt with in the framework of the EC Treaties. The legal basis for co-operation is Article 220 of the Treaty on the Functioning of the EU. The CoE's focus on human rights led to close co-operation between both institutions, which developed over decades to include democratic institution building, legal affairs, social and health matters, education and culture, heritage and the environment, local government and the protection of national minorities.

571. This broad relationship was based on an exchange of letters between the Secretary General of the CoE, the President of the Commission of the European Economic Community (EEC) and the President of the European Atomic Energy Community which spelled out the modalities of relations between the three institutions. In addition to regular exchanges of information it was agreed that experts from the Commission could be invited to the CM debates on any item of interest to the Commission.

572. In 1987, co-operation became more structured through an Arrangement between the European Commission and the CoE providing for the convening of high-level meetings to discuss and assess co-operation in areas of mutual interest, and the European Commission was invited to take part in all meetings of the CM and its subsidiary bodies (Ministers' Deputies, Rapporteur Groups, et al.).

573. 1989 saw another important development with the decision to set up regular political-level Quadripartite meetings bringing together, on the one hand, the EU Presidency and the Commission and, on the other hand, the CoE Chairmanship and Secretary General. These meetings constitute the main framework for political dialogue between the EU and the CoE enabling both parties to exchange views on matters of common interest and to identify new areas of co-operation. The meetings are also intended to provide an opportunity for both parties to evaluate the advantages of their co-operation and avoid duplication or overlap in the work of the two institutions.

574. In 2001, a Joint Declaration on Co-operation and Partnership by the CoE and the European Commission provided the framework and principles guiding co-operation and called for meetings at the level of senior officials to 'draw up objectives, plan activities, monitor joint programmes and evaluate their implementation'. It confirmed the determination of both sides to deepen the partnership and to enhance co-operation bearing in mind the recent events in Eastern Europe and the consequent changing priorities.

575. 1989 had, of course, been an important catalyst for the EC/CoE partnership with both the CoE and the European Commission deploying important programmes in support of the efforts of numerous countries towards democracy, human rights and the rule of law. Since 1993, co-operation in this area has taken the form of joint programmes co-financed by the European Commission and the CoE, of which there have been more than 180 to date. Most of the first joint programmes were country-specific (and ran for two to three years),[520] aimed at facilitating institutional reform and support for the legal system to facilitate co-operation with countries which had joined the CoE since 1989.

576. It is against this background of longstanding co-operation that, in the light of the decisions taken at the Third CoE Summit, a Memorandum of Understanding was concluded by the CoE and the EU in May 2007 in order to consolidate present co-operation and to pave the way for a strengthened relationship in the future. The Memorandum of Understanding led not only to the intensification and multiplication of country-specific joint programmes and actions, but also to a greater emphasis on thematic programmes, covering areas ranging from support for national minorities, awareness-raising on the abolition of the death penalty, the fight against organized crime and corruption, the development of independent and multidisciplinary ethics committees for review of biomedical research and action to promote the European Social Charter, to a programme to strengthen democracy and constitutional development in central and eastern Europe with the CoE's Venice Commission.

577. The global financial volume of contracts being implemented in 2012 reached more than EUR 100 million that year. In the last few years, the EU has also funded a CoE Facility with the countries of the EU Eastern Partnership through a series of multilateral activities. Joint activities to support reform processes in countries of the Mediterranean area and Central Asia have also been developed in the framework of the policy of the CoE towards neighbouring regions, mainly through a multi-million EU-financed programme for the Southern Mediterranean.

578. Apart from Joint Programmes, the CoE and the European Commission have continued to strengthen other forms of co-operation, for example in the field of civil law. These joint activities include regular contact, organization of common conferences and working together to ensure consistency of legal instruments and non-binding instruments. Co-operation between the CoE and the EU at various levels has developed considerably in a number of areas in the last few years, notably anti-discrimination, gender equality and the fight against ill-treatment in particular, children's rights, the Roma, the independence and efficiency of the judiciary, the fight against corruption and money laundering, cybercrime and the protection of minorities. Communication between the CoE and EU institutions is also increasing as regards media and freedom of expression activities and, more specifically, Internet Governance.

520. The first joint programmes involved cooperation with Albania (since 1993), Armenia (since 1999), Azerbaijan (since 1999), Bosnia and Herzegovina (since 2003), Bulgaria, Croatia, Estonia, 'the Former Yugoslav Republic of Macedonia', Georgia (since 1999), Latvia, Lithuania, Moldova (since 1997), Montenegro (since 2001), the Russian Federation (since 1996), Serbia (since 2001), Turkey (since 2001), Ukraine (since 1995), as well as certain CoE non-Member States.

579. The EU has also increasingly supported a number of CoE instruments, *inter alia*, the Convention for the protection of individuals with regard to automatic processing of personal data ('Convention 108'), the Convention on preventing and combating violence against women and domestic violence (Istanbul Convention), the Convention on action against trafficking in human beings, the Convention for the protection of children against sexual exploitation and sexual abuse, the CoE Guidelines on child-friendly justice and the Budapest Convention on cybercrime, which is mentioned in the EU cyber-security strategy as a model for drafting national cybercrime legislation and a basis for international co-operation in this field.

580. As concerns legal and human rights issues and the need to ensure coherence between the two organizations' standards, CoE and EU leaders have reiterated their strong commitment to a successful conclusion of the negotiations on the Lisbon-Treaty-mandated accession by the EU to the ECHR. In January 2013, the Secretary General recalled that 'It will bring everyone in Europe under the same set of rules and the same Court. This will in turn create the basis for a dialogue, on an equal footing among all geopolitical players in Europe'.[521] However, following the negative opinion of the European Court of Justice of 18 December 2014, the European Commission is currently completing its analysis of legal issues raised by the Court, and accession negotiations are on ice.

581. A common attitude towards the situation in Belarus and possible joint activities such as strengthening civil society forces, is also part of the regular exchanges that take place between the CoE Secretariat and Commission's officials in view of the preparation of country reports and action plans.

582. With regard to the development of the EU neighbourhood policy with Mediterranean partners, the CoE's North-South Centre in Lisbon has been instrumental in providing possibilities for dialogue, information and training in the Council's core values with all partners in the Mediterranean of the Quadrilogue (representatives of governments, parliaments, local and regional authorities and civil society, and in particular youth) in the past. Co-operation currently builds more on joint programmes and on the Parliamentary Assembly's Partnership for Democracy.

583. The EU has constantly been involved in the CoE's Partial Agreements and intergovernmental activities. Among others, the EC is an active member of the European Audiovisual Observatory (16 November 2000) and of the European Pharmacopoeia (21 June 1994).

584. The European Commission has been taking part in the work of the Venice Commission since 1994 and fruitful co-operation has been developed over the years. This is also the case for questions covered by former Title VI of the Treaty

521. Ministers' Deputies, CM Document (2013) 43 of 22 Apr. 2013, 'Co-operation with the European Union – Summary report'.

on EU (co-operation in the fields of justice and home affairs).[522] This takes the form of regular exchanges of views between the Troika of the Article 36 Committee (which comprises the Union Presidency, the incoming Presidency, the European Commission and the Secretariat of the Council) and a CoE delegation.

585. There have been regular covenants between the European Commission and the Youth Directorate covering close co-operation in the youth field activities (training for trainers, validation of qualifications and youth research). The practice of an informal dialogue with the competent committees of the Council of the EU in the fields of education, culture, asylum and migration is now firmly established.

§3. Relations with the OSCE

586. Since the inception of the Helsinki process the CoE, and in particular the Parliamentary Assembly, followed closely the work of the CSCE, which led to the conclusion of the *Helsinki Final Act* in 1975 and was to become the OSCE in 1994. Between 1975 and the systemic changes in the Central and Eastern European countries, the Helsinki process and the CoE existed in parallel without institutional relations. When in the historic year of 1989 the CoE embarked on fulfilling its pan-European vocation by opening its doors to Central and Eastern European states, the requirement 'to apply and implement the Helsinki Final Act and the instruments adopted at the CSCE conferences' was one of the conditions for granting 'special guest status' to the national legislative assemblies of these countries in the CoE's Parliamentary Assembly.

587. The first official participation of the Council of the Europe in the CSCE process occurred in November 1989 on the occasion of the Special meeting convened by the French President, Francois Mitterrand. The CoE was subsequently represented at the CSCE Summit in Paris in November 1990 (where the Charter of Paris for a New Europe was adopted) and at other meetings which followed. Institutional relations started and rapidly developed in pursuit of more synergy, better coordination, co-operation and coherence. The question of pragmatic and increased co-operation between the CoE and the CSCE/OSCE has thus regularly been on the agenda of the CM. A special ad hoc working party of the Ministers' Deputies on relations between the CoE and the CSCE (later called the GR-OSCE and covered by the GR-EXT mandate today) has been active since April 1994.

588. At the Second CoE Summit held in October 1997 in Strasbourg, Member States gave their full support to the CoE with a view to intensifying its contribution to cohesion, stability and security in Europe and they welcomed the development of

522. With the entry into force of the Treaty of Lisbon, the provisions of Title VI have been replaced by provisions of Chs 1, 4 and 5 of Title V of Part Three of the Treaty on the Functioning of the European Union.

the CoE's co-operation with other European and transatlantic organizations, in particular the EU and the OSCE. Indeed, it can be said that the democratic institution-building process and the promotion and protection of human rights in the European continent are all common achievements of the various organizations working together towards the same goal.

589. The OSCE with its human dimension (as part of its comprehensive concept of security), shares the CoE's principles of democracy, human rights and the rule of law. However, the two Organizations differ in terms of mandates, membership and working methods.

590. The relations between the CoE and the OSCE were formalized in April 2000 in the 'Common Catalogue of Co-operative Modalities' to ensure that existing good practice continues, to help avoid duplication, and to pave the way for future action. It was the first formal agreement on the inter-institutional relationship between the CoE and the OSCE, and provided a good basis for further strengthening co-operation between the two organizations. In 2005, this was followed by a joint Declaration on enhanced co-operation between the CoE and the OSCE, adopted at the Warsaw Summit and marking the establishment of the CoE-OSCE Coordination Group. The Joint Statement and the Declaration on Co-operation between the CoE and the OSCE of 2005 are still today the latest political guidelines for relations between the two organizations.

591. There are three main forms of co-operation between the two organizations: (a) High-level political contacts and meetings at senior officials level; (b) Joint activities carried out in the framework of the Coordination Group and beyond; (c) Co-operation 'in the field'. High-level political contacts take the form of participation of the respective Secretaries General in the Ministerial sessions of the CoE CM and the OSCE Ministerial Councils and exchanges of views between the CoE CM' Deputies/the OSCE Permanent Council and the Chairpersons-in-Office, the Secretaries General, the CoE senior officials (the Human Rights Commissioner, the Secretary of the Venice Commission, etc.) or the Heads of the OSCE Institutions and Missions, in particular the Director of ODIHR.

592. The CoE-OSCE Coordination Group discusses co-operation in four agreed priority areas: (1) the protection of the rights of persons belonging to national minorities; (2) the promotion of tolerance and non-discrimination; (3) the fight against terrorism; (4) the fight against trafficking in human beings.

593. The CoE has good co-operation with OSCE field missions and with ODIHR in the context of electoral assistance. In the field of election observations, PACE has an institutional co-operation with the two bodies of the OSCE-ODIHR and the Parliamentary Assembly of the OSCE. This co-operation takes place in the framework of the International Election Observation Mission. Since 2011, the CoE Liaison Offices in Vienna and Warsaw facilitate the co-operation between the two organizations.

§4. Relations with the UN

594. The CoE and the UN share many areas of common interest. The most important areas of co-operation are: human rights, humanitarian issues and refugees, legal co-operation, social policy, culture and education. As already stated, co-operation between the CoE and the UN began with the Agreement between the Secretariat of the CoE and the Secretariat of the UN of 15 December 1951.

595. This Agreement was updated on 19 November 1971 through the arrangements on co-operation between the Secretariats of the CoE and of the UN. These were concluded in the form of an exchange of letters between the Secretary Generals of both organizations. Under this agreement, periodic high-level contacts, Tripartite UN/COE/OSCE High-Level Meetings, meetings of Experts, exchanges of views, reciprocal participation in meetings and conferences between the CoE and the UN take place regularly.

596. On 17 October 1989, the United Nations General Assembly (UNGA) adopted a resolution granting observer status to the CoE in the UN General Assembly (Resolution 44/6 of 17 October 1989). As an observer the CoE regularly participates in the sessions of the General Assembly.

597. Since 2000 (every second year since 2004), the General Assembly of the UN adopts a Resolution on co-operation between the UN and the CoE to coincide with its debate on co-operation with regional and other organizations.[523] A draft of such a Resolution is prepared and adopted by the CM in Strasbourg. The CM Chair is then asked to table the draft with the UN in New York and to hold the necessary consultations towards its adoption by the UNGA, preferably without vote.

598. The UN is a major partner for the CoE and an ideal platform for global outreach. The universality of values shared by the Member States of the CoE constitutes the basis for co-operation. Due to its global nature, both in thematic and geographical terms, the UN constitutes an 'across-the-board' partner for the CoE: For the UN, the CoE is 'a key partner in our shared quest … united behind the principle of all human rights for all people … and a beacon of democracy'.[524] The mutual interest in co-operation is reflected in regular contacts, consultations and dialogue between the Secretaries General, the Deputy Secretaries General and the UN Under-Secretaries General about current political or thematic issues. In recent years, co-operation has focused on achieving the UN Sustainable Development Goals, many of which fall squarely within the mandate of the CoE – the CoE runs activities in thirteen of the seventeen areas covered by the Goals.

523. The Secretary General has also on several occasions addressed the UN Security Council, to which the Council of Europe was invited for the first time in October 2005.
524. Speech by UN SG Ban Ki-Moon on the occasion of the ceremony to mark sixtieth anniversary of the ECHR, Strasbourg 19 Oct. 2010.

599. The CoE also works closely with a large number of UN bodies, including the UNHCR,[525] OHCHR,[526] UNICEF,[527] OCHA,[528] UNDP,[529] UNECE,[530] UNESCO,[531] WHO,[532] etc. There has indeed been a marked increase in CoE involvement in the work of the UN at the technical and working levels (for instance on counter-terrorism, combating violence against children, or the Protection and Promotion of the Rights and Dignity of Persons with Disabilities).

600. The relations between both organizations are focused on, but not limited to human rights in a broad sense. Emphasis is given to co-operation with the Human Rights Council in particular in the framework of the Universal Periodic Review, in which the CoE contributes actively as regards the situation of human rights in its Member States. Increased co-operation in the field of human rights is also demonstrated by the signature on 26 September 2013 in New York by the Secretary General of the CoE and the United Nations High Commissioner for Human Rights (UNHCHR) of the Joint Declaration on the reinforcement of co-operation between the CoE Secretariat and the Office of the UNHCHR.

601. The UN is also involved in promoting accession of CoE non-Member States to the CoE conventions with global vocation (e.g., the CoE Conventions on Action against Trafficking in Human Beings, on preventing and combating violence against women and domestic violence, on cybercrime, on MEDICRIME, etc.) or supporting their implementation.

602. High-level Tripartite meetings between the CoE, UN Office in Geneva and the OSCE were instituted in 1994 to exchange information and to promote coordination of activities of common concern (conflicts in South-Eastern Europe, refugee problems, fight against international crime and terrorism). Tripartite Target-oriented working level Meetings on specific issues of common interest are held whenever the need arises. Since their opening, respectively in 2010 and 2011, the CoE offices in Geneva and Vienna, acting as CoE Permanent Delegations to the UN Offices in both cities, strongly contributed to the enhancement of relations with the UN, as well as to the increased visibility of the CoE among UN Member States.

603. The PACE follows closely the work of the UN and its relations with the CoE. The Parliamentary Assembly holds regular debates on the activities of the UN, while representatives of the latter and its agencies regularly attend the Assembly's committees. The competent Assembly committees pay regular visits to the UN in New York and Geneva.

---

525. United Nations High Commissioner for Refugees.
526. Office of the United Nations High Commissioner for Human Rights.
527. United Nations Children's Fund.
528. United Nations Office for the Co-ordination of Humanitarian Affairs.
529. United Nations Development Programme.
530. United Nations Economic Commission for Europe.
531. United Nations Educational, Scientific and Cultural Organization.
532. World Health Organization.

604. The CoE has also engaged in joint programmes with the UN. It has co-operated with the UN Interim Administration Mission in Kosovo (UNMIK), most notably in human rights, legal reforms, education and culture. It has also been involved in the observation of the electoral process for Kosovo municipal and Assembly elections. Likewise the CoE worked closely with the United Nations Mission to Bosnia and Herzegovina (UNMIBH), in particular on legal and human rights programmes, implementation of the ECHR, and local prison reform.

605. The CoE participates actively in Special Sessions of the UN General Assembly including those on Women, Social Development, Habitat, and Children and it also participated in or contributed to the UN Conference against Racism, Racial Discrimination, Xenophobia and Related Intolerance, the Summit on Sustainable Development and the World Summit on the Information Society. The CoE's regular participation in the annual sessions of the UN Commission on the Status of Women, the organization of side events on that occasion and the presentation of keynote speeches confirm high-level, pragmatic and target-oriented relations with UN Women.

606. Finally, increased co-operation in the field of democracy is worth mentioning, demonstrated by the contribution to the UN efforts to promote and consolidate new or restored democracies or by regular UN participation in the CoE Forum for the Future of Democracy, as well as by the acceptance by Mr Ban Ki-moon to make a keynote address at the opening of the first Strasbourg World Forum for Democracy (Strasbourg, 8 October 2012).

§5. Relations with NGOs

607. The CoE's work benefits extensively from contacts and co-operation with civil society, as represented by NGOs. One of the main challenges currently facing the organization is to strengthen NGOs and civil society in the new Member States and to develop participatory democracy on a pan-European basis. The CoE's co-operation programmes rely on partner NGOs and focus on democratic reform.

608. The CoE's formalized relationship with NGOs is based on the Council's Conference of INGOs which is made up of INGOs which have been granted participatory status. Through this status, the CoE includes INGOs in intergovernmental activities and encourages dialogue between MPs as well as local and regional authorities with associations on major social issues.

609. INGOs have been able to acquire consultative status with the organization since 1952. In November 2003, this was upgraded to participatory status for international NGOs, recognizing their significance in CoE policy-making. This status is governed by CM' Resolution (2003)8. INGOs wishing to obtain such status must be particularly representative in their field(s); they must share the Council's objectives for Europe and contribute actively to its work. To date, approximately 400

INGOs hold such status. They form the Conference of INGOs of the CoE, which meets once a year to decide on general lines of action.

610. A Liaison Committee elected by the Conference meets regularly, promoting permanent dialogue and co-operation between the Council's Secretariat and the INGOs. It maintains close contact with the Council's political bodies – the CM, the Parliamentary Assembly, the Congress of Local and Regional Authorities and the Commissioner for Human Rights.

611. Co-operation with INGOs takes many forms, from simple consultation to full-scale co-operation on specific projects. INGO experts may participate in various projects as consultants; they may contribute to the work of intergovernmental committees on an institutionalized or ad hoc basis, prepare memoranda for the Secretary General, make oral or written statements to the committees of the Parliamentary Assembly and the Congress of Local and Regional Authorities and address seminars and other meetings organized by the CoE. INGOs enjoying participatory status also disseminate information about the CoE's aims and activities among their constituencies.

612. In November 2003, the participatory status for international NGOs was supplemented by a partnership between the CoE and national NGOs (Resolution (2003)9) reflecting their vital role in strengthening a democratic and open society in all Member States, and their active and constructive contribution to the CoE's work programme.

§6. Relations with Non-member States

613. The number of countries worldwide which are in touch with the CoE has increased significantly over the years. This is due to increased interest in the role of the CoE, particularly in the field of democracy and human rights. It is also due to the increasing number of Conventions which are open to signature by all states.

614. In the 1990s the CoE introduced Observer Status for like-minded countries wishing to follow the work of the Council. This has now been granted to Canada, the Holy See, Japan, Mexico and the US. These countries are able to participate in most CoE meetings including those of the Ministers' Deputies. These countries also often make generous voluntary contributions to the Organization's budget to support its work in areas in which they have a particular interest.

615. At the level of the Parliamentary Assembly, three parliaments hold observer status: Canada, Israel and Japan. In 2009, the status of Partner for Democracy was created through the adoption of Resolution 1680(2009). The national parliaments of all southern Mediterranean and Middle Eastern countries participating in the Union for the Mediterranean-Barcelona Process (including the Palestinian Legislative Council), and of central Asian countries participating in the OSCE (Kazakhstan, Kyrgyzstan, Tajikistan, Turkmenistan and Uzbekistan), are eligible to request this status with the Assembly.[533] The following parliaments have been granted this status: the parliament of Morocco (2011), the Palestinian National Council (2011), the Parliaments of the Kyrgyz Republic (2014) and of Jordan (2016).

616. The CoE also maintains relations with third countries through co-operation with other international organizations. This is the case for instance in the area of intercultural and interreligious dialogue where in recent years the Council has begun to work more closely with bodies such as the League of Arab States, the Organization of the Islamic Conference and their respective educational, cultural and scientific agencies, The Arab League Educational, Cultural and Scientific Organization (ALECSO) and The Islamic Educational, Scientific and Cultural Organization (ISESCO).

617. Today it is increasingly recognized that the challenges for Europe's future stability lie both within and without its borders. Geopolitical realities across the world can impact on the very values on which the CoE is based. If Europe is to enjoy a peaceful and secure future it will do so only if it learns to live with its neighbours. Over the coming years both Europe's relations, and those of the CoE, with the rest of the world will determine our future and the kind of society in which we live.

533. However, requests from parliaments of other states may also be considered if the Bureau of the Assembly so decides.

Chapter 2. The CoE Today and the Perspectives for the Future

Matjaz Gruden, updated by Tanja E.J. Kleinsorge

§1. Introduction

618. Every year in January, the Secretary General of the CoE delivers the annual communication to the members of the Parliamentary Assembly. This practice has gradually become known as 'The State of the CoE' and the purpose is for the Secretary General to report on how the CoE has done in the year that passed, and to speak about the prospects for the Future. In his 2013 State of the CoE speech, Secretary General Thorbjørn Jagland concluded that, while the political and economic situation in Europe was worrying, there should be no room for pessimism:

> After all, the construction of Europe has its origins in a far bleaker period in almost every aspect. Its founders saw the co-operation and integration based on trans-European solidarity as a way to overcome the economic, social, political and security challenges of the post-war era. It worked at the time and it can work again. We simply have to recapture the meaning of European solidarity. And the perspective must be pan-European. It is in everybody's interest that the EU overcomes its economic crisis. At the same time we have to keep in mind that Europe is more than the EU and more than economy. Without common values that are for all, Europe will not be held together.
>
> What Europe needs is a pan-European alliance based on common values interpreted through commonly agreed standards and supervised by common mechanisms in which every partner has the same rights and the same responsibilities. What Europe needs is the CoE.

619. In the next few pages, we shall look into key characteristics of the CoE, namely its membership, mandate, working methods and external relations, and try to identify risks and opportunities for the organization against the background of the rapidly changing international context in which it operates.

§2. Membership

I. The End of Enlargement

620. The enlargement of the CoE is all but complete. Belarus is the only European[534] country without an imminent prospect of joining the CoE. This is of great significance for the future of the organization which is no longer growing but has to manage its enlarged membership instead.

534. A country within the boundaries of Europe as defined by the Parliamentary Assembly's Recommendation 1247(1994) on the enlargement of the Council of Europe.

621. This is a complicated task, because for more than a decade, the enlargement dominated every aspect of the CoE's work. Considering its historic importance, this is not surprising. We should not forget that the CoE was the first European institution to invite former communist countries to join, and therefore provided them with the first tangible political recognition of their new status in Europe. Every successive accession was an achievement in itself, keeping busy all parts of the organization, from the Parliamentary Assembly, which took upon itself the leading role in the examination of membership requests, to the CM with the responsibility for taking the formal decision to invite a new member to join.

II. From More to Better

622. Today, the focus is back on members, not candidates, and while this shift of emphasis is not an easy one, it provides new opportunities for the CoE. In other words, even if quantitative enlargement has come to an end, the 'qualitative' one, measured in the level of Member States' compliance with the organization's standards, will continue on a new basis, with the CoE again more present in the so-called old Member States.

623. This 'return to origins' will challenge, and hopefully change, the perception that human rights issues in Europe are limited to recent democracies. This is of course far from being true. The Secretary General expressed his conviction that:

> the Council of Europe has come to a crossroad. There are a number of human rights and rule of law problems in several of our member countries. Actually there are problems in every member country. If we cannot prove that we are able to provide an effective response, we will slowly undermine the credibility of the organisation and the Convention system. Therefore we have to differentiate between the member states which clearly recognise that they have shortcomings and want to work with us to find remedies and those who have problems, but on the contrary do not recognise it and do not want to commit to concrete action plans.[535]

624. The priority now is to live up to this statement. The end of enlargement is an opportunity for the CoE to consolidate its role as the organization for Europe as a whole, responding to the real needs and interests of all Europeans, regardless of where they live.

III. Europe's Neighbours in the Mediterranean and Central Asia

625. The fact that the enlargement of the CoE is almost completed does not mean that the organization is not open to closer co-operation with its non-European neighbours especially in the Mediterranean basin and in Central Asia. In May 2011,

535. State of the Council of Europe speech, to PACE, 22 Jan. 2013.

the Ministerial Session of the CM endorsed the creation of the CoE Neighbourhood Policy. The Secretary General advocated the introduction of such a policy by stressing that, while the mandate of the CoE would remain geographically focused on Europe, many of its priority activities, including most of its key recent conventions, were aimed at extending co-operation also beyond the borders of our continent. Moreover, he underlined that many of the core issues under the CoE mandate were influenced by developments outside Europe, and notably in our immediate neighbourhood, in the Mediterranean region, the Middle East and in Central Asia.[536]

626. The Secretary General's policy paper which was the basis for the Ministers' decision defined the following key features of the future policy:

- flexibility – allowing for the implementation to be tailored to specific national situations, in order to take into account the difference in political situation, state of existing relations, geographic proximity and other parameters influencing the modalities and intensity of future relations;
- content driven by demand;
- respect for Europe's neighbours – stipulating that CoE relations with the countries concerned and our action should be perceived and accepted as genuine co-operation and assistance, not interference;
- close co-operation and coordination with other international partners; the CoE would focus on areas in which it has a clear and unparalleled added value.

The framework for co-operation would consist of:

- Neighbourhood Co-operation Dialogue – a framework for political dialogue between the country concerned and the CoE, identifying the main priority areas and modalities for co-operation.
- Neighbourhood Co-operation Action Plan – an agreement on specific co-operation activities during a two-year period, concluded between the country concerned and the CoE, in consultation with other possible international partners and financial contributors.

627. Three years later, through a report to the 123rd session of the CM in Vienna in May 2014, the Ministers were informed that:

> after three years of existence, concrete and significant progress has been made with respect to its two key components: the Neighbourhood Co-operation Dialogue and the Neighbourhood Co-operation Priorities setting out specific activities to be carried out in the fields of human rights, democracy and the rule of law.

536. SG/Inf(2011)7 Rev 2 19 Apr. 2011.

Neighbourhood Co-operation Dialogue was carried out by the CM, the Secretary General and the Deputy Secretary General, in the countries concerned and in Strasbourg. This dialogue has so far involved the authorities of Morocco, Tunisia, Jordan, Israel, the Palestinian National Authority, Kazakhstan and Kyrgyzstan.

Neighbourhood Co-operation Priorities (NCPs) designed for 2012–2014 have been implemented with Morocco, Tunisia and Jordan. The successful implementation of these priorities was made possible thanks to the partnership with the EU, whose political and financial support remains vital. These NCPs were financed for the most part by a three-year Joint EU/CoE EUR 4.8 million programme ('Strengthening democratic reform in the Southern Neighbourhood') aimed in particular at supporting efforts undertaken to reform the judiciary, as well as to fight corruption and money laundering. Moreover, it allowed for a series of activities, including at the regional level, to promote human rights and democratic values. The NCPs have also been implemented thanks to the support of a number of Member States which have contributed notably to the implementation of Venice Commission's actions in the region as well as of other CoE's projects to combat violence against women and children, of Pompidou Group projects through the Mediterranean Network for Co-operation on Drugs and Addictions (MedNET) and of activities on freedom of expression.

§3. Mandate

I. The Warsaw Declaration

628. Even if the mandate of the CoE is spelled out in its Statute in precise and unequivocal terms, the organization's terms of reference have been animatedly debated throughout its five decades of existence. Perhaps responding to this quest for greater clarity, the Warsaw declaration, adopted at the Third Summit of the CoE in May 2005, defined the mandate by stating that:

> The Council of Europe shall pursue its core objective of preserving and promoting human rights, democracy and the rule of law. All its activities must contribute to this fundamental objective. We commit ourselves to developing those principles, with a view to ensuring their effective implementation by all Member States. In propagating these values, we shall enhance the role of the Council of Europe as an effective mechanism of pan-European co-operation in all relevant fields.

II. Core Issues and Enabling Factors

629. In real terms, the definition brought little relief to the debate between the Member States which are partisans of the 'core issues', advocating a greater, if not exclusive, focus on human rights, democracy and the rule of law, and others who want to maintain, if not further develop, other activities in areas such as youth and sport, culture, social cohesion and the environment. The latter, and the list is not exhaustive, are often described as enabling factors.

630. To complicate things further, the Summit resulted in an action plan containing a long and diverse list of priorities, while at the same time calling to further 'strengthen and streamline' the organization's activities, structures and working methods.

III. Focus on Core Issues in a Broader Sense

631. The debate between the advocates of core issues and partisans of enabling factors continued unabated until the election of the new Secretary General Thorbjørn Jagland in 2009. His position was that the debate on core issues and enabling factors was largely a false dilemma. A prominent part of his broad programme of reforms was therefore a reorganization of both the programme and budget, but also the administrative set-up reflecting the new concept. The CoE was to concentrate on democracy, human rights and the rule of law.

§4. Working Methods

632. But the aim of the reforms was not only to clarify and sharpen the CoE's focus, but also to reform, revitalize and render more effective the Organization's working methods.

633. The starting point was the belief that the CoE, as the guardian of the ECHR, is the principal operator and ultimate guarantor of the effectiveness, authority and sustainability of the European model for the protection, enforcement and promotion of human rights, democracy and the rule of law.

In this context, the ECtHR, as the unique international court allowing individual petitions against states and issuing legally binding judgments, is the key part of an overall, mutually reinforcing system, composed of all CoE conventions, bodies and programmes, including its monitoring mechanisms. The purpose of the monitoring is to identify any shortcomings, but also good practices in the compliance with the CoE standards. The monitoring also serves to indicate appropriate remedies and possible need for CoE assistance in their implementation.

634. A reform of the monitoring was therefore chosen as a natural and indispensable next step of the reform process. The aim was to strengthen the monitoring activities in order to better identify shortcomings in individual as well as Member States' general trends in Europe.

As a result, the Secretary General during 2013 introduced a number of measures to better coordinate the work of different monitoring and evaluation mechanisms. These included the creation of a shared monitoring-visits calendar for a better coordination of visits, including the possibility of joint visits.

635. The second segment of changes focused on ways to reinforce the follow-up to the findings of the monitoring and evaluation mechanisms. The key objective was to improve the relevance and the effectiveness of our activities, especially our assistance programmes, through a better processing of monitoring and evaluation data. This was to be done in two ways, through a country-by-country matrix and a Europe-wide report on the state of democracy, human rights and the rule of law.

636. The matrix, first announced in the Secretary General's speech to PACE in January 2013, was based on the following principles:

- identification of key challenges in each Member State;
- a dialogue on appropriate remedies with the Member States concerned; and
- identification of possible assistance from the CoE.

The objective is not to shame and blame any country for any shortcomings, but rather to establish a constructive dialogue on the basis of the findings of various monitoring and evaluation bodies.

The starting point is that none of our Member States is immune to occasional difficulties in meeting the CoE standards and that none of our Member States would be opposed to acknowledging and responding to such difficulties.

637. The method is based on the following principles:

- equality of treatment and non-discrimination;
- impartiality, quality of data and reliability of sources;
- no finger-pointing at Member States' performance;
- dialogue and confidence.

638. The country-by-country analysis remains a working tool of the Secretary General. However, an integrated analysis showing the trends at the level of all forty-seven Member States was also carried out and resulted in the Report on the State of Democracy, Human Rights and the Rule of Law in Europe, presented by the Secretary General to the Ministerial session of the CM in Vienna in May 2014.[537] This integrated analysis could and should be made public in the form of an annual report on the state of human rights, democracy and the rule of law. This report had a clear positive impact on the visibility of the CoE and its action, but most of all, on the prominence of democratic and human rights values in Europe. Five editions of the report have now been published.

639. Drawn up at the request of the CM, the report provides an in-depth analysis of the state of human rights, democracy and the rule of law in Europe. It also critically examines the CoE's capacity to assist Member States in complying with the ECHR and the standards derived from it.

537. SG(2014)1 – Final.

640. The report lists a large number of concrete challenges to human rights, democracy and the rule of law in Europe, and recommends actions to meet them.

§5. CONCLUSION

641. In conclusion, we would offer the words of the Secretary General from the introduction to the 2018 Report on the State of democracy, Human Rights and the Rule of Law in Europe. It reflects both the challenges, the uncertainties but also ways forward for the CoE:

> The five chapters look at the key building blocks of democratic security: efficient, impartial and independent judiciaries; freedom of expression; freedom of assembly and freedom of association; democratic institutions; and inclusive societies. In line with previous editions, this report finds many good examples of Council of Europe member states carrying out reforms in line with their obligations and to the direct benefit of their citizens. The Council of Europe and the European Court of Human Rights (the Court) remain the bedrock of human rights, democracy and the rule of law in Europe. Their positive impact can be very easily taken for granted, but read this report – or others from this Organisation – and the proof is vivid and clear.[538]
>
> Nonetheless, this report also brings into sharp relief the challenges facing the Council of Europe. (…)
>
> In last year's report, we outlined the challenge posed by the rise of populism and asked how strong Europe's checks and balances are. It is of little surprise that just 12 months later we are still living with this resurgence. But this year's report draws attention to one of its disturbing outcomes.
>
> Our human rights, democracy and the rule of law depend on the institutions that give them form. But for populists, who invoke the proclaimed 'will of the people' in order to stifle opposition, these checks and balances on power are often seen as an obstacle that should be subverted. This year's report finds nascent trends – illuminated by alarming examples – of exactly this. There have been attempts to undermine institutions at the European level, namely the Council of Europe and the European Court of Human Rights themselves, and at the level of member states which, under the principle of subsidiarity, are at the vanguard of upholding our laws, standards and values. (…)
>
> The Council of Europe has equipped member states to take on many significant challenges in the past. Together, we can also address the challenges outlined in this report. That requires a recommitment to our shared values, reflected in the terms of the Convention and the judgments of the Court,

---

538. SG report of 18 May 2018, State of democracy, human rights and the rule of law, Role of institutions, Threats to institutions, at: https://rm.coe.int/prems-199318-gbr-1201-rapport-sg-2018-web-a4/168090361c.

including the defence of our institutions. Such a recommitment is in the interests of every European. It is our means to prevent the ghouls of the past returning to torment us, and a way to provide one another with the freedom and security we all deserve.

Selected Bibliography

§1. Books in the English Language

Bullock, A. *Ernest Bevin – Foreign Secretary 1945–51*. London: Heinemann, 1983.
Churchill, R.S. *The Sinews of Peace, Post-War Speeches by Winston S. Churchill*. London: Cassell, 1948.
Churchill, W. *The Second World War*. Six Volumes, vol. IV. London: Cassell, 1948–1954.
Colville, J. *Downing Street Diaries*. German edn. Berlin: Siedler Verlag, 1988/1991.
Council of Europe. *Filling the Frame; Five Years of Monitoring the Framework Convention for the Protection of National Minorities*. Strasbourg: Council of Europe Publishing, 2004.
Council of Europe. *Framework Convention for the Protection of National Minorities; Collected Texts*. 3rd edn. Strasbourg: Council of Europe Publishing, 2005.
Council of Europe. *From Theory to Practice: The European Charter for Regional or Minority Languages*. Strasbourg: Council of Europe Publishing, 2003.
Council of Europe. *Mechanisms for the Implementation of Minority Rights*. Strasbourg: Council of Europe Publishing, 2005.
Eden, A. *Freedom and Order*. London: Faber & Faber, 1957.
European Commission for Democracy through Law. *Xth Anniversary of the European Commission for Democracy Through Law (Venice Commission), Speeches*. Strasbourg: Council of Europe Publishing, 1990–2000.
European Yearbook of Minority Issues. Vols 1–5. Leiden & Boston: Martinus Nijhoff Publisher, 2001–2006.
Gladwyn (Lord) (Gladwyn Jebb). *The European Idea*. London: Weidenfeld & Nicholson, 1966.
Gladwyn (Lord) (Gladwyn Jebb). *The Memoirs*. London: Weidenfeld & Nicholson, 1972.
Haller, B. *An Assembly for Europe –The Council of Europe's Parliamentary Assembly 1949–1989*. Strasbourg: Council of Europe Publishing, 2006.
Huber, D. *A Decade that Made History – The Council of Europe 1989–1999*. Strasbourg: Council of Europe Publishing, 1999.
Lamberton Harper, J. *American Visions of Europe. Franklin D. Roosevelt, George F. Kennan, and Dean G. Acheson*. Cambridge: Cambridge University Press, 1996.

Letschert, R.M. & J. Lamberton Harper. *The Impact of Minority Rights Mechanisms*. The Hague: T.M.C Asser Press, 2005.
Lipgens, W. (ed.). *Documents on the History of the European Integration Volume 2, Plans for European Union in Great Britain and in Exile, 1939–45*. Berlin & New York: De Gruyter Verlag, 1986.
Morgan, R. & M. Evans. *Combating Torture in Europe*. Strasbourg: Council of Europe Publishing, 2001.
Murdoch, J. *The Treatment of Prisoners: European Standards*. Strasbourg: Council of Europe Publishing, 2006.
Notter, H.A. *Postwar Foreign Policy Preparation 1939–1945*. Washington: Department of State Publications, 1949.
Pentassuglia G. *Minorities in International Law*. Strasbourg: Council of Europe Publishing, 2002.
Salmon, T. & W. Sir Nicoll. *Building European Union – A Documentary History and Analysis*. Manchester & New York: Manchester University Press, 1997.
Thornberry P. & M.A. Estebanez. *Minority Rights in Europe*. Strasbourg: Council of Europe Publishing, 2004.
Weller, M. (ed.). *The Rights of Minorities; A Commentary on the European Framework Convention for the Protection of National Minorities*. Oxford & New York: Oxford University Press, 2005.
Zurcher, A.J. *The Struggle to Unite Europe, 1940–58*. New York: New York University Press, 1958.

§2. Articles in the English Language

Foreign Relations of the United States. *Diplomatic Papers*, 1943. Vol. 1. Washington: Government Printing Office, 1963, 624et seq.
Bartole, S. 'Final Remarks: The Role of the Venice Commission'. *Review of Central and East European Law* 26 (2000): 3, 351 et seq.
Bindig, R. & Kleinsorge, T.E.J. 'Monitoring the Compliance of Member States with Obligations and Commitments: The Case of Estonia'. In *Law in Greater Europe – Towards a Common Legal Area*, edited by B. Haller, H.-C. Krüger & H. Petzold. The Hague & London: Kluwer Law International, 2000, 102–130.
Hammarberg, T. & I. Gachet, 'Human Rights Diplomacy and the Council of Europe Commissioner for Human Rights'. In *Human Rights Diplomacy: Contemporary Perspectives,* edited by O'Flaherty, M. et al. Leiden: Brill, 2011, 101–128.
Jowell, J. 'The Venice Commission: Disseminating Democracy Through Law'. *Public Law* (Winter 2001): 675–683.
McCauley, M. 'Yalta, Potsdam and the Emergence of the Cold War: An Overview from the United Kingdom in the Light of the Latest Research'. In *Crossroads of European Histories, Multiple Outlooks on Five Key Moments in the History of Europe*, edited by Stradling. Strasbourg: Council of Europe Publishing, December 2006, 251–259.
UK Labour Party. 'Manifesto on the Peace Aims'. *The Times*, 9 February 1940.

§3. Books in Other Languages

Benoît-Rohmer, F. *Les minorités, quels droits?* Strasbourg: Council of Europe Publishing, 2000.

Bitsch, M.-T. *Histoire de la construction européenne de 1945 à nos jours*. 2nd edn. Bruxelles: Éditions Complexe, 1999.
Bonnefous, E. *La construction de l'Europe par l'un de ses initiateurs*. Paris: Presses Universitaires de France, 2002.
Bonnefous, E. *L'idée européenne et sa réalisation*. Paris: Editions du Grand Siècle, 1950.
Burckhardt, C.J. *Vier historische Betrachtungen*. Zürich: Manesse Verlag, 1953.
Coudenhove-Kalergi, R. *Kampf um Europa*. Zürich: Atlantis Verlag, 1949.
Fleury, A. & L. Jilek. *Le plan Briand d'Union fédérale européenne*. Bern: Éditions Lang, 1998.
Haller, B. *Une Assemblée au service de l'Europe, L'Assemblée parlementaire du Conseil de l'Europe 1949–1989*. Strasbourg: Éditions du Conseil de l'Europe, janvier 2006.
Herriot, E. *Europe*. Paris: Rieder, 1930.
Leone, U. *Le origine diplomatiche del Consiglio d'Europa*. Milano: Giuffrè, 1966.
Melandri, P. *Les Etats-Unis face à l'unification de l'Europe 1945–1954*. Paris: Editions Pédone, 1980.
de Molènes, C.M. *L'Europe de Strasbourg – une première expérience de parlementarisme international*. Paris: Rondil, 1971.
Näf, W. *Abrüstungsverhandlungen im Jahr 1931*. Bern: Lang, 1931.
Raue, J. *Der Europarat als Verfassungsgestalter seiner neuen Mitgliedsstaaten: Vom Beobachter zum Reformer in Osteuropa?* Zürich: Juristische Medien, Schweizer Studien zum Internationalen Recht, Band 126, 2006.
Rülke, S. *Venedig-Kommission und Verfassungsgerichtsbarkeit: Eine Untersuchung über den Beitrag des Europarates zur Verfassungsentwicklung in Mittel- und Osteuropa* (Diss.). Köln, Berlin, Bonn & München: Göttinger Studien zum Völkerund Europarecht, Band 1, 2003.
Salinas Alcega, S. *La Comision para la democracia a traves del derecho (Comision de Venecia), Una Accion, en el Marco del consejo de europa, para el desarrollo y la extension de los valores democraticos*. Zaragoza: Monografias del Real Instituto de Estudios Europeos, 1999.
Unger, G. *Aristide Briand – le ferme conciliateur*. Paris: Éditions Fayard, 2005.

§4. Articles in Other Languages

Buquicchio, G. & P. Garrone. 'L'harmonisation du droit constitutionnel européen: la contribution de la commission européenne pour la démocratie par le droit'. *Uniforme Law Review*, NS 3 (1998): 2/3.
Buquicchio, G. & P. Garrone. 'Vers un espace constitutionnel commun? Le rôle de la Commission de Venise'. In *Law in Greater Europe – Towards a Common Legal Area, Studies in Honour of Heinrich Klebes*, edited by Haller, Krueger & Petzold. Den Haag & London: Kluwer Law International, 2000, 3 et seq.
Cornides, W. 'Das Problem der europäischen Sicherheit auf der Berliner Viermächtekonferenz 1954'. *Europa-Archiv* (1954): 6489 et seq.
Cornides, W. 'Der Straßburger Europarat in der Perspektive der Vorschläge Briands von 1929'. *Europa-Archiv* 17 (1949): 2417–2420.
Cornides, W. & H. Volle. 'Die Vorgeschichte des Brüsseler Fünfmächte-Pakts'. *Europa-Archiv* (1949): 1755–1767.

Selected Bibliography

Coudenhove-Kalergi, R. *Paneuropa* (periodical). No. 4/1933, 97–101.

Coudenhove-Kalergi, R. 'La paix de demain'. *Politique étrangère* 4 (1939).

Garrone, P. 'La Commission de Venise à la veille de son dixième anniversaire'. *Rivista di studi politici internazionali* 66 (1999): 527 et seq.

Garrone, P. 'Le patrimoine électoral européen'. *Revue du droit public* 5 (2001): 1417 et seq.

Haller, B. 'L'Assemblée parlementaire et les conditions d'adhésion au Conseil de l'Europe'. In *Law in Greater Europe – Towards a Common Legal Area*, edited by Haller, Krüger & Petzold. The Hague & London: Kluwer Law International, 2000, 27–79.

Jilek, L. 'Projets d'Assemblée européenne en 1946–48, rôle des associations militantes'. In *Jalons pour une histoire du Conseil de l'Europe*, actes du colloque de Strasbourg (8–10 June 1995), 17–37 et seq., Bern: Lang, 1997.

Malinverni, G. 'La Commission de Venise et l'ingénierie constitutionnelle au bénéfice des nouveaux adhérents du Conseil de l'Europe', Intervention a l'occasion de la 13ieme Académie européenne d'été de Grenoble 'L'Europe en transition'. 16–27 Septembre 2002.

Matscher, F. 'Demokratie durch Recht'. *Salzburger Nachrichten*, Ausgabe vom 1. Juli 2000.

Näf, W. 'Versuche gesamteuropäischer Organisation und Politik in den ersten Jahrzehnten des 19. Jahrhunderts'. In *Staat und Staatsgedanke, Vorträge zur neueren Geschichte*. Bern: Stümpfli Verlag, 1935.

Podevin, R. 'Die europapolitischen Initiativen Frankreichs des Jahres 1950 – aus einer Zwangslage geboren?'. In *Vom Marshallplan zur EWG*, edited by Herbst, Bührer & Sowade. München: Oldenbourg Verlag, 1990, 257–262.

Puttkamer, E. v. 'Der Briand Plan – Vorbote der europäischen Einigung?'. In *Festschrift für Carl Friedrich Ophüls aus Anlass seines 70. Geburtstags*, edited by Hallstein, Ophüls & Schlochauer. Karlsruhe: Verlag C.F. Müller 1965, 143–151.

Robert, J. 'L'ingénierie constitutionnelle et l'Europe de l'est: Le rôle de la Commission européenne pour la démocratie par le droit'. In *La réinvention de l'Etat: démocratie politique et ordre juridique en Europe centrale et orientale*, edited by S. Milacic. Bruxelles: Bruylant, 2003, 195 et seq.

Schuman, R. 'L'Europe est une Communauté spirituelle et culturelle'. *European Yearbook*. Vol. I. The Hague: Council of Europe, Martinus Nijhoff, 1955, 18–24.

Schwimmer, W. 'Der Einfluss der Parlamentarischen Versammlung auf die Konventionen des Europarats'. In *Law in Greater Europe – Towards a Common Legal Area*, edited by Haller, Krüger & Petzold. The Hague & London: Kluwer Law International, 2000, 377–406.

Uerpmann-Wittzack, R., 'Europarat', in Hatje, A. & Müller-Graff, P.-C., (eds.), *Europäisches Organisations- und Verfassungsrecht*, Enzyklopädie Europarecht, 1, Baden-Baden, Nomos, 2014, 1071–1103.

Zeeman, B. 'Der Brüsseler Pakt und die Diskussion um einen westdeutschen Militärbeitrag'. In *Vom Marshallplan zur EWG*, edited by Herbst, Bührer & Sowade. München: Oldenbourg Verlag, 1990, 350–441.

§5. Resolutions, Recommendations and Reports in the English Language

Jagland, T. *State of Democracy, Human Rights and Rule of Law in Europe*.
Report by the Secretary General of the Council of Europe, April 2014, SG (2014) 1 – Final.
Report by the Secretary General of the Council of Europe, 18 May 2018.
Juncker, J.-C. *Council of Europe – European Union: A Sole Ambition for the European Continent*. Report by the Prime Minister of the Grand Duchy of Luxembourg to the attention of the Heads of State or Government of the Member States of the Council of Europe, Doc. 10897 of the Parliamentary Assembly, 11 April 2006.
Marty, D. *Alleged Secret Detentions and Unlawful Inter-state Transfers of Detainees Involving Council of Europe Member States*. Doc. 10957 of the Parliamentary Assembly, led to the adoption of Resolution 1507 (2006) and Recommendation 1754.
Marty, D. *Secret Detentions and Illegal Transfers of Detainees Involving Council of Europe Member States: Second Report*. Doc. 11302 of the Parliamentary Assembly, led to the adoption of Resolution 1562 (2007) and Recommendation 1801 (2007).
Muižnieks, N. Commissioner for Human Rights, *Annual Activity Report 2013*, Council of Europe, April 2014.
Schieder, P. *The Institutional Balance at the Council of Europe*. Doc. 11017 of the Parliamentary Assembly, 18 September 2006, led to the adoption of Recommendation 1763 (2006) of the Parliamentary Assembly (reply by the Committee of Ministers: Doc. 11222 of the Parliamentary Assembly).
Valsecchi, F. (for the Council of Europe). *Working Group on History and Political Institutions*. Council of Europe Doc. TR/Etude (55)2.
Resolution (99)50 *on the Council of Europe Commissioner for Human Rights*, adopted by the Committee of Ministers, at its 104th Session, Budapest, 7 May 1999.

§6. Other Sources

Annuaire de l'Institut de Droit International, session de Lausanne, 1947.
Bevin, E. (then foreign minister of the United Kingdom). Speech before the House of Commons of 22.1.1948.
Churchill, W. (then no longer prime minister of the United Kingdom). Speeches in Fulton (March 1946) and in Zürich (September 1946).
Posselt, M. *Richard Coudenhove-Kalergi und die Europäische Parlamentarier-Union, 1946–52*. Doctoral thesis, University of Graz, 1984.
Schuman, R. 'Speech on the Occasion of the 10th Anniversary of the Council of Europe'. 20 April 1959, Council of Europe document A.46.544, 34–37.

Selected Bibliography

Index

The numbers here refer to paragraph numbers.

Index

Index

Council of Europe (CoE)

Third Edition

Tanja E.J. Kleinsorge

This book was originally published as a monograph in the International Encyclopaedia of Laws/Intergovernmental Organizations.

Founding Editor: Roger Blanpain
General Editor: Frank Hendrickx
Volume Editor: Jan Wouters

Wolters Kluwer

Published by:
Kluwer Law International B.V.
PO Box 316
2400 AH Alphen aan den Rijn
The Netherlands
E-mail: international-sales@wolterskluwer.com
Website: lrus.wolterskluwer.com

Sold and distributed in North, Central and South America by:
Wolters Kluwer Legal & Regulatory U.S.
7201 McKinney Circle
Frederick, MD 21704
United States of America
Email: customer.service@wolterskluwer.com

Sold and distributed in all other countries by:
Air Business Subscriptions
Rockwood House
Haywards Heath
West Sussex
RH16 3DH
United Kingdom
Email: international-customerservice@wolterskluwer.com

Printed on acid-free paper

ISBN 978-94-035-1342-3

e-Book: ISBN 978-94-035-1364-5
web-PDF: ISBN 978-94-035-1394-2

Printed in the United Kingdom.

Dedicated to the late Heinrich Klebes, former Secretary General of the Council of Europe's Parliamentary Assembly

Made in the USA
Monee, IL
18 October 2026

66041408R10149